CYBERB

The   eer-
revie   s to
make   the
prob   ides
a tho   dis-
cusse   it.

W   ventions   ods
and   ders
with   nal
insig   as:
how   hat
its ne   and
conte   ting
bully   tion
from

C   and
resea   will
also   mi-
natin

Trijn   ver-
sity o

Fran   Uni-
versit

Conor Mc Guckin is Assistant Professor, School of Education, Trinity College Dublin, Ireland.

Current Issues in Social Psychology

Series Editor: Arjan E. R. Bos

Current Issues in Social Psychology is a series of edited books that reflect the state-of-the-art of current and emerging topics of interest in basic and applied social psychology.

Each volume is tightly focused on a particular topic and consists of seven to ten chapters contributed by international experts. The editors of individual volumes are leading figures in their areas and provide an introductory overview.

Example topics include: self-esteem, evolutionary social psychology, minority groups, social neuroscience, cyberbullying and social stigma.

Self-Esteem
Edited by Virgil Zeigler-Hill

Social Conflict within and between Groups
Edited by Carsten K. W. De Dreu

Power and Identity
Edited by Denis Sindic, Manuela Barret and Rui Costa-Lopes

Cyberbullying
From theory to intervention
Edited by Trijntje Völlink, Francine Dehue and Conor Mc Guckin

CYBERBULLYING

From theory to intervention

*Edited by Trijntje Völlink, Francine Dehue
and Conor Mc Guckin*

Routledge
Taylor & Francis Group

LONDON AND NEW YORK

First published 2016
by Routledge
2 Park Square, Milton Park, Abingdon, Oxon, OX14 4RN

and by Routledge
711 Third Avenue, New York, NY 10017

Routledge is an imprint of the Taylor & Francis Group, an informa business

British Library Cataloguing in Publication Data
A catalogue record for this book is available from the British Library

Library of Congress Cataloging-in-Publication Data
Cyberbullying (Psychology Press)
  Cyberbullying : from theory to intervention / edited by Trijntje Völlink, Francine Dehue and Conor Mc Guckin.
    pages cm
  1. Cyberbullying. 2. Cyberbullying—Prevention. I. Völlink, Trijntje. II. Dehue, Francine. III. Mc Guckin, Conor. IV. Title.
  HV6773.15.C92C936 2016
  302.34'3—dc23
  2015017283

ISBN: 978-1-848-72339-9 (hbk)
ISBN: 978-1-848-72338-2 (pbk)
ISBN: 978-1-315-68035-4 (ebk)

Typeset in Bembo
by Apex CoVantage, LLC
Printed and bound in Great Britain by Ashford Colour Press Ltd, Gosport, Hampshire

CONTENTS

CONTRIBUTORS

Sara Bastiaensens, Department of Communication Studies, University of Antwerp, Belgium

Ilse De Bourdeaudhuij, Department of Movement and Sport Sciences, Ghent University, Belgium

Francine Dehue, Faculty of Psychology and Educational Science, Open University of the Netherlands, The Netherlands

Ann DeSmet, Department of Movement and Sport Sciences, Ghent University, Belgium

Sibylle Enz, University of Bamberg, Germany

Nicole Gunther, Faculty of Psychology and Educational Science, Open University of the Netherlands, The Netherlands

Niels C. L. Jacobs, Faculty of Psychology and Educational Science, Open University of the Netherlands, The Netherlands

Lilian Lechner, Faculty of Psychology and Educational Science, Open University of the Netherlands, The Netherlands

Tanya Lereya, Department of Psychology, The University of Warwick, United Kingdom

Conor Mc Guckin, School of Education, Trinity College Dublin, Ireland

Ersilia Menesini, Department of Educational Science and Psychology, University of Florence, Italy

Annalaura Nocentini, Department of Educational Science and Psychology, University of Florence, Italy

Benedetta Emanuela Palladino, Department of Educational Science and Psychology, University of Florence, Italy

Karolien Poels, Department of Communication Studies, University of Antwerp, Belgium

Margaritis Samaras, Economic and Social Sciences, University of Macedonia, Greece

Maria Sapouna, Faculty of Education, Health and Social Science, University of the West of Scotland (UWS), United Kingdom

Neil Tippett, Department of Psychology, The University of Warwick, United Kingdom

Katrien Van Cleemput, Department of Communication Sciences, University of Antwerp, Belgium

Heidi Vandebosch, Department of Communication Sciences, University of Antwerp, Belgium

Trijntje Völlink, Faculty of Psychology and Educational Science, Open University of the Netherlands, The Netherlands

Dieter Wolke, Department of Psychology, The University of Warwick, United Kingdom

PART I
State of the art

1

AN INTRODUCTION IN CYBERBULLYING RESEARCH

Trijntje Völlink, Francine Dehue, Conor Mc Guckin and Niels C. L. Jacobs

Online Internet activities of children and adolescents

The Internet and information communication technologies (ICT) are becoming a natural part of everyday life for children and adolescents. Many researchers refer to the generation born after 1980 as 'the always-on generation': this generation is growing up in a world that offers them instant access nearly everywhere to a huge amount of human knowledge. They have access to a wide range of social media that offer them the opportunities to connect, create and collaborate with each other. They can play, watch and/or create games, make videos and photos, and buy the products they want online. The down-side of these growing opportunities is that they also create more possibilities for negative experiences such as online bullying. Online bullying, mostly referred to as cyberbullying, is described as ". . . bullying and harassment of others by means of new electronic technologies, primarily mobile phones and the internet" (Smith, Steffgen, & Sittichai, 2013, p.3). Over the last 10 years, many studies have been published about cyberbullying that have provided increased insight into the prevalence, determinants, coping strategies, and (health) consequences related to cyberbullying.

However, while the research field of cyberbullying is growing, more critical studies are appearing about the uniqueness of cyberbullying: is it just a form or an extension of traditional bullying, or is it a completely new phenomenon? In addition, recent critical papers have been published concerning the different definitions of cyberbullying, instruments to measure cyberbullying and the poor theoretical background of most available studies.

This book brings together these different insights from international researchers involved in (cyber)bullying research. Part I will give a thorough overview of the state of the art concerning cyberbullying research (e.g., what is cyberbullying, what is the overlap with traditional bullying, and how is it related to negative consequences?). Part II will give an overview of the development and content of evidence-based ICT interventions aimed at preventing and combating (cyber) bullying. In addition, some of the important outcomes of the effect evaluations will be described. The final chapter concludes with feedback on the interventions based on the recommendations that resulted from Part I.

Online Internet activities of children and adolescents

For a better understanding of the main topics and different perspectives in cyberbullying research, this chapter starts with a brief overview of cyberbullying studies from the start, around 2004, until now. Since cyberbullying can only happen when young people connect with each other online, we give a brief overview of children's online activities and the relation with cyberbullying.

In many studies, researchers state that 'staying in contact with friends through social media' is one of the most important activities of children and adolescents on the Internet. However, what do we actually know from the main online activities of children, and are these activities age-dependent? The 2011 EU Kids Online study measured the frequencies and duration of online activities of 25.142 European children, between 9 and 16 years of age, from 25 different countries (see www.eukidsonline.net). The results showed that 33% of the children between 9 and 10 years old, and 80% of the adolescents between 15 and 16 years old, were online daily. The same age pattern was visible for the number of different activities children performed online: younger children were involved on average over five activities while teenagers performed eight or nine activities. When the same children were asked about what kind of activities they did, they spontaneously mentioned using the Internet for homework (85%), playing games (83%), and watching video clips (76%). Counterintuitively, social media (e.g., instant messaging) was ranked fourth (62%). Fewer children mentioned posting images (39%), messages (31%), sharing files (16%) or writing blogs (11%). Nevertheless, online chatting and texting was an important activity for the young people, often combined with doing homework. The time spent online and having a social network profile increases with age (Ólafsson, Livingstone, & Haddon, 2014). When the time spent online and using social networks increases, the occurrence of cyberbullying increases, too (Ybarra & Mitchell, 2004).

First studies on cyberbullying

Fifteen years ago, Finkelhor, Mitchell and Wolak (2000) were probably the first to publish a report about online harassment. In the Netherlands, the first report, 'Online bullying: harm is right', was published in 2005 by Van den Akker. In 2006 and 2008, two large-scale studies on the prevalence of cyberbullying appeared (Dehue, Bolman & Völlink, 2008; van den Eijnden, Verhulst, Rooy & Meerkerk, 2006). Around 2006, studies appeared on a large scale in several European countries that explicitly dealt with cyberbullying: see, for instance, a review by Kiriakidis and Kavoura (2010). In 2007, the first special issue (i.e., 'Youth Violence and Electronic Media: Similar behaviors, different Venues?') on online bullying was published. Since then, many studies about cyberbullying have been published all over the world. The prevalence of cyberbullying, the overlap with traditional bullying, the relation with parenting and mediation styles, coping strategies, health and (mental) well-being, as well as other negative consequences, have been studied intensively.

Prevalence of cyberbullying

The prevalence of cyberbullying varies considerably, depending on how it is defined and measured. Tokunaga (2010) reported average prevalence rates between 20% and 40% of youth being cyberbullied at least once in their lifetime. When more restricted time frames (i.e., 2 or 3 times a month in the past year) are used, the prevalence of cyberbullying reduces to an average between 3% and 10% (Olweus, 2012; Smith et al., 2008; Tokunaga, 2010; Williams & Guerra, 2007; Ybarra, Mitchell, Wolak, & Finkelhor, 2006). Cyberbullying experiences rise from 3% for 9- to 10-year-old children to 8% for 15- to 16-year-olds (Livingstone, Haddon, Görzig, & Olafsson, 2011). Furthermore, longitudinal data about trends in cyberbullying between 2010 and 2013/2014 shows a slight increase in receiving hate messages (from 13% to 20%) and being cyberbullied (from 7% to 12%) (Hasebrink, 2014). However, there are still many more children involved in traditional, or offline, bullying compared to cyberbullying: in a recent meta-analysis by Modecki and colleagues (2014), of 80 studies that measured both cyber- and traditional bullying, mean prevalence rates of 35% for traditional bullying and 15% for cyberbullying involvement were found.

An interesting fact that needs to be known is that children do not see all specific negative online behaviours, as measured by many cyberbullying questionnaires, as cyberbullying. For example in their focus group study with 66 adolescents aged between 12 and 15 years, Jacobs, Goossens, Dehue, Völlink and Lechner (2015) found that name-calling was considered as 'normal' communication (i.e., even friends call each other names) and being lied to was not perceived as cyberbullying. Vandebosch and Van Cleemput (2008) found that it depends on the power imbalance and intention to hurt as to whether or not an online experience is seen as cyberbullying. These findings show that there is a difference between children's and researchers' perception of which behaviours can be labelled as cyberbullying. As a consequence, higher scores on a cyberbullying scale may not always mean that these children are in need of help. Yet, it is very important that children be aware of the fact that (repeated) aggressive coping strategies or actions to combat cyberbullying makes them a bully-victim, although they might perceive their actions as a justified defence. Furthermore, if an intervention aims to reach a broad category of children with negative online experiences, it seems more effective not to speak about victims but about experiences with negative online behaviour.

Main streams in cyberbullying research

Researchers who study cyberbullying can usefully be divided into two groups. In the first of these groups are researchers who examine cyberbullying as one of the online risks, divided into three main types: (a) content risk (e.g., violent and/ or pornographic content); (b) conduct risk (e.g., threats, vulgar language, things that can damage your reputation); and (c) contact risk (e.g., grooming) (see for instance Livingstone, Kirwil, Ponte, & Staksrud, 2014; Mesch, 2009; Staksrud & Livingstone, 2009; Valkenburg & Peter, 2011). In the second group are researchers who examine cyberbullying in relation to traditional bullying (see for instance Cassidy, Faucher, & Jackson, 2013; Li, 2007; Hemphill et al., 2012; Olweus, 2012). The first group of researchers more thoroughly examines the pros and cons of online communication for adolescents (see Valkenburg & Peter, 2011), possibilities for the prevention of online risks (i.e., cyber safety), variables that make children more vulnerable for online risks in general, and opportunities for parents, teachers and policy makers to mediate and minimize online risks for children. An important study about online risk and parental mediation is that by Mesch (2009). He concluded that having a social network site and having high scores on willingness to provide personal information both offline and online increases the risk of being bullied online. It also increases the risk of meeting offenders who use the personal information found on social network sites to threaten and humiliate a victim. Furthermore, in this study it was found that evaluative mediation (i.e., setting rules and talking to children about the online risks) decreases the risk of exposure to online bullying. In a more recent study by Livingstone et al. (2014), it was found that for the children who live in the Northern European high-risk countries (due to high levels of Internet access), the frequency of exposure to online risk is fairly high, although most of these children adopt positive coping strategies such as ignoring, blocking the sender or seeking help from friends. The researchers conclude that risk-free Internet for children is an illusion and that we should help children to cope adequately with, and to develop their resilience for, the negative impact of online risks.

Regarding the second group of researchers, in recent studies those in this group are examining the prevalence and overlap between traditional and cyberbullying. One of the first studies, by Li (2007), entitled 'New bottle but old wine: A research of cyberbullying in schools', shows that 54% of the 177 seventh-grade students in Canada had been bullied offline, and 25% had been bullied online. About one third of the victims that had been bullied offline reported that they also had been bullied online. In a study among 1221 Dutch children aged 10 to 14 years it was found that 7% of the children were only involved in cyberbullying, 30% were involved in only traditional bullying and 31% were involved in both forms of bullying (Dehue, Bolman, Völlink & Pouwelse, 2012). In their meta-analysis, Modecki et al. (2014) found a strong correlation between offline and online perpetration and victimization. They also found strong behavioural similarities across online and offline settings. However, Ybarra, Diener-West and Leaf (2007) found that among the less frequently cyberbullied children (a few times a year or less) in their study, the overlap between being traditionally and being cyberbullied was much lower. Because of these contrasting findings, more information about the similarities and differences between traditional and cyberbullying is needed.

Although most researchers in this area agree that traditional and cyberbullying are (tightly) interwoven (i.e., at least for the frequently involved children) and share some important background variables, there is still a lot of discussion going on about the uniqueness of cyberbullying, the prevalence of cyberbullying and whether or not cyberbullying needs specific interventions.

Coping, cyberbullying and negative consequences

In most studies it is found that being (cyber)bullied can have tremendous negative (long term) consequences on, for example, children's (mental) well-being, social functioning and school results (see Chapter 4). According to many researchers, effective coping can help to avoid escalation of cyberbullying and/or can help to buffer against the negative impact of (cyber)bullying (see for instance Völlink, Bolman, Eppingbroek, & Dehue, 2013). Lazarus and Folkman (1987) postulate that coping has two main functions: (1) to change the actual terms of the troubled person-environmental relationship (i.e., problem-focused coping); and (2) to regulate emotional distress (i.e., emotion-focused or cognitive coping). In a study by Völlink, Bolman, Dehue and Jacobs (2013), it was found that coping strategies in daily life are highly correlated to cyber specific coping strategies: bully-victims more frequently react to stressful situations in an aggressive way and passive victims use more avoidance and depressive coping to combat stressful situations. These results suggest that children use the same coping styles on- and offline. Does this mean that we need a broader intervention to help children to react more adequately to stressful situations in general? Or is it more effective to develop specific interventions for cyberbullying, and for traditional bullying?

Interventions to prevent and combat cyberbullying

Many professional groups like educators, teachers and healthcare workers are aware of the negative consequences of (cyber)bullying experiences on health and well-being. On the Internet, these professionals, as well as hands-on experts, express their worry and their belief that it is vital to stop cyberbullying and to help the victims. A host of sites with tips, advice and recommendations regarding cyberbullying are provided, and there is a proliferation of prevention and intervention programs regarding both traditional and cyberbullying. The problem is, however, that many of these materials and programs, whilst well intentioned, do not have a theoretical base, nor has the effectiveness of their materials been investigated. Hence, there is an urgent need for prevention and intervention programs on cyberbullying which are developed on the basis of scientific theories and research, and whose effectiveness is scientifically investigated. Only by doing so can we be confident that our well-intentioned efforts to help are targeted in an evidence-informed manner.

On a positive note, intervention programs specially developed to tackle traditional bullying based on scientific theories and tested for effectiveness exist already. For example, the peer support intervention approach (Cowie, 2000) and the Olweus Bullying Prevention Program (OBPP) (Olweus & Limber, 2010). However, the results of the peer support intervention are not unequivocal. According to Menesini, Codecasa, Benelli, and Cowie (2003), the intervention seems to prevent the escalation of negative behaviours and negative attitudes. Cowie and Olafsson (2000), on the other hand, found significant increases in bullying behaviour among students who received the peer support intervention, a result that is corroborated by Ttofi and Farrington's (2011) scholarly review. The OBPP is a "whole school" based intervention and seems to be more effective in reducing bullying. Findings from the initial study, the First Bergen Project Against Bullying (Olweus, 1994), and from the six follow-up evaluations in Norway, demonstrated a decrease in teachers' ratings and students' self-reports of being bullied and bullying others (Olweus & Limber, 2010).

Many other bullying prevention programs are based on the OBPP. One of them is the Flemish Anti-Bullying Intervention (Stevens & Van Oost, 1994). A study on the effectiveness of this intervention in primary and secondary schools showed no effects on self- and teacher-reported victimization and positive interactions between pupils, and only a decrease in self- and teacher-reported bullying in primary schools (Stevens, De Bourdeaudhuij, & Van Oost, 2000). In a second study with two post-tests, Stevens, Van Oost, and De Bourdeaudhuij (2000) found that in primary schools, seeking a teacher's help decreased and support for victims increased in the second post-test. However, in secondary schools, the positive results on attitudes found in the first post-test were not evident in the second post-test. KiVa, an intervention developed in Finland (Salmivalli, Kärnä & Poskiparta, 2010), is also a whole school approach that is based on the developers' research-based view of bullying as a group process, and is focused on the bystanders of bullying behaviour. A study on the effects of KiVa shows that the KiVa program is effective in reducing bullying and victimization, but effect sizes are small. For peer-reported victimization and bullying, they were .33 and .14, and for self-reported victimization and bullying, they were .17 and .10 (Kärnä et al., 2011). This means that although the difference in bullying frequency between the experimental group and control group(s) is significant, the intervention does not influence bullying behaviour that much. A second study that has explored the effects of KiVa compared the effects on 9 different forms of bullying. Results of the study showed a decrease in percentage of victimization ranging from 0.3% on material bullying to 0.8% on cyberbullying and 2.1% on verbal bullying (Salmivalli, Kärnä, & Poskiparta, 2011). Williford et al. (2012) further investigated the effect of the KiVa program on cyberbullying and found an effect size of .14 for victimization. The effect of KiVa for bullying depended on age: no effect was found for children above 12.9 years but for younger children they found an effect size of .29.

Other whole school approaches often have been compared in meta-analytic studies. Smith, Schneider, Smith, and Ananiadou (2004), for example, conducted a meta-analysis of 14 studies from 10 countries on whole school interventions and concluded that the majority of these studies did not find significant results with regards to self-reported bullying and victimization experiences. On the other hand, Vreeman and Caroll (2007) found that out of 10 studies, seven revealed a decrease in bullying, but that the decrease was less profound among younger children. Ttofi, Farrington, and Baldry (2008) concluded that the effectiveness of whole school programs varies and seems to depend on the way the interventions are implemented. Programs in which implementation was systematically monitored seemed to be more effective than programs without systematic monitoring (Smith, Schneider, Smith, & Ananiadou, 2004). In addition, according to Vreeman and Caroll (2007), the involvement of schools is directly related to the effectiveness of the intervention. Indeed, Olweus and Limber (2010, p. 379) state that teachers are "key agents of change with regard to adoption and implementation of the OBPP". Apparently, whole school interventions require a serious investment by schools: all children, staff, and parents need to be involved and motivated, teachers need to be trained, activities need to be planned on a school-wide, classroom-wide and individual level, and activities should start in primary grades and continue throughout all school years (National Safe Schools Framework, 2011). Hence, it is highly likely that not all schools can meet these requirements, which may explain the conflicting results.

Until now it has been unclear whether these whole-school approaches are also effective in decreasing or preventing cyberbullying. In the above-mentioned interventions, almost no attention is paid to the effects on cyberbullying. Consequently, there is hardly any evidence that these interventions are also effective in preventing bullying through the Internet and other communication methods. Some advocates of whole-school interventions state that bullying behaviour has many forms and that cyberbullying is just one form of bullying (e.g., Olweus, 2012). Salmivalli et al. (2011) also consider cyberbullying as one of the nine forms of bullying. This approach corresponds to the first approach described by Menesini, Nocentini, and Palladino in Chapter 2 of this book.

A lot of questions remained unanswered in the brief introduction of cyberbullying research we summarized above. Based on the interpretation of available research, this book provides answers and recommendations that will increase insight into the characteristics and the consequences of cyberbullying. In addition we describe in detail evidence-based ICT interventions to prevent and combat cyberbullying that will help to improve future intervention methods.

Overview of the book content

In Chapter 2 Menesini, Nocentini, and Palladino summarise recent studies regarding the definition of cyberbullying. They discuss aspects of the overlap and distinctions in the theoretical definitions of traditional and cyberbullying. Additionally, they outline the impact of several definitions for the empirical findings related to the prevalence of cyberbullying. In Chapter 3, Wolke, Lereya, and Tippett explore the findings of recent studies to determine key similarities and differences between traditional and cyberbullying. They assess whether cyberbullying arises from a unique set of social and individual risk factors, or results from similar circumstances to traditional bullying, and can therefore be considered as an extension of traditional bullying behaviours. Based on these findings they discuss whether interventions should specifically tackle cyberbullying, or address this as just a component of traditional bullying behaviour among peers. In Chapter 4, Gunther, DeSmet, Jacobs, and De Bourdeaudhuij describe the current research on the negative outcomes of traditional and cyberbullying concerning psychological health, physical health, social functioning, and behaviour problems. They explore these problems from the perspective of bullies, victims, bully-victims, and bystanders, and discuss whether the impact of cyberbullying compared to traditional bullying on the outcomes is equal, less, or more severe. Furthermore, they discuss the interrelatedness between (cyber) bullying and negative (health) outcomes.

In Part II of this book, four interventions aimed at reducing and/or preventing (cyber)bullying are explored. Each of these interventions have several common features: (a) they focus on cyberbullying as well as on traditional bullying; (b) they are theoretically based; (c) they use aspects of interventions developed for traditional bullying; (d) they do not require a substantial investment from schools; and (e) they use electronic communication tools.

The first intervention (Chapter 5), written by Sapouna, Enz, Samaras and Wolke, is a game that focuses on the reduction of victimization by letting the participant "experience" victimization and by giving them an active role: children are asked to help the victims and the game shows them the effects of their support. The intervention consists of a virtual simulation of a primary school environment in which cartoon-like virtual characters can take the role of a bully, victim, bully-assistant, victim-defender, or bystander. It is based on the proven benefits of experiential learning and on the assumption that children learn to cope effectively with bullying by role-playing different coping strategies.

The second (Chapter 6) intervention is a serious game for bystanders of bullying. It is an online, one-player puzzle game with a virtual character and virtual bullying experience scenarios in which players can choose a role and several behavioural alternatives, like ignoring the bully, standing up for the victim, etc. Thereafter, they receive immediate feedback about the consequences of the choice they made.

The third intervention (Chapter 7) has been developed for victims and bully-victims of cyberbullying, and contains three online tailored modules. The first module aims to teach participants about the connection between thoughts and behaviour. In the second module participants learn effective coping strategies in order to stop the (cyber)bullying and to decrease negative effects of victimization. In the third module participants learn how to use the Internet in a safe and secure manner and how to prevent/solve cyberbullying experiences.

The second and third interventions were developed via the Intervention Mapping protocol. This protocol consists of six steps that can be used as an iterative process for theory- and evidence-based development of health promotion interventions (Bartholomew, Parcel, Kok, Gottlieb, & Fernández, 2011). The six steps include: (a) conducting a needs assessment of the problem and the at-risk group and forming a logic model of the health problem based on the PRECEDE/PROCEED model (Green & Kreuter, 2005); (b) defining performance objectives for the intervention participants and combining them with relevant determinants to form change objectives; (c) translating change objectives into practical strategies by selecting theory-based intervention methods; (d) developing, selecting, testing, and producing intervention components in which all strategies are integrated; (e) planning for adoption and implementation of the program; and (f) anticipating the process and effect evaluation of the program.

The fourth intervention again focuses on bystanders of bullying behaviour (Chapter 8). The intervention is based on the assumption that peers learn from and influence each other, and aims to change group norms through peer interactions. Peer educators are selected by nomination and are trained in communication and social skills in real and virtual situations, and in empathy and adaptive coping strategies.

The last chapter of the book (Chapter 9) will be devoted to an integration of Part I and Part II. It will combine the 'know-how' of Part I with the practical applications of Part II. The main topics that are discussed are (a) the adequacy of the definition of cyberbullying for the selection of children who need help; (b) the differences in methods, practical applications, and content of the four intervention programs; and (c) the effects of the four interventions on the harmful effects of cyberbullying.

This book gives an in-depth and up-to-date overview of what is known about cyberbullying based on research of the past decade. It also shows the challenges that remain in understanding the cyberbullying phenomenon, in helping children to stop cyberbullying, and in developing children's resilience against the negative impact of cyberbullying.

References

Bartholomew, L. K., Parcel, G. S., Kok, G., Gottlieb, H. H., & Fernández, M. A. (2011). *Planning health promotion programs: An intervention mapping approach*. San Francisco: Jossey-Bass.

Cassidy, W., Faucher, C., & Jackson, M. (2013). Cyberbullying among youth: a comprehensive review of current international research and its implications and application to policy and practice. *School Psychology International, 34*(6), 575–612. doi:10.1177/0143034313479697

Cowie, H. (2000). Bystanding or standing by: Gender issues in coping with bullying in English schools. *Aggressive Behavior, 26*, 85–97. doi:10.1002/(SICI)1098-2337(2000)26

Cowie, H., & Olafsson, R. (2000). The Role of Peer Support in Helping the Victims of Bullying in a School with High Levels of Aggression. *School Psychology International, 21*(1), 79–95.

Dehue, F., Bolman, C., & Völlink, T. (2008). Cyberbullying: youngsters' experiences and parental perception. *Cyberpsychology & Behavior: The Impact of the Internet, Multimedia and Virtual Reality on Behavior and Society, 11*(2), 217–23. doi:10.1089/cpb.2007.0008

Dehue, F., Bolman, C., Völlink, T., & Pouwelse, M. (2012). Cyberbullying and traditional bullying in relation with adolescents' perception of parenting. *Journal of CyberTherapy & Rehabilitation, 5*(1), 25–34.

David-Ferdon, C., & Feldman Hertz, M (Eds) (2007). Youth Violence and Electronic Media: Similar Behaviors, Different Venues? *Journal of Adolescent and Health.*

Eijnden, R., van den, Vermulst, A., Rooy, T., van, & Meerkerk, G. J. (2006). *Monitor internet en jongeren: Pesten op internet en het psychosociale welbevinden van jongeren.* Factsheet van IVO: wetenschappelijk bureau voor onderzoek, expertise en advies op het gebied van leefwijzen, verslaving en daaraan gerelateerde maatschappelijke ontwikkelingen.

Finkelhor, D., Mitchell, K. J., & Wolak, J. (2000). *Online victimization: A report on the nation's youth (NCMEC 6–00–020).* Alexandria, VA: National Center for Missing & Exploited Children.

Green, L. W., & Kreuter, M. W. (2005). *Health program planning: An educational and ecological approach* (4th ed.) New York: McGraw Hill Professional.

Hasebrink, U. (2014). Children's changing online experiences in a longitudinal perspective. London, UK: EU Kids Online. http://eprints.lse.ac.uk/60083/.

Hemphill, S. A., Psych, A. K.D., Tollit, M., Smith, R., Herrenkohl, T. I., Toumbourou, J. W., & Catalano, R. F. (2012). Longitudinal predictors of cyber and traditional bullying perpetration in Australian secondary schools students. *Journal of Adolescent Health, 51*, 59–65. doi:10.1016/j.jadohealth.2011.11.019

Jacobs, N. C. L., Goossens, L., Dehue, F., Völlink, T., & Lechner, L. (2015). Dutch cyberbullying victims' experiences, perceptions, attitudes and motivations related to (coping with) cyberbullying: Focus group interviews. *Societies, 5*(1), 43–64. doi:10.3390/soc5010043

Kärnä, A., Voeten, M., Little, T. D., Poskiparta, E., Kalijonen, A., & Salmivalli, C. (2011). A large scale evaluation of the KiVa antibullying program: Grades 4–6. *Child Development, 82*, 311–330. doi:10.1111=j.1467-8624.2010.01557.x

Kiriakidis, S. P., & Kavoura, A. (2010). A review of the literature on harassment through the Internet and other electronic means. *Family & Community Health, 11*(2), 82–93.

Lazarus, R. S., & Folkman, S. (1987). Transactional theory and research on emotions and coping. *European Journal of Personality, 1*(3), 141–169. doi:10.1002/per.2410010304

Li, Q. (2007). New bottle but old wine: A research of cyberbullying in schools. *Computers in Human Behavior, 23*(4), 1777–1791. doi:10.1016/j.chb.2005.10.005

Livingstone, S., Haddon, L., Görzig, A., & Olafsson, K. (2011). *Risks and safety on the internet: the perspective of European children: full findings and policy implications from the EU Kids Online survey of 9–16 year olds and their parents in 25 countries.* London, UK: EU Kids Online. http://eprints.lse.ac.uk/33731/

Livingstone, S., Kirwil, L., Ponte, C., & Staksrud, E. (2014). In their own words: what bothers children online? *European Journal of Communication, 29*(3), 271–288. doi:10.11 77/0267323114521045

Menesini, E., Codecasa, E., Benelli, B., & Cowie, H. (2003). Enhancing children's responsibility to take action against bullying: Evaluation of a befriending intervention in Italian middle schools. *Aggressive Behavior, 29*, 1–14. doi:10.1002/ab.80012

Mesch, G.S. (2009). Parental mediation, online activities, and cyberbullying. *CyberPsychology & Behavior,12*(4), 387–393. doi:10.1089/cpb.2009.0068

Modecki, K. L., Minchin, J., Harbaugh, A. G., Guerra, N. G., & Runions, K. C. (2014). Bullying prevalence across context: a meta-analysis measuring cyber and traditional bullying. *Journal of Adolescents Health, 55*, 602–611. doi.org/10.1016/j.jadohealth.2014.06.007

National Safe Schools Framework. (2011). Anti-Bullying policy–school audit checklist and support information. Retrieved January 31, 2014, from http://www.decd.sa.gov.au/speced2/files/links/Draft_for_web_Anti_bullyin.pdf.

Ólafsson, K., Livingstone, S., & Haddon, L. (2014). *Children's Use of Online Technologies in Europe. A review of the European evidence base* (Rev. ed.). LSE, London: EU Kids Online.

Olweus, D. (1994). Annotation: Bullying at school: Basic facts and effects of a school based intervention program. *Journal of Child Psychology and Psychiatry, 35*, 1171–1190.

Olweus, D. (2012). Cyberbullying: An overrated phenomenon? *European Journal of Developmental Psychology, 9*(5), 1–19.

Olweus, D., & Limber, S.P. (2010). The Olweus Bullying Prevention Program: Implementation and evaluation over two decades. In S.R. Jimerson, S.M. Swearer, & D.L. Espelage (Eds.) *The handbook of school bullying: An international perspective* (pp. 377–402). New York, NY: Routledge.

Salmivalli, C., Kärnä, A., & Poskiparta, E. (2010). From peer putdowns to peer support: A theoretical model and how it translated into a national anti-bullying program. In S. Shimerson, S. Swearer, & D. Espelage (Eds.) *The handbook of bullying in schools: An international perspective* (pp. 441–454). New York, NY: Routledge.

Salmivalli, C., Kärnä, A., & Poskiparta, E. (2011). Counteracting bullying in Finland: The KiVa program and its effects on different forms of being bullied. *International Journal of Behavioral Development, 35*, 405–411. doi:10.1177=0165025411407457

Smith, J. D., Schneider, B. H., Smith, P. K., & Ananiadou, A. (2004). The effectiveness of whole-school anti bullying programs: a synthesis of evaluation research. *School Psychology Review, 33*(4), 547–560.

Smith, P. K., Mahdavi, J., Carvalho, M., Fisher, S., Russell, S., & Tippett, N. (2008). Cyberbullying: its nature and impact in secondary school pupils. *Journal of Child Psychology and Psychiatry, and Allied Disciplines, 49*(4), 376–85. doi:10.1111/j.1469-7610.2007.01846.x

Smith, P. K., Steffgen, G., & Sittichai R. (2013). The nature of cyberbullying, and an international network. In P. K. Smith, & G. Steffgen (Eds.), *Cyberbullying through the new media. Findings from an international network.* London: Psychology Press.

Staksrud, E., & Livingstone, S. (2009). Children and online risk. Powerless victims or resourceful participants? *Information, Communication & Society, 12*(3), 364–387. doi:10.10 80/13691180802635455

Stevens, V., De Bourdeaudhuij, I., & Van Oost, P. (2000). Bullying in Flemish schools: An evaluation of anti-bullying intervention in primary and secondary schools. *British Journal of Educational Psychology, 70*, 195–210. doi: 10.1348/000709900158056

Stevens, V. & Van Oost, P. (1994). *Pesten op School: een actieprogramma.* Kessel-Lo: Garant Uitgevers.

Stevens, V., Van Oost, P., & De Bourdeaudhuij, I. (2000). The effects of an anti-bullying intervention program on peers' attitudes and behavior. *Journal of Adolescence, 23*(1), 21–34.

Tokunaga, R.S. (2010). Following you home from school: A critical review and synthesis of research on cyberbullying victimization. *Computers in Human Behavior, 26*(3), 277–287. doi:10.1016/j.chb.2009.11.014

Ttofi, M.M., & Farrington, D.P. (2011). Effectiveness of school-based programs to reduce bullying: a systematic and meta-analytic review. *Journal of Experimental Criminology, 7*, 27–56. doi:10.1007/s11292-010-9109-1

Ttofi, M.M., Farrington, D.P., & Baldry, A.C. (2008). *Effectiveness of programmes to reduce bullying.* Stockholm, Sweden: Swedish National Council for Crime Prevention.

Valkenburg, P. M., & Peter, J. (2011). Online communication among adolescents: an integrated model of its attraction, opportunities, and risks. *Journal of Adolescent Health, 48*, 121–127. doi:10.1016/j.jadohealth.2010.08.020

Van den Akker, H., (2005). Online pesten: Geintje of kwetsend? [Online bullying: a joke or harm?] (Retrieved July 10, 2009, from: http://www.planet.nl/upload/1539825_8482_ 1115049310581-Persrapport_pestonderzoek.pdf).

Vandebosch, H., & Van Cleemput, K. (2008). Defining cyberbullying: a qualitative research into the perceptions of youngsters. *Cyberpsychology & Behavior: The Impact of the Internet, Multimedia and Virtual Reality on Behavior and Society, 11*(4), 499–503. doi:10.1089/ cpb.2007.0042

Völlink, T., Bolman, C. A. W., Dehue, F., & Jacobs, N. C. L. (2013). Coping with cyberbullying: Differences between victims, bully-victims and children not involved in bullying. *Journal of Community & Applied Social Psychology, 23*(1), 7–24. doi:10.1002/casp.2142

Völlink, T., Bolman, C. A. W., Eppingbroek, A., & Dehue, F. (2013). Emotion-focused coping worsens depressive feelings and health complaints in cyberbullied children. *Journal of Criminology, 2013*, 1–10. doi:10.1155/2013/416976

Vreeman, R. C. & Caroll, A. E. (2007). A systematic review of school-based interventions to prevent bullying. *Archives of Pediatrics & Adolescent Medicine, 161*, 78–88. doi: 10.1001/ archpedi.161.1.78

Williams, K. R., & Guerra, N. G. (2007). Prevalence and predictors of internet bullying. *Journal of Adolescent Health, 41*, 14–21. doi:10.1016/j.jadohealth.2007.08.018

Williford, A., Boulton A. I., Noland B., Little T. D., Kärnä A., & Salmivalli C. (2012). Effects of the KiVa anti-bullying program on adolescents' depression, anxiety, and perception of peers. *Journal of Abnormal Child Psychology, 40*(2), 301–302.

Ybarra, M. L., Diener-West, M., & Leaf, P. J. (2007). Examining the overlap in Internet harassment and school bullying: implications for school intervention. *Journal of Adolescent Health 41*, S42–S50. http://dx.doi.org/10.1016/j.jadohealth.2007.09.004

Ybarra, M. L., & Mitchell, K. J. (2004). Youth engaging in online harassment: associations with caregiver-child relationships, Internet use, and personal characteristics. *Journal of Adolescence, 27*(3), 319–36. doi:10.1016/j.adolescence.2004.03.007

Ybarra, M. L., Mitchell, K. J., Wolak, J., & Finkelhor, D. (2006). Examining characteristics and associated distress related to Internet harassment: findings from the Second Youth Internet Safety Survey. *Pediatrics, 118*(4), e1169–77. doi:10.1542/peds.2006-0815

2

CYBERBULLYING

Conceptual, theoretical and methodological issues

Ersilia Menesini, Annalaura Nocentini and Benedetta Emanuela Palladino

Introduction

Our relationships, interpersonal interactions and daily activities are heavily changed through the internet and the introduction of Smart phones. One of the main reasons people use the Internet and ICT is to create and maintain interpersonal relationships through chat, e-mails, and sharing photographs. This is even more evident for young people, the so-called always-on generation. The current use of new ICT, the increasingly young age at which people start using them, and the consistent amount of time spent online (Livingstone, Haddon, Görzig, & Ólafsson, 2011) are clear indications that young people benefit from the use of new technologies. However, this does not mean that they are necessarily aware of the risks involved, nor that they master the most appropriate strategies to be safe when online. Young people online can be exposed to inappropriate material (e.g., sexually explicit content, violence), sexual predators seeking to build relationships with children (i.e., paedophilia, cyber-stalking), theft of personal information, and to online forms of harassment by peers such as cyberbullying. Within the more general framework of Internet-associated risk for children, cyberbullying is included in the cluster of risks perpetrated by peers in which children can be actors as well as victims (Livingstone et al., 2011).

Internet harassment (Ybarra & Mitchell, 2004), online harassment (Finkelhor, Mitchell, & Wolak, 2000), and electronic aggression (Pyżalski, 2012) are all terms used to define aggressive acts conducted on the Internet or through ICT. Although these terms can include (and partly overlap) cyberbullying attacks, they do not necessarily coincide exactly with cyberbullying, which usually also includes features derived from the literature on traditional bullying, such as the intentionality of the perpetrators, the power imbalance between the actors and victims and the repetition of the attack.

Bullying is often defined as an intentional and aggressive act or behaviour carried out by a group or an individual repeatedly and over time against a victim who cannot easily defend him- or herself (Olweus, 1993). Three criteria are relevant in order to define an aggressive behaviour as bullying: intentionality, repetition, and imbalance of power. Extending the definition of traditional bullying to the virtual environment, cyberbullying has been defined as ". . . an aggressive, intentional act carried out by a group or individual, using electronic forms of contact, repeatedly and over time against a victim who cannot easily defend him or herself" (Smith et al., 2008, p. 376). Considering the ICT context, new criteria have been added and discussed, such as the anonymity that occurs when the victim does not know the identity of the bully, the publicity that characterises the acts where a large audience is involved, the permanent trace of online activities (e.g., the impossibility of removing permanently anything shared online), and the lack of supervision (Dooley, Pyżalski, & Cross, 2009; Hinduja & Patchin, 2007; Kowalski & Limber, 2007; Menesini & Nocentini, 2009; Menesini et al., 2012; Nocentini et al., 2010; Palladino, Nocentini, & Menesini, 2011; Tokunaga, 2010; Wingate, Minney, & Guadagno, 2013). Several researchers have also discussed the specific meaning of the criteria associated with traditional bullying in the cyber context and in the definition of cyberbullying (Menesini et al., 2012; Nocentini et al., 2010; Sticca & Perren, 2013). Although having a clear definition is essential to get insight into the magnitude of the problem and the consequences, unfortunately, we are far from a unanimous consensus regarding the criteria that are essential for the definition of cyberbullying.

Given the relevance of the association between cyberbullying and traditional bullying, we will discuss the areas of overlap and distinction between the two constructs, considering the following level of analysis:

a   The theoretical-definitional criteria;
b   The empirical evidence related to the measurement;
c   The empirical evidence related to prevalence.

a. The theoretical-definitional criteria

As Wingate and colleagues assert (Wingate, Minney, & Guadagno, 2013 p. 88), "The cyberbullying literature has suffered from the absence of a 'gold standard' definition." Researchers have differed significantly in their inclusion of the criteria used to define traditional bullying in their operational definitions of cyberbullying and in the specific meaning they assume in the cyber context (Dooley et al., 2009; Smith et al., 2008; Willard, 2007). At the same time, new criteria that are specific to the ICT environment and can be considered to define cyberbullying, such as anonymity and publicity, have also been implemented (Menesini et al., 2012).

In a qualitative cross-cultural study (Nocentini et al., 2010), the issue of "intention to harm," a main characteristic of all aggressive acts (e.g., Berkowitz, 1993), appears to be an important criterion for bullying as it is strictly related to the effects on the victim. Without "intention to harm," the behaviour is perceived as a joke. Intentionality was the second most important criterion to define cyberbullying in a cross-cultural study by Menesini et al. (2012) regarding how adolescents perceive the definition of cyberbullying. Overall, we can conclude that the criterion of intentionality needs to be included in the definition of cyberbullying. The important question is whether to measure this characteristic using the perpetrator's or the victim's perspective (e.g., "wants to hurt" versus "felt hurt"). If we look at the cyberbully's perspective, his/her level of awareness is very important. If we look at the victim's perspective, the psychological and perceived consequences matter the most. In this regard, the victim's perception of the attack can be close to and partly overlap the other important criterion: the imbalance of power. In fact the perception of the perpetrator's intention and the personal difficulties in reacting can elicit a growing sense of helplessness from the victim.

Although it is neither easy nor clear to determine whether someone is considered powerless in relation to someone else in cyberspace, the relevance of the criterion of "imbalance of power" is strongly confirmed across all the countries involved in Menesini's study (2012) and across all types of behaviour (Menesini et al., 2012). The imbalance of power causes a feeling of powerlessness for the victim and also makes it difficult to defend oneself (Olweus, 1993; Smith & Brain, 2000). In our view, a view supported by other researchers (e.g., Langos, 2012), the meaning of this criterion is not altered in the cyber context, signifying that cyberbullying, just like traditional bullying behaviour, puts the victim in a position where he/she cannot easily defend himself/herself. What is different in the cyber context, however, is the way in which this powerlessness comes about. In the traditional context, this is a consequence of physical, social and psychological strength of the bullies. In the virtual domain, the imbalance of power is mainly due to psychological threats and attacks often happening in a public context. At the same time the perception of loneliness and of the social impact on the victim can be amplified by the public exposure of the victim (number of comments, sharing, visualizations and "likes" on the web). In conclusion, power imbalance remains an essential criterion in defining cyberbullying.

The relevance of repetition in cyberbullying seems to be still open, albeit not appearing so significant from a qualitative study by us (Menesini et al., 2012). This criterion can partly be useful to determine the difference between cyberbullying and aggression as it is in face-to-face context. Bullying is repeated by definition whereas aggressive behaviours can happen just once (Dooley et al., 2009; Menesini & Nocentini, 2009; Nocentini et al., 2010). Langos (2012) clarified further the role of repetition in relation to direct and indirect forms of cyberbullying. Direct cyberbullying occurs when the cyberbully attacks the victim directly (private e-mail or chat), as opposed to indirect cyberbullying when communications are posted to more public areas of cyberspace (e.g., public forums such as social media sites, blogs, web pages, video-sharing web sites). Repetition is needed in the direct cyberbullying context, whereas in indirect cyberbullying, repetition occurs by virtue of the arena in which the behaviour takes place since the post or the message can stay on the web for a long time and many people can see it.

With respect to "anonymity," results from both qualitative and quantitative studies (Nocentini et al. 2010; Menesini et al. 2012) suggest that this criterion is not a requisite for labelling an action as cyberbullying, yet it is relevant because it can reveal the nature and the severity of the attack and the victim's reaction. Similarly, the criterion of publicity was not considered as necessary to define cyberbullying. However, when there is a public cyberbullying attack, the huge audience, the number of views and comments can contribute to the severity of the situation and make the victim feeling extremely hurt and rejected.

Overall, we can conclude that there is wide agreement in the literature on the definition of cyberbullying based on two main criteria of intentionality and power imbalance. Therefore, a workable definition should include these two characteristics. More controversial is the consideration of repetition in the virtual domain and of the two cyber-specific criteria: publicity and anonymity, although they add information about the perceived severity of the acts.

b. The empirical evidence related to the measurement

Problems regarding the definition of cyberbullying have subsequently triggered problems in the measurement of the phenomenon. With regard to cyberbullying and its relation to the measurement of traditional bullying, the literature demonstrates two different approaches. The first approach measures cyberbullying with one or two items as a form of bullying behaviour. The second approach measures cyberbullying as a separate construct through multiple items specifically aimed at analysing the different aspects of the problem.

The first approach considers bullying as a broad construct empirically defined by different types of behaviours: physical bullying, verbal bullying, relational bullying, and cyberbullying. This approach is based on the consideration that cyberbullying is strictly related to traditional bullying and that the definitional criteria of the two constructs are the same. For example, in the Olweus Bully/ Victim Questionnaire (OBVQ: Olweus, 2012a), following provision of a definition of bullying, students respond to a global question about whether they had been bullied in the past couple of months. This general question is followed by eight questions about various forms or ways of being bullied covering the four main categories of verbal, physical, indirect, or relational bullying, and finally two questions on cyberbullying via mobile phone or the Internet (Olweus, 2012a). This approach implies that children and adolescents recognise and are able to provide answers about the general category of bullying and cyberbullying instead of specific behaviours included under this umbrella.

The second approach considers cyberbullying as a separate construct from traditional bullying, although correlated with it. It measures specifically and more analytically different types of behaviours regarding relational cyberbullying, verbal or visual attacks, technically sophisticated cyberbullying, bullying by mobile phone, and bullying by Internet (Berne et al., 2013). Studies have shown that different types of cyberbullying can be classified according to specific criteria, such as the covert or overt nature of the acts, the electronic devices/media used, or the specific behaviours involved (e.g., exclusion, verbal attack, photos, theft of personal information) (Menesini et al., 2012; Nocentini et al., 2010; Schultze-Krumbholz & Scheithauer, 2009; Slonje et al., 2013; Slonje & Smith, 2008; Spears, Slee, Owens, & Johnson, 2009). This last classification based on specific behaviours is the same type of classification used for traditional bullying, where verbal, physical, and relational types of behaviours are generally differentiated.

Both approaches show strengths and limitations (Menesini & Nocentini, 2009). The strength of the first approach (a macro-category of bullying comprising also cyberbullying) is that it ensures that we are referring to the correct definition of cyberbullying, including the three criteria of traditional bullying. By contrast, when using cyberbullying as a separate construct, the relevant criteria of traditional bullying need to be reported explicitly. In their review, Berne et al. (2013) found that most definitions used in 44 different instruments focused on the fact that cyberbullying behaviour occurs through electronic devices/media and mentions the criterion of the intention to harm another person. The other bullying criteria (repetition and imbalance of power) were emphasised much less while the specific cyberbullying criteria were not present at all. The first approach does not consider cyberbullying as a multidimensional construct, which can limit the understanding of the phenomenon and the reliability of the measurement (Menesini & Nocentini, 2009). For instance, literature underlined the question of whether consequences in terms of psychological symptoms can be different as a result of different acts (e.g., verbal attack versus sending a compromising picture or video), or whether the definitional criteria can be relevant only for specific cyberbullying acts (Menesini & Nocentini, 2009). These considerations underscore the relevance of having a more complex definition and taking into account the different types of cyberbullying behaviours.

The practical implications of these two different approaches become relevant for interventions. For example, which measures have to be used to assess the need for intervention? We can answer this question by taking into consideration different types of interventions. The first approach – that is, the global question about having been cyberbullied or being a cyberbully – is more person-oriented. Through this measure we can detect those who are aware that they are cyberbullies or cybervictims. Generally, this measure implies a higher level of severity of behaviours as compared to the multiple-item scale, normally due to a higher level of involvement in the phenomenon and a certain degree of personal awareness of the problem. Consequently, we think that this approach can be used to detect more serious cases of young people involved and to plan secondary and tertiary prevention interventions for students at risk.

On the contrary, the second approach (the multiple-item scale) is more behaviour-oriented and relevant to detecting both the least and the most frequent forms of cyberbullying as well as the early manifestations of cyberbullying. For instance, we can detect those specific behaviours that may have occurred only once or twice and often are not well recognized and categorized as cyberbullying. At the same time, if the scale reports a specific cut-off, it allows us to classify people as involved or not, and we can also have a measure of involvement in terms of frequency and seriousness. Through this approach, we are able to select the most and the least serious cases of cyberbullying and to plan accordingly selected interventions for those young people who are highly involved and universal, primary prevention interventions for those who are less involved.

All of these types of measurements are conducted by self-report measures. Problems related to the effects of social desirability on self-report measurements suggest the need for other informants. To date, it has been difficult to measure the nature and extent of cyberbullying using other informants. Since cyberbullying, by its nature, is less visible and children often do not talk about it with adults (Slonje, Smith, & Frisén, 2013), it can be less accurately detected by peers and by adults, such as teachers and parents (Menesini et al., 2012). Therefore detecting the involvement of children in cyberbullying or cybervictimisation using adult informants is difficult, especially with older children, because their online activity is less monitored. Peer evaluation is also quite difficult to detect reliably, since cyberbullying occurs by definition across different online formats and with various groups of peers. It is not sufficient to use classmates' information as we do with traditional bullying.

c. The empirical evidence related to prevalence

An important implication of definitional clarity is related to measurement problems, as was summarised by Olweus (2012a) in his provocatively titled article "Cyberbullying: An overrated phenomenon?" Olweus claimed that cyberbullying is characterised by low prevalence rates and is completely absorbed by the traditional roles of bullying, given that it has not given rise to "new" victims and bullies that were not already involved in some form of traditional bullying, and, overall, is an exaggerated phenomenon. The question becomes: is this provocative assertion true?

It is a difficult question to answer because the phenomenon was investigated using different instruments focused on partially different operationalisations of different definitions of the construct, even with different labels used to name it (e.g., electronic bullying, online aggression, country-specific labels) (Berne et al., 2013; Menesini & Nocentini, 2009; Nocentini et al., 2010; Tokunaga, 2010; Wingate et al., 2013). However, when searching for a realistic estimate of the presence of cyberbullying, we should be aware that the instruments developed use different time frames (e.g., the past couple of months, in the last year, during your life) (Hinduja & Patchin, 2012; Menesini, Nocentini, & Calussi, 2011; Menesini & Nocentini, 2009; Tokunaga, 2010). We should also consider that the ICTs are evolving quickly and, for example, since the launch of smart phones, the initial distinction between mobile phone and Internet cyberbullying is no longer supported by evidence (Slonje, Smith, & Frisén, 2013). Results of a review of cyberbullying prevalence rates show a significant presence of cyberbullying in all countries analysed (Garaigordobil, 2011): approximately 40% to 55% of students are involved in some way (victims, perpetrators, or observers); between 20% and 50% reported experiences of victimisation; and only between 2% and 7% have suffered severely, with variation according to the country, ages of the samples, and the time frame in which information was requested. Reviewing available data, Tokunaga (2010) stresses that cyberbullying victimisation is not limited to an insignificant portion of children and teens. He reports that an average of 20% to 40% of youths were cybervictimised during their life, while, limiting the time frame (e.g., the last year), the figure naturally decreases. In contrast, he reports that data from a national telephone survey (YISS) showed an incidence rate of cybervictimisation of around 6.5% (Ybarra, 2004; Ybarra & Mitchell, 2004), suggesting that this deflated result could be caused by the use of two dichotomous items about Internet harassment. Reviewing 35 papers published in peer-reviewed journals, Sabella, Patchin, and Hinduja (2013) reported that, on average, 24% of students had been cyberbullied and 17% admitted to having engaged in cyberbullying behaviours during their lifetime.

In the face-to-face context, the literature shows higher estimates of bullying and victimisation. In the World Health Organization's Health Behaviour in School-Aged Children Survey (HBSC: see Craig & Harel, 2004), the average prevalence of victims and bullies across the 35 countries involved for the past couple of months prior to survey administration was 34% and 35% respectively for the less severe forms and 11% for the most severe. Rigby and Smith (2011) explored a possible longitudinal trend in prevalence between 1990 and 2009, analysing studies in different countries that collected data over time and making use of the same questionnaire. Despite the same methodological issues implied in these studies, they reported a decrease in the prevalence of victimisation, although in a minority of countries this was not the case. They also showed some indications that cyberbullying had increased during the period of 1999 to 2006. The authors attributed the decreasing trend in bullying to the effectiveness of interventions or to the different and more restricted definition of bullying widely adopted by researchers.

All the cited studies underline the importance of taking into consideration cyberbullying as a specific dimension of bullying, but Olweus's provocative statement still cannot be completely rejected. In attempts to disentangle the possible conceptual overlap, some studies have been conducted in order to analyse the co-occurrence of both bullying and cyberbullying and the differences in predictors (Gradinger, Strohmeier, & Spiel, 2009; Kowalski & Limber, 2013; Low & Espelage, 2013). Gradinger and colleagues (2009) analysed the co-occurrence by creating groups of bullies (e.g., traditional, cyber, or both), victims (e.g., traditional, cyber, or both), and bully-victims and tested gender differences. The authors highlight the presence of an overlap between traditional and cyber forms of victimisation for both genders, while for the traditional and cyber forms of bullying they found the same overlap only for males. Dehue et al. (2012) showed that 40.1% of the youths were not involved in either form of bullying behaviour, 7.1% of all youths were involved in only cyberbullying, 30.1% were involved in only traditional bullying, and 22.8% were involved in both forms of bullying behaviour as either bully, victim, or bully-victim. Looking at possible outcomes of the involvement in bullying in both contexts, we still found controversial results. Categorising the participants as belonging to one of four groups (victims, bullies, bully-victims, and not involved) for both bullying and cyberbullying, Kowalski and Limber (2013) found a substantial overlap in the involvement in both forms, with bully-victim groups, particularly in the cyber context, having the most negative scores on most measures of psychological health, physical health, and academic performance. By contrast, Low and Espelage (2013), analysing the impact of different predictors on both phenomena, found that at only a simple, bivariate level did cyberbullying appear to have significant overlap with non-physical bullying, while longitudinal analyses reveal less overlap.

In conclusion, some findings lead us to consider cyberbullying as a logical extension of traditional bullying, which means we can apply our knowledge of traditional bullying to cyberbullying. Other findings suggest that, although sharing certain features, cyberbullying and traditional bullying are distinct types of bullying. It is possible to agree with Olweus that data do not support the mass media-endorsed idea of an increase in the presence of cyberbullying and its extreme pervasiveness, even more so than bullying (Hinduja & Patchin, 2012; Olweus, 2012a), but at the same time it is hard to agree with a complete denial of this phenomenon (Smith, 2012). Perhaps the best approach is to give it the right value (Menesini, 2012). In this view, the prefix "cyber" could be seen as the context of bullying, thus placing cyberbullying research in the "proper context" along with traditional bullying, as asserted by Olweus (2012b) in his replies to the comments regarding his article questioning whether cyberbullying is an overrated phenomenon. Getting back to our working definition, we can assume that cyberbullying fits under the broad banner of bullying, given the strong relevance of intentionality and power imbalance. At the same time, other cyber-specific features like anonymity and publicity should be considered to understand the context and the phenomenon.

Concluding remarks

The present review supports a definition of cyberbullying as a highly correlated although distinct phenomenon when compared to traditional bullying. Although the overlap between the two constructs in terms of definitional criteria, measurement instruments, and prevalence is large, we think that cyberbullying maintains certain specificities that need to be considered. Recognising both overlap and differences is important for the implications in terms of intervention.

In particular, as reported by Sabella et al. (2013), interventions focused on cyberbullying as a priority at the expense of traditional bullying are not justified. Both problems are different manifestations of the same underlying construct, and thus both phenomena should be considered in interventions.

The virtual domain has certain characteristics and specificities that need to be taken into consideration, however, in order to promote specific useful coping strategies. For example, blocking or banning a cyberbully, changing personal account details, or adopting safer online behaviours are all specific cyber-coping strategies (Slonje, Smith, & Frisén, 2013). However, this might not be enough: given that the roots of cyberbullying lie in the face-to-face context, more efforts are needed to examine the general processes of bullying and coping strategies, such as possible behaviours of bystanders and the idea of searching for social support to defend victims.

In order to detect the behaviours of cyberbullies and cybervictims and to target them through intervention, the scale approach seems to be more useful and effective. At the same time other measures able to grasp the role of bystanders and to understand which is their function in cyber-attacks can help in understanding how to involve these participants and how to develop better preventive approaches to this problem.

References

Berkowitz, L. (1993). *Aggression: Its causes, consequences, and control.* New York: McGraw-Hill.

Berne, S., Frisén, A., Schultze-Krumbholz, A., Scheithauer, H., Naruskov, K., Luik, P., Katzer, C., Erentaite, R., & Zukauskiene, R. (2013). Cyberbullying assessment instruments: A systematic review. *Aggression and Violent Behavior, 18*, 320–334.

Craig, W. M., & Harel, Y. (2004). Bullying, physical fighting and victimization. In C. Currie, C. Roberts, A. Morgan, R. Smith, W. Settertobulte, & O. Samdal, et al. (eds.), *Young people's health in context: Health Behaviour in School-aged Children (HBSC) study: International report from the 2001/2002 survey* (pp. 133–144). Copenhagen, Denmark: World Health Organization, Regional Office for Europe.

Dehue, F., Bolman, C., Völlink, T., & Pouwelse, M. (2012). Cyberbullying and traditional bullying in relation with adolescents' perception of parenting. *Journal of CyberTherapy & Rehabilitation, 5*(1), 25–34.

Dooley, J. J., Pyżalski, J., & Cross, D. (2009). Cyberbullying versus face-to-face bullying: A theoretical and conceptual review. *Zeitschrift fur Psychologie/Journal of Psychology, 217*(4), 182–188.

Finkelhor, D., Mitchell, J. K., & Wolak, J. (2000). *Online victimization: A report on the nation's youth.* National Center for Missing and Exploited Children.

Garaigordobil, M. (2011). Prevalencia y consecuencias del cyberbullying: una revisión. *International Journal of Psychology and Psychological Therapy, 11*(2), 233–254.

Gradinger, P., Strohmeier, D., & Spiel, C. (2009). Traditional Bullying and Cyberbullying. *Zeitschrift Für Psychologie / Journal of Psychology, 217*(4), 205–213. doi:10.1027/0044-3409.217.4.205

Hinduja, S. & Patchin, J. W. (2007). Offline consequences of online victimization: School violence and delinquency. *Journal of School Violence, 6*(3), 89–112.

Hinduja, S., & Patchin, J. W. (2012). Cyberbullying: Neither an epidemic nor a rarity. *European Journal of Developmental Psychology, 9*(5), 539–543. doi:10.1080/17405629.2012.706448

Kowalski, R. M., & Limber, S. P. (2007). Electronic bullying among middle school students. *Journal of Adolescent Health, 41*, S22–30.

Kowalski, R. M., & Limber, S. P. (2013). Psychological, physical, and academic correlates of cyberbullying and traditional bullying. *Journal of Adolescent Health, 53*(1 Suppl), S13–20. doi:10.1016/j.jadohealth.2012.09.018

Langos, C. (2012). Cyberbullying: The challenge to define. *Cyberpsychology, Behavior & Social Networking, 15*(6), 285–289.

Livingstone, S., Haddon, L., Görzig, A., & Ólafsson, K., with members of the EU Kids Online network (2011). *Risks and safety on the internet. The perspective of European children. Full findings and policy implications from the EU Kids Online survey of 9–16 year olds and their parents.* LSE, London: EU Kids Online.

Low, S., & Espelage, D. (2013). Differentiating cyber bullying perpetration from non-physical bullying: Commonalities across race, individual, and family predictors. *Psychology of Violence, 3*(1), 39–52. doi:10.1037/a0030308

Menesini, E. (2012) Cyberbullying: the right value of the phenomenon. Comments on the paper "Cyberbullying: An over-rated phenomenon?". *European Journal of Developmental Psychology, 9*(5), 544–552.

Menesini, E., & Nocentini, A. (2009). Cyberbullying definition and measurement: Some critical considerations. *Zeitschrift fur Psychologie/Journal of Psychology, 217*(4), 230–232.

Menesini, E., Nocentini, A., & Calussi, P. (2011). The measurement of cyberbullying: Dimensional structure and relative item severity and discrimination. *Cyberpsychology, Behavior and Social Networking, 14*(5), 267–274.

Menesini, E., Nocentini, A., Palladino, B. E., Frisén, A., Berne, S., Ortega Ruiz, R., Calmaestra, J., Scheithauer, H., Schultze-Krumbholz, A., Luik, P., Naruskov, K., Blaya, C., Berthaud, J., & Smith, P. K. (2012). Cyberbullying definition among adolescents: A comparison across six European countries. *Cyberpsychology, behavior and social networking, 15*(9), 455–463.

Nocentini, A., Calmaestra, J., Schultze-Krumbholz, A., Scheithauer, H., Ortega, R., & Menesini, E. (2010). Cyberbullying: Labels, behaviours and definition in three European countries. *Australian Journal of Guidance & Counselling, 20*(2), 129–142.

Olweus, D. (1993). *Bullying in school: What we know and what we can do.* Oxford: Blackwell.

Olweus, D. (2012a). Cyberbullying: An overrated phenomenon? *European Journal of Developmental Psychology, 9*(5), 520–538. doi:10.1080/17405629.2012.682358

Olweus, D. (2012b). Comments on cyberbullying article: A rejoinder. *European Journal of Developmental Psychology, 9*(5), 559–568. doi:10.1080/17405629.2012.705086

Palladino, B. E., Nocentini, A., & Menesini, E. (2011). Definition of cyberbullying among Italian adolescents: to what extent do criteria and type of behaviour matter? An investigation through COST scenarios. *Giornale di Psicologia dello sviluppo – Journal of Developmental Psychology, 100*, 94–103.

Pyżalski, J. (2012). From cyberbullying to electronic aggression: Typology of the phenomenon. *Emotional and Behavioral Difficulties, 17*(3–4), 305–317.

Rigby, K., & Smith, P. K. (2011). Is school bullying really on the rise? *Social Psychology of Education, 14*(4), 441–455. doi:10.1007/s11218-011-9158-y

Sabella, R. A, Patchin, J. W., & Hinduja S. (2013). Cyberbullying myths and realities. *Computers in Human Behavior, 29*(6), 2703–2711.

Schultze-Krumbholz, A., & Scheithauer, H. (2009). Social-behavioral correlates of cyberbullying in a German student Zeitschrift für Psychologie/Journal of Psychology, Vol 217(4), 2009, 224-226. http://dx.doi.org/10.1027/0044-3409.217.4.224sample.

Slonje, R., & Smith, P. K. (2008). Cyberbullying: Another main type of bullying? *Scandinavian Journal of Psychology, 49*, 147–154.

Slonje, R., Smith, P. K., & Frisén, A. (2013). The nature of cyberbullying, and strategies for prevention. *Computers in Human Behavior, 29*, 26–32.

Smith, P. K. (2012). Cyberbullying: Challenges and opportunities for a research program – A response to Olweus (2012). *European Journal of Developmental Psychology, 9*(5), 553–558.

Smith, P. K., & Brain, P. (2000). Bullying in schools: Lessons from two decades of research. *Aggressive Behavior, 26,* 1–9.

Smith, P. K., Mahdavi, J., Carvalho, M., Fisher, S., Russell, S. N., & Tippett, N. (2008). Cyberbullying: its nature and impact in secondary school pupils. *Journal of Child Psychology & Psychiatry, 49,* 376–385.

Spears, B., Slee, P., Owens, L., & Johnson, B. (2009). Behind the scenes and screens: Insights into the human dimension of covert and cyberbullying. *Zeitschrift für Psychologie/Journal of Psychology, 217*(4), 189-196. http://dx.doi.org/10.1027/0044-3409.217.4.189

Sticca, F., & Perren, S. (2013). Is cyberbullying worse than traditional bullying? Examining the differential roles of medium, publicity, and anonymity for the perceived severity of bullying. *Journal of Youth and Adolescence, 42*(5), 739–50. doi:10.1007/s10964-012-9867-3.

Tokunaga, R.S. (2010). Following you home from school: A critical review and synthesis of research on cyberbullying victimization. *Computers in Human Behavior, 26*(3), 277–287. doi:10.1016/j.chb.2009.11.014

Willard, E.N. (2007). *Cyberbullying and cyberthreats: Responding to the challenge of online social aggression, threats, and distress.* Illinois, USA: Malloy, Inc.

Wingate, V.S., Minney, J. A., & Guadagno, R. E. (2013). Sticks and stones may break your bones, but words will always hurt you: A review of cyberbullying. *Social Influence, 8*(2–3), 87–106. doi:10.1080/15534510.2012.730491

Ybarra, M.L. (2004). Linkages between depressive symptomatology and Internet harassment among young regular Internet users. *Cyberpsychology & behavior: the impact of the Internet, multimedia and virtual reality on behavior and society, 7*(2), 247–57. doi:10.1089/109493104323024500

Ybarra, M. L., & Mitchell, J. K. (2004). Online aggressor/targets, aggressors, and targets: A comparison of associated youth characteristics. *Journal of Child Psychology and Psychiatry, 45*(7), 1308–1316.

3

INDIVIDUAL AND SOCIAL DETERMINANTS OF BULLYING AND CYBERBULLYING

Dieter Wolke, Tanya Lereya and Neil Tippett

Introduction

Delineating the risk factors for involvement in cyberbullying is crucial for identifying those who are in need of support, and enables interventions to be developed and targeted towards specific at-risk groups. Some researchers argue that it
is incorrect to consider cyberbullying as a distinct phenomenon; rather cyberbullying is a part of, or an extension of, traditional bullying behaviours (Li, 2007;
Olweus, 2012). Hence, it is important to compare risk factors for cyberbullying with those for traditional bullying to identify key similarities and differences
between the behaviours, determining whether cyberbullying is due to a unique
set of individual and social risks, or arises from similar circumstances as found
for traditional bullying. Identifying these similarities and differences can help in
developing targeted interventions that go beyond the school environment, and
may provide greater encouragement for anti-bullying and anti-cyberbullying programs to work together to eradicate all forms of bullying.

This chapter considers individual and social risk factors that have been associated with involvement in both traditional and cyber forms of bullying. Five
main groups of risk factors which have been previously considered in relation
to traditional bullying (Wolke & Stanford, 1999) are addressed: (a) demographic
characteristics including age, sex, and ethnicity; (b) psychological characteristics
including self-esteem, internalising behaviours, empathy, and aggression; (c) family and household factors such as parenting, socioeconomic status, and sibling relationships; (d) school and peer factors such as school climate and peer relationships;
and finally (e) availability and use of technology, which considers the frequency,
patterns, and nature of children's electronic interactions.

In reviewing factors that may be differentially related to traditional and cyberbullying, there is a clear need to establish whether these are two separate types of

bullying, or whether cyberbullying is simply an extension of traditional bullying, which is used to attain the same aims (e.g., social dominance, peer acceptance, and access to resources) (Volk, Camilleri, Dane, & Marini, 2012), but carried out through different means. Evidence tends to suggest the latter, as many studies report a significant overlap between involvement in traditional and cyber forms of bullying (Beran & Li, 2008; Dehue, Bolman, & Völlink, 2008; Gradinger, Strohmeier, & Spiel, 2009; Li, 2007; Raskauskas & Stoltz, 2007; Smith et al., 2008; Ybarra & Mitchell, 2004a). Few children appear to only be involved in cyberbullying; many also experience traditional forms of bullying at school. Dehue, Bolman, Völlink, and Pouwelse (2012) found among a sample of adolescents that only 7.1% were exclusively involved in cyberbullying, while 22.8% had experienced both cyberbullying and traditional bullying, as either a victim, bully, or bully-victim. Furthermore, roles taken in traditional bullying appear to transfer over into cyberbullying, whereby victims at school are more likely to be cybervictims, and school bullies more often perpetrate cyberbullying (Raskauskas & Stoltz, 2007; Smith et al., 2008; Vandebosch & Van Cleemput, 2009). For example, Smith et al. (2008) found that over 80% of cybervictims were traditional victims, and three quarters of cyberbullies were also traditional bullies. Raskauskas and Stoltz (2007) compared roles of involvement in traditional and cyberbullying, finding that 85% of cybervictims were also traditional victims, and 94% of cyberbullies were traditional bullies. Olweus (2012) reports that only 10% of children involved in cyberbullying have not experienced traditional bullying, and argues that few new victims or bullies are created by cyberbullying – rather, bullying is just transferred from one setting (the school) to another (the virtual world).

As such, the strongest risk factor for involvement in cyberbullying is whether children participate in traditional bullying. Juvonen and Gross (2008) found that after controlling for other risk factors, the experience of being bullied at school led to a seven-fold increase in the risk of being victimised online. While much of the literature suggests that bullying roles remain consistent across settings, an additional link between traditional victimisation and cyberbullying perpetration has been speculated, whereby children who are victimised at school enact revenge on their attackers from the safety of their own home. First suggested by Ybarra and Mitchell (2004a) this has come to be termed as the "revenge of the nerds hypothesis" (Vandebosch & Van Cleemput, 2009). There appears to be some support for this; among 65 cyberbullies identified by Smith et al. (2008), almost two thirds were also victimised at school. The authors suggest that many of these may have been traditional bully-victims, and this is supported by Dehue et al. (2012), who found that a greater proportion of traditional bully-victims cyberbullied others when compared with traditional victims. Despite this, other studies have reported no association between traditional victimisation and cyberbullying perpetration (Raskauskas & Stoltz, 2007; Slonje & Smith, 2008).

Although there is still some debate over the exact relationship between roles in traditional and cyberbullying, it is clear that there is a significant overlap, and the two forms of victimisation are strongly linked. Many incidents of cyberbullying can be seen to originate within the school environment, as most victims of cyber-bullying know their attacker in real life (Mishna, Khoury-Kassabri, Gadalla, & Daciuk, 2012; Slonje & Smith, 2008; Smith et al., 2008). As the findings suggest, cyberbullying is not a new type of bullying, but rather a continuation of traditional bullying behaviours, which is carried out through virtual rather than face-to-face interactions. Considering traditional and cyberbullying as extensions of the same behaviour has two important implications in identifying potential risk factors. Firstly, we would expect risk factors to be associated with traditional and cyberbullying roles in fairly similar ways. Secondly, valid conclusions are only possible if comparisons can be made between those who are involved in only traditional or only cyberbullying, and those involved in both traditional and cyberbullying. Such comparisons have rarely been performed, and where this has been attempted, there have been too few cases of children only involved in cyberbullying to allow for any meaningful comparisons (Dehue et al., 2012; Gradinger et al., 2009). Thus, these two considerations need to be kept in mind when examining existing research on risk factors.

Demographic characteristics

Age

Self-reports of traditional victimisation steadily decrease with age (Craig et al., 2009; Olweus, 1993; Solberg & Olweus, 2003). More children report being victims at primary school than at secondary school (Finkelhor, Ormrod, Turner, & Hamby, 2005; Nansel et al., 2001), and this decrease has been attributed to older children acquiring social skills and coping strategies that enable them to deal more effectively with incidents of bullying (Smith, Madsen, & Moody, 1999). The most recent data from a United Kingdom household survey (Tippett, Wolke, & Platt, 2013) shows a similar trend of reducing victimisation over time during adolescence in traditional bullying. Similarly, the number of bully-victims has been found to decline with increasing age (Solberg, Olweus, & Endresen, 2007). Rates of bullying perpetration vary less by age, and reach their peak during early adolescence (Analitis et al., 2009; Nansel et al., 2001; Scheithauer, Hayer, Petermann, & Jugert, 2006), which may result from the tendency of bullies to pick on children who are younger than themselves (Smith et al., 1999).

Although a strong determinant of traditional bullying, the relationship between age and cyberbullying is less clear due to a lack of consistent findings. Most studies report no association with cybervictimisation (Beran & Li, 2008; Patchin & Hinduja, 2006; Wolak, Mitchell, & Finkelhor, 2007). For example, a comparative study of cyberbullying in Italy, England, and Spain found that rates of victimisation through both mobile phones and the Internet did not differ across a sample of 12 to 16 year old adolescents (Genta et al., 2011). Others, however, find significant variation by age, indicating that victimisation either increases with age, reaching its peak at around 13 to 14 years (Kowalski & Limber, 2013; Ybarra, Mitchell,

Wolak, & Finkelhor, 2006) or shows a similar decline to traditional victimisation, occurring more frequently among primary than secondary school children (Dehue et al., 2008; Mishna et al., 2012; Slonje & Smith, 2008). A meta-synthesis suggests a curvilinear relationship, whereby rates of victimisation (not including bully-victims) increase up until the ages of 12 to 14 years and then gradually decline thereafter (Tokunaga, 2010).

Fewer studies have considered cyberbullying perpetration. However, Mishna et al. (2012) found self-reported rates of cyberbullying perpetration increased with age among a sample of middle and high school students, despite younger students more often being victims of cyberbullying. Similarly, Kowalski and Limber (2007) found 7th to 8th graders (aged 12 to 14 years) were twice as likely to cyberbully others than 5th graders (aged 10 to 11 years). This increase across early-to-mid-adolescence is reported in several studies (Hinduja & Patchin, 2008b; Wolak et al., 2007); however, by late adolescence rates of cyberbullying perpetration appear to decline substantially (Williams & Guerra, 2007). Despite only limited findings, a similar effect has been found for cyber bully-victims, with self-report rates highest among mid-adolescents (Mishna et al., 2012; Sourander et al., 2010). An additional consideration concerns the type of media used for cyberbullying, as this may vary with age. Smith et al. (2008) found that older students were more likely to have cyberbullied others using text messages, photo/video clips, and instant messaging, but less so through other means.

Sex differences

Early studies found that males were more often involved in traditional bullying than females (Boulton & Underwood, 1992; O'Moore & Hillery, 1989; Whitney & Smith, 1993); however, more recent research suggests that these sex differences are less clear than first thought (Seals & Young, 2002; Stassen Berger, 2007). Boys do appear more likely to be bullies and bully-victims (Haynie et al., 2001; Nansel et al., 2001; Scheithauer et al., 2006), but are as likely, or only slightly more likely, than girls to be victimised (Analitis et al., 2009; Espelage, Mebane, & Swearer, 2004; Veenstra et al., 2005). A meta-analysis by Cook, Williams, Guerra, Kim, and Sadek (2010) found bully and bully-victim roles to be moderately associated with the male sex, but only a weak relationship was observed for victimisation. Type of bullying is an important consideration; young males have been found to use direct forms of bullying (Wolke, Woods, Stanford, & Schulz, 2001) and to be more often physically bullied by their peers (Finkelhor et al., 2005; Nansel et al., 2001), while females more often bully others and are bullied through indirect forms (Craig, 1998; Crick & Grotpeter, 1996; Nansel et al., 2001). These sex differences are only found in younger children, however, and disappear by around 12 years of age (Analitis et al., 2009; Wolke et al., 2001). Meta-analytic evidence suggests that most of those who are involved in one form of bullying (e.g., direct) are also involved in other forms (e.g., indirect or relational), with adolescent girls tending to use relational means slightly more often (Card, Stucky, Sawalani, &

Little, 2008). Thus, the empirical evidence for sex differences in traditional bully-ing, at least in adolescence, is less clear than often portrayed.

The nature of online communication led to initial speculation that cyber-bullying may hold greater appeal for girls, as it offers them the opportunity to carry out indirect methods of aggression, such as spreading rumours and gos-sip. Some confirmation has been found for this, with girls reporting greater rates of cybervictimisation than boys (Dehue et al., 2012; Genta et al., 2011; Kowalski & Limber, 2007; Li, 2006). However, findings are not consistent, with other studies finding that males are more often victims of cyberbullying (Aricak et al., 2008; Slonje & Smith, 2008), or that both males and females are victimised at fairly similar rates (Beran & Li, 2008; Patchin & Hinduja, 2006; Smith et al., 2008; Wolak et al., 2007; Ybarra et al., 2006). Tokunaga (2010) concludes that, overall, the research shows there are no predominant sex differ-ences in cybervictimisation. Fewer studies report on bullies or bully-victims; however, current findings suggest that females are equally as likely, and in some cases more likely, to perpetrate cyberbullying (Hinduja & Patchin, 2008b; Riv-ers & Noret, 2010; Smith et al., 2008), or to report being cyber bully-victims (Mishna et al., 2012).

Ethnicity

Examining the relationship between traditional bullying and ethnicity has been a problematic issue, compounded by the difficulty in obtaining representative samples which enable comparisons between individual ethnic groups. Studies which used class- or school-based samples generally found no difference in rates of victimisation or bullying perpetration between ethnic groups (Durkin et al., 2012; Eslea & Mukhtar, 2000; Monks, Ortega-Ruiz, & Rodríguez-Hidalgo, 2008; Siann, Callaghan, Glissov, Lockhart, & Rawson, 1994). However, more recent research using larger, representative samples have found significant differences, which indicate that ethnic minority children may be more likely to participate in bullying others, but are at no greater risk of being victimised than the ethnic majority (Carlyle & Steinman, 2007; Sawyer, Bradshaw, & O'Brennan, 2008; Tip-pett et al., 2013; Wang, Iannotti, & Nansel, 2009).

At present, there is very limited evidence on ethnicity and cyberbullying. Hinduja and Patchin (2008b) examined the association between ethnicity and cyberbullying, and found no significant differences in either cybervictimisation or bullying perpetration. Similarly Ybarra, Diener-West, and Leaf (2007) reported no difference in the frequency of Internet harassment between youths who were either White, Black, or of mixed ethnicity. In contrast, Wang et al. (2009) com-pared involvement in four types of bullying among ethnic groups using a nation-ally representative sample of US schoolchildren, finding that compared to White youth, African Americans were more likely to be cyberbullies, while Hispanic students were more likely to be cyber bully-victims. Adolescents in the combined "Other" ethnic group more often reported being victims of cyberbullying. The limited studies to date suggest there may be small differences in the likelihood of being victimised or perpetrating cyberbullying according to ethnic group.

Psychological characteristics

Aggression and anti-social behaviour

A strong association has been found between traditional bullying involvement and aggressive or anti-social behaviour. Bullying perpetration is strongly linked to delinquent behaviour (Barker, Arseneault, Brendgen, Fontaine, & Maughan, 2008; Perren & Hornung, 2005), and both bullies and bully-victims display greater levels of aggression from a young age (Carney & Merrell, 2001; Griffin & Gross, 2004; Perren & Alsaker, 2006). Examining a range of individual and social risk factors for bullying perpetration, Farrington and Baldry (2010) found that anti-social and troublesome behaviour between the ages of 8 and 10 years most strongly predicted bullying perpetration at age 14. There is substantial evidence that children who endorse aggressive beliefs are more likely to engage in peer aggression and traditional bullying, as both bullies and bully-victims (Bentley & Li, 1996; Huesmann & Guerra, 1997; McConville & Cornell, 2003), and in particular, positive attitudes towards aggression have been reported to predict pure bully roles (McConville & Cornell, 2003). Similarly Salmivalli and Voeten (2004) found that pro-bullying attitudes were able to moderately predict whether children perpetrated acts of traditional bullying. Boulton, Bucci, and Hawker (1999) found that although the majority of children believe that bullying is wrong and exhibit anti-bullying attitudes, children that express the weakest anti-bullying attitudes are more often nominated as bullies and bully-victims by their peers. In contrast, there appears to be little association between aggression and pure victim roles. Victims show similar levels of aggression as children not involved in bullying (Salmivalli & Nieminen, 2002), and are less likely than bullies and bully-victims to endorse aggression-supporting beliefs (Bentley & Li, 1996).

While similar evidence regarding cyberbullying is limited, studies have found that children who cyberbully others score higher on measures of aggression, and exhibit greater levels of anti-social or delinquent behaviour (Beran & Li, 2008; Dilmac, 2009; Ybarra & Mitchell, 2004a). Both Schultze-Krumbholz and Scheithauer (2009) and Sontag, Clemans, Graber, and Lyndon (2011) found that cyberbullying perpetrators scored higher on measures of proactive and reactive aggression. Taking into consideration the strong links between traditional and cyberbullying, Gradinger et al. (2009) found that children who were both traditional and cyberbullies reported the highest levels of reactive and instrumental aggression, while traditional and cyber bully-victims scored higher on both measures when compared to uninvolved students or only traditional bully-victims. Furthermore, cyberbullying perpetrators have been found to display more aggressive attitudes. Williams and Guerra (2007), using multiple indicators to measure moral approval of bullying, found a single point increase raised the odds of being an Internet bully by 24%, and similarly Calvete, Orue, Estévez, Villardón, and Padilla (2010) reported that children who engaged in cyberbullying were more likely to believe that the use of violence was justifiable.

Internalising behaviour

Children with internalising problems, such as withdrawal, anxiety, and depression, show an increased risk for being traditionally bullied in childhood (Hawker & Boulton, 2000; Reijntjes, Kamphuis, Prinzie, & Telch, 2010). It has been suggested that the behaviour exhibited by anxious and depressed children may send signals to their peers that they are easy targets, and will not retaliate against acts of aggression (Arseneault, Bowes, & Shakoor, 2010). Although some find internalising problems to be an antecedent to bullying, evidence from longitudinal research also shows that the experience of victimisation in adolescence can significantly predict internalising problems in both the short and long term (Reijntjes et al., 2010; Sweeting, Young, West, & Der, 2006). This suggests the two are locked in a vicious circle, whereby internalising problems can be a cause for, but also an outcome of, victimisation by peers (Kaltiala-Heino, Rimpelä, Rantanen, & Rimpelä, 2000; Reijntjes et al., 2010). Bully-victims have also been found to display internalising behaviour, including anxiety and depression (Kaltiala-Heino et al., 2000), and to score higher than all other bullying roles on psychosocial adjustment problems (Klomek, Marrocco, Kleinman, Schonfeld, & Gould, 2007).

Similar associations with internalising problems have been found in studies on cyberbullying. Raskauskas and Stoltz (2007) found that victims of cyberbullying were more likely to report feeling sad, hopeless, or anxious than non-victims, and to score highly on measures of depression (Ybarra & Mitchell, 2004b). In addition, Navarro, Yubero, Larrañaga, and Martínez (2012) found that internalising problems, which included social anxiety, poor social skills, and difficulties communicating with peers and friends, all increased the likelihood of children being victims of cyberbullying. Similar to traditional bully-victims, cyber bully-victims also appear to show significant internalising problems, and have been found to display significantly poorer psychosocial functioning (e.g., depressive symptoms) than both cybervictims and cyberbullies (Ybarra & Mitchell, 2004b).

Self-esteem

Self-esteem has been identified as both a risk factor and an outcome of traditional bullying. Victimisation in particular is associated with low self-esteem (Egan & Perry, 1998), and both victims and bully-victims have been found to report substantially lower self-esteem than their peers (Egan & Perry, 1998; O'Moore & Kirkham, 2001; Wild, Flisher, Bhana, & Lombard, 2004). The relationship with bullying perpetration is less clear; while some studies found bullies exhibited lower self-esteem than non-involved children (Frisén, Jonsson, & Persson, 2007; Jankauskiene, Kardelis, Sukys, & Kardeliene, 2008), others suggest that bullies have the highest levels of self-esteem within their whole peer group (Rigby & Slee, 1991). Salmivalli, Kaukiainen, Kaistaniemi, and Lagerspetz (1999) found that levels of self-esteem predicted children's roles in traditional bullying, with bullies scoring high on measures of defensive egotism and self-concept, while victims scored low across all measures. Self-esteem itself can act as a protective factor against involvement in traditional bullying by reducing the negative effects of being bullied (Sapouna & Wolke, 2013), and improving individuals' self-esteem has been identified as a potential route for intervention programmes (O'Moore & Kirkham, 2001).

Similar associations have been found between cyberbullying and self-esteem. Katzer, Fetchenhauer, and Belschak (2009) found that children who were victimised through chatrooms had a significantly lower self-concept than their non-involved peers, and Patchin and Hinduja (2010) reported moderate negative associations between self-esteem and cyberbullying victimisation and perpetration. Brighi et al. (2012) compared the self-esteem of adolescents involved in cyberbullying across three European countries and found that victims of cyberbullying reported significantly lower self-esteem than non-victims. Additionally, concurrent involvement in traditional bullying was also considered, with the findings indicating that children who were victims of both traditional and cyberbullying scored significantly lower on measures of global self-esteem than those who were victimised only traditionally or only online. Sticca, Ruggieri, Alsaker, and Perren (2013) assessed cyberbullying over a six-month period. Although no association between cyberbullying perpetration and self-esteem was found at time 2, cyberbullies scored significantly lower on self-esteem at time 1. Similarly, a moderate negative correlation was found between self-esteem and the experience of cybervictimisation.

Empathy

Empathy can be divided into two major dimensions: affective empathy, which is the ability to experience and share the emotions of others, and cognitive empathy, which is the ability to understand the emotions of others (Ang & Goh, 2010). Empathy differs significantly across roles in traditional bullying. Jolliffe and Farrington (2006) found that bullies had significantly less affective empathy than those who did not bully, or had only bullied others once or twice. Similarly, Shechtman (2002) reported that boys who bullied others showed lower affective empathy than non-bullies, although there were no differences in levels of cognitive empathy. There is some debate in the literature over whether bullies have high or low levels of cognitive empathy. Some argue that bullies lack social skills or social understanding (Crick & Dodge, 1999), and therefore continue to bully as they do not understand the pain that it causes. Endresen and Olweus (2001) found that a positive attitude toward bullying mediated the association between empathic concern and the frequency of bullying others. In other words, children with high empathic concern tended to view bullying as negative, hence they bullied less. In contrast, others argue that bullies are in fact skilled manipulators, who possess good cognitive empathy, and are highly attuned to the feelings of others, which they use to their advantage (Sutton, Smith, & Swettenham, 1999). Woods, Wolke, Nowicki, and Hall (2009) found that bullies did not differ from either victims or non-involved children on measures of both cognitive and affective empathy. While much of the research has focused on bullying perpetration, there has been little consideration of other roles. Victims have been found to show similar empathic levels to children not involved in bullying (Woods et al., 2009), but no studies report levels of empathy among bully-victims.

A number of studies have similarly looked at the association between empathy and cyberbullying, finding some evidence that lower empathy is related to cyberbullying perpetration. Steffgen, König, Pfetsch, and Melzer (2011) found that cyberbullies demonstrated lower empathic responsiveness, and suggest that a lack of empathy may be considered a risk factor for cyberbullying behaviour. Similarly, longitudinal research by Sticca et al. (2013) found that children who cyberbullied others scored significantly lower on empathic concern, and this association was found to be stable across the six-month period of the study. No similar association was found for victims of cyberbullying, whose level of empathic concern did not differ from non-involved children. Other studies, however, report contrasting results. Almeida, Correia, and Marinho (2009) found that although cyberbullies tended to score lower than non-bullies on measures of empathy, these differences were not significant. Victims of cyberbullying appeared more likely to exhibit both cognitive and affective empathic skills, whereas cyber bully-victims scored significantly lower on all empathic measures. A summary of individual psychological characteristics and involvement in either traditional or cyberbullying as victim, bully-victim, or bully is given in Table 3.1.

Family and household factors

Parenting characteristics

Parenting shows strong links to traditional bullying, and the way in which children are parented can significantly impact on the likelihood of being victimised or of bullying others. From a social learning perspective (Bandura, 1977) parenting is seen as a key influence upon children's peer relationships, as the child-rearing behaviour that they experience serves as a model for their own social behaviour (Ladd, 1992). Similarly, family system theory proposes that conflict within one or more of the intra-family relationships increases the likelihood of children's conflict with peers (Ingoldsby, Shaw, & Garcia, 2001).

All roles in traditional bullying have shown links to particular parenting practices. Children who are victimised by peers tend to experience maladaptive parental practices, which include harsh discipline and abuse (Baldry, 2003; Duncan, 1999; Schwartz, Dodge, Pettit, & Bates, 2000), overprotection (Rigby, Slee, & Martin, 2007; Veenstra et al., 2005), and authoritarian parenting practices (Baldry &

TABLE 3.1 Psychological characteristics associated with traditional and cyberbullying

	Traditional Bullying			Cyberbullying		
	Victim	Bully-victim	Bully	Victim	Bully-victim	Bully
Aggression	Low aggression	High aggression Aggressive attitudes	High aggression Aggressive attitudes	?	High aggression	Highest aggression Aggressive attitudes
Internalising Problems	Display range of internalising symptoms	Display range of internalising symptoms	No association	Display range of internalising symptoms	Display range of internalising symptoms	No association
Self-esteem	Low self-esteem	Low self-esteem	Unclear association	Low self-esteem	?	Low self-esteem
Empathy	No association	?	Low empathy	?	Low empathy	Low empathy

Farrington, 1998). These characteristics are to an extent shared among bully-victims, who also have been found to experience harsh punishment and abuse (Schwartz, Dodge, Pettit, & Bates, 1997), poor parental attachment, and a lack of parental involvement or supervision (Bowes et al., 2009; Marini, Dane, Bosacki, & Cura, 2006). A meta-analysis of research by Lereya, Samara, and Wolke (2013) found that both victims and bully-victims were more likely than non-victims to experience negative parenting behaviours, including abuse, neglect, and maladaptive practices. In addition, victims were also more likely to have overprotective parents. In contrast, parental characteristics such as good communication, warm and affectionate relationships, and adequate supervision protected children against the risk of traditional victimisation.

Traditional bullying perpetration is also linked with certain parental behaviours, including poor relationships and a lack of supervision (Pepler, Jiang, Craig, & Connolly, 2008). In particular, bullies report problematic and conflicted relationships with their parents, characterised by a lack of warmth and support (Bowes et al., 2009; Perren & Hornung, 2005), poor supervision (Smith & Myron-Wilson, 1998), and harsh or infrequent discipline and maltreatment (Carney & Merrell, 2001; Shields & Cicchetti, 2001).

Few studies have explored the association between parenting and cyberbullying. Initial research has found that both cyberbullies and bully-victims experienced less parental monitoring and reported poorer emotional bonds with their parents than children not involved in cyberbullying (Ybarra et al., 2007; Ybarra & Mitchell, 2004a). Wang et al. (2009) assessed parental support in relation to cyberbullying using four measures: (a) whether parents provided help when needed, (b) were loving, (c) understood children's problems, and (d) were able to make them feel better when upset. The authors found both cyberbullies and cyber-victims experienced significantly less parental support than children not involved in bullying, but no significant differences were observed for cyber bully-victims. Additionally, the effect of parenting style on involvement in cyberbullying has been considered. Dilmaç and Aydoğan (2010) found that both authoritarian and protective parenting styles were associated with cybervictimisation, while only authoritarian parenting was related to bullying perpetration. Dehue et al. (2012) examined the relationship between cyberbullying and parenting characteristics, while adjusting for children's involvement in traditional bullying. Children who were involved in both traditional and cyberbullying, as victims, bullies, or bully-victims, reported having parents who were less responsive to their needs, but were also more demanding. Additionally, cyber and traditional bullies were more likely to have neglectful parents, while cyber and traditional victims more often reported having authoritarian or neglectful parents. Interestingly, most children who participated in cyberbullying were also involved in traditional bullying; there were too few only cyber bullies or victims for any meaningful analysis.

Overall, the findings suggest that parenting characteristics are related to roles in traditional and cyberbullying in similar ways, with bullies tending to experience more neglectful parenting practices, while victims are more often exposed to authoritarian or restrictive parenting styles. One additional factor identified through the research that specifically relates to cyberbullying is the extent to which parents monitor children's use of technology and have an element of control over their child's online behaviour. Twyman, Saylor, Taylor, and Comeaux (2010) found that victims of cyberbullying were more likely to have an e-mail account not accessible to parents, and it appears that cyberbullying more often occurs where parents do not have control over their child's online activities. Sengupta and Chaudhuri (2011) report that using the Internet in private, without parents being able to monitor activity, is associated with a 60% increase in the likelihood of being cyberbullied on social networking sites. In terms of protective factors, Mesch (2009) found that setting rules appeared to be particularly effective; although parental mediation in online behaviour and the use of filters to block access to certain websites were not related to victimisation, setting rules which identified sites children were allowed to visit significantly decreased the risk of online victimisation.

Domestic and sibling violence

Literature on traditional bullying suggests there is an association between exposure to violence at home and involvement in traditional bullying. Children who witness harsh discipline and violent behaviour at home are more likely to engage in bullying at school (Bowes et al., 2009; Lereya, Winsper, et al., 2013; Lereya & Wolke, 2013; Smith & Myron-Wilson, 1998). Baldry (2003) found that, after controlling for child abuse, which in itself is a risk factor, both traditional bullies and victims were more likely to have been exposed to inter-parental violence. Sibling violence has also been associated with traditional bullying roles. Youth who are victimised by siblings are more often victims of bullying by peers, while those who bully their siblings are more likely to be traditional bullies or bully-victims at school (Duncan, 1999; Tippett & Wolke, submitted; Wolke & Samara, 2004). A longitudinal study on sibling and peer violence found that anti-social behaviour between siblings at age 3 predicted bullying of peers at age 6, indicating that experiencing violence within the home at a young age can increase the risk of later involvement in peer bullying (Ensor, Marks, Jacobs, & Hughes, 2010).

As yet there is little concurrent research on cyberbullying. However, Calvete et al. (2010) examined the relationship between cyberbullying perpetration and a combined measure of violence exposure which considered whether children were exposed to violence across four settings: the school, the neighbourhood, at home, and on television. Cyberbullying perpetration was significantly associated with greater exposure to violence across all settings. Although this does not identify whether domestic violence in itself is a risk factor for cyberbullying, it suggests there may be some association, and future research is needed to identify whether inter-parental or sibling violence increases the risk of children of cyberbullying involvement.

Socioeconomic status

Several studies have explored the association between traditional bullying and socioeconomic status. However, findings differ greatly between studies, depending upon the sample and which socioeconomic measure was used. In general, both victims and bully-victims are more likely to come from low socioeconomic families (Alikasifoglu, Erginoz, Ercan, Uysal, & Albayrak-Kaymak, 2007; D. Jansen, Veenstra, Ormel, Verhulst, & Reijneveld, 2011; P. W. Jansen et al., 2012). However, not all studies confirm this association (Garner & Hinton, 2010; Ma, 2001). Similarly, while several studies report that perpetrators of traditional bullying more often come from low socioeconomic households (D. Jansen et al., 2011; Wolke et al., 2001), others find no evidence of this association (Ma, 2001; Veenstra et al., 2005). A meta-analysis of research by Tippett and Wolke (in press) finds that both victims and bully-victims are slightly associated with low socioeconomic status. However, no association was found for bullying perpetration, with bullies likely to be found among all socioeconomic strata.

Several studies on cyberbullying have included measures which pertain to socioeconomic status, and as with traditional bullying, it appears that this relationship varies greatly between studies. Ybarra and Mitchell (2004a) compared roles in cyberbullying on household income and found no significant difference between cybervictims, bullies, or bully-victims compared to non-involved children. Similarly, Sengupta and Chaudhuri (2011) found no significant association with rates of cybervictimisation in their study, which used both parental education and household income as measures of socioeconomic status. In contrast, other studies have found a link between cybervictimisation and measures of low socioeconomic status, including low household income (Ybarra et al., 2007) and poor parental education (Mesch, 2009). The associations between individual, family, and household factors and involvement in either traditional or cyberbullying are summarised in Table 3.2.

School and peer factors

School climate

Students who report being traditionally victimised feel less safe in school (Varjas, Henrich, & Meyers, 2009) or perceive their school as less harmonious (Wong, 2003). Yoneyama and Rigby (2006) showed that victims perceived both school and classroom climate negatively. Furthermore, Lee and Wong (2009) found that students' experience of harmony within school was an important predictor of bullying behaviour. Traditional bullying has been found to be more prominent in high-conflict and disorganised schools (Kasen, Berenson, Cohen, & Johnson, 2004). Additionally, low levels of supervision within school settings have also been associated with higher rates of bullying (Craig, Pepler, & Atlas, 2000).

TABLE 3.2 Family and household factors associated with traditional and cyberbullying

	Traditional Bullying			Cyberbullying		
	Victim	Bully-victim	Bully	Victim	Bully-victim	Bully
Parenting	Parental maltreatment Over protection	Parental maltreatment	Parental maltreatment Poor relationships with parents	Parental maltreatment Over protection	Parental maltreatment	Parental maltreatment
Domestic violence	Parental and sibling violence	Sibling violence	Parental and sibling violence	?	?	Exposure to violence
SES	Low SES	Low SES	No association	Low SES	No association	No association

Given the strong association between bullying at school and cyberbullying, the school environment itself may be considered a risk factor. Although limited, there is some evidence that a poor school climate is associated with greater rates of cyberbullying. Sourander et al. (2010) incorporated measures of school environment in their research, finding that cybervictims, bullies, and bully-victims all felt significantly less safe at school, and were more likely to report that their teachers did not care about them. Bayar and Ucanok (2012) found that adolescents involved in cyberbullying perceived their schools and teachers less positively. In addition, Williams and Guerra (2007) found that rates of cyberbullying perpetration were lower among youth who rated the school climate as trusting, fair and pleasant, and who perceived themselves as being connected to the school. On the other hand, Varjas et al. (2009) found only limited evidence to support the association between cyberbullying and feeling less safe at school.

Peer relationships

Studies that have investigated the association between traditional bullying involvement and friendships have shown that victims as well as bully-victims usually have few friends (Boulton & Underwood, 1992; Rigby, 2007; Wolke, Woods, & Samara, 2009) and suffer more often than those not involved in bullying from long-lasting social isolation and loneliness (Cook et al., 2010; Juvonen, Graham, & Schuster, 2003; Veenstra et al., 2005). Hodges, Malone, and Perry (1997) have argued that there are three factors that prolong the duration of victimisation: (a) few friends, (b) the quality of friends, and (c) general standing in the peer group (extent of peer rejection). Indeed, positive friendships have been found to act as a protective factor against peer victimisation (Bollmer, Milich, Harris, & Maras, 2005). Rigby (2005) demonstrated that Australian elementary and middle school students' negative attitudes toward the victim was significantly associated with bullying behaviour, whereas friendships were protective against victimisation. Similarly, Boulton, Trueman, Chau, Whitehand, and Amatya (1999) reported that young people without a best friend were at risk of being bullied at school. Bullies have also been identified as being friendless, lonely, and rejected by their peers (Salmivalli, Lagerspetz, Björkqvist, Österman, & Kaukiainen, 1996; Warden & Mackinnon, 2003). However, there is also evidence suggesting that bullies are perceived as cool and popular and even leaders in their peer culture (Juvonen et al., 2003). Although these results may seem contradictory, it is possible that bullies may be rejected (disliked by the victims) but still perceived as popular by most classmates (Estell, Farmer, Pearl, Van Acker, & Rodkin, 2008; Rodkin, Farmer, Pearl, & Van Acker, 2006). Moreover, in some studies, bullies were only rejected by children who represented a potential threat (Veenstra, Lindenberg, Munniksma, & Dijkstra, 2010). Furthermore, it has been suggested that although bullies tend to be popular in earlier grades, this popularity declines in later years (Olweus, 1997).

Although findings on cyberbullying are limited, it appears that children involved in cyberbullying share similar peer relationship problems to those involved in traditional bullying. Victims of cyberbullying have been found to rate their friendships as being less trusting, caring, and helpful (Williams & Guerra, 2007) than children not involved in bullying, and both cybervictims and bully-victims score significantly higher than non-involved children on peer relationship problems (Sourander et al., 2010). In contrast, cyberbullies showed good peer relationships, but along with cyber bully-victims, scored significantly lower on measures of prosocial behaviour. While these findings reflect those observed for traditional bullying roles, other studies find little evidence of an association between cyberbullying and peer problems. Katzer et al. (2009) report that although victims of chatroom bullying rated themselves as less popular, they were no less socially integrated than their peers within the school. Furthermore, no association between cybervictim or bully roles and loneliness (Şahin, 2012) or peer rejection or social acceptance (Calvete et al., 2010) have been reported. A longitudinal study on the stability of cybervictimisation found no evidence that victims of cyberbullying were less popular, or perceived themselves to be less popular, than non-victims (Gradinger, Strohmeier, Schiller, Stefanek, & Spiel, 2012). A summary of the associations between school and peer factors and involvement in either traditional or cyberbullying is shown in Table 3.3.

Use of technology

Unsurprisingly, the way children use technology appears to be a key determinant for whether they experience cyberbullying. In particular, which technologies children use, the frequency of use, and the ways in which they are used all appear to increase the risk of being victimised or of bullying others online.

Firstly, the amount of time that children spend using technology significantly increases the risk of their becoming involved in cyberbullying. Smith et al. (2008) found that victims of cyberbullying used the Internet more often than those who were not victims, with high Internet usage in particular associated with victimisation through websites, chatrooms, e-mail, and instant messaging. Similar results have been observed elsewhere, with victims found to engage in high levels of Internet use (Wolak et al., 2007) and to spend more hours per day using a computer than those who are not victimised (Mishna et al., 2012).

Furthermore, this association appears to extend across all roles in cyberbullying. Twyman et al. (2010) reported that youths who were identified as either cyber bullies, victims, or bully-victims spent a greater amount of time on the computer engaging in computer-based social activities, including e-mailing, instant messaging, and posting in chatrooms. The authors suggest that the more time spent online by an individual, the more likely they are to communicate with others, and, as result, are exposed to a greater risk of being targeted or of targeting others online.

The way in which children communicate online also matters. Comparing rates of victimisation across different online activities, Mesch (2009) found that participating in social networking sites and chatrooms significantly increased the

TABLE 3.3 School and peer factors associated with traditional and cyberbullying

	Traditional Bullying			Cyberbullying		
	Victim	*Bully-victim*	*Bully*	*Victim*	*Bully-victim*	*Bully*
School Climate	Less safe, less harmonious schools	?	High conflict Disorganised schools	Less safe	Less safe	Less safe
Peer Relationships	Few friends, lonely	Few friends, lonely	Few friends, lonely, controversial but popular	Peer relationship problems	Peer relationship problems	Good peer relationships

risk of children being bullied online. Furthermore, Twyman et al. (2010) report that children who had a social network profile, a personal website, or a personal e-mail account that was not monitored by parents, were at greater risk of being involved in cyberbullying. Posting detailed personal information online offers greater opportunities for being cyberbullied, and having a social networking profile appears to be a particular risk, as it enables aggressors to easily obtain personal information and contact details of their victim, and use this material to abuse, threaten, or make fun of them (Mesch, 2009). The risk of cyberbullying is not simply limited to social networking; it extends to cybervictimisation and bullying perpetration in relation to instant messaging programs (Dehue et al., 2008; Smith et al., 2008; Ybarra & Mitchell, 2004a), e-mails (Aricak et al., 2008; Kowalski & Limber, 2007), mobile phone calls or text messages (Smith et al., 2008), and chatrooms (Kowalski & Limber, 2007; Walrave & Heirman, 2011).

Furthermore, the way in which children use technology increases the risk of cyberbullying. In particular, engaging in risky online behaviour, such as posting private information, sharing passwords, or interacting with anonymous strangers, can significantly increase the risk of children being victimised online. Among several forms of risky behaviour, Mesch (2009) reports that children's disclosure of private information significantly increased the risk of being cyberbullied. Similarly, Vandebosch and Van Cleemput (2009) found that indicators of risky online behaviour, including talking to people who were only known online, posting personal information, and passing on a password to a friend were all associated with an increased risk for victimisation. One study which examined the association between cyberbullying and social networking sites reported that it was not use of social networking, but rather participants' online behaviour, including posting pictures, disclosing information about their school or home, and flirting with unknown people, that significantly increased the risk of being victimised (Sengupta & Chaudhuri, 2011).

While the findings suggest that children involved in cyberbullying are more likely to engage in risky behaviour, it may in fact be that they are not sufficiently aware of the risks that their behaviour entails. One study which examined children's perception of online risky behaviour found that those who were more often cyberbullied were less aware of the risks associated with using the Internet, including sharing passwords with others or talking with individuals they did not know in their offline lives (Hinduja & Patchin, 2008a). Similarly, Mishna et al. (2012) found that victims of cyberbullying were more likely to share their passwords with friends, which the authors suggest is indicative of a lack of awareness of online safety and of the dangers entailed in sharing private information. That victims of cyberbullying are more likely to be unaware of the risks associated with online behaviour suggests that large-scale awareness campaigns are likely to be an effective route in preventing cyberbullying (Vandebosch & Van Cleemput, 2009).

A further interesting finding concerns children's technological ability and their skill in using the Internet and other social media. Compared to victims of cyberbullying, cyberbullies appear to be much more capable at using technology.

Ybarra and Mitchell (2004a) found that cyberbullies were twice as likely to rate themselves as almost expert or expert at using the Internet. Cyberbullies generally appear to be heavy Internet users, using the Internet more frequently, and rating their technological skills more highly than non-involved children (Vandebosch & Van Cleemput, 2009; Walrave & Heirman, 2011). Walrave and Heirman (2011) suggest that the amount of time cyberbullies spend online allows them to improve their skills, becoming adept users who are then able to utilise their technological skills to create an imbalance of power over the less capable victim.

Conclusion

In summary, research on cyberbullying has identified a range of factors that can increase the risk of children becoming involved in cyberbullying, ranging from individual traits through children's home and school environments. The literature is far from comprehensive. Only a few studies have specifically investigated a comprehensive range of risk factors, and there is a lack of longitudinal research that could identify the pathways to children being cyberbullied or cyberbullying others. The strongest risk factor for involvement in cyberbullying that has been identified is being involved in traditional bullying; many cybervictims are also traditional victims, and many cyberbullies also perpetrate traditional bullying at school. Furthermore, the risk factors for traditional and cyberbullying are similar. Traditional and cybervictims tend to lack self-esteem, have internalising problems and problematic peer relationships, and experience maladaptive parenting practices which impact on their ability to form and maintain positive relationships with peers. Bullies, both traditional and cyber, are more aggressive, and experience more harsh or neglectful home environments. There is still less research on traditional or cyber bully-victims, although findings indicate that they experience significant individual and environmental difficulties.

That the same factors predict involvement in both traditional and cyberbullying further supports the view that these are *not* separate phenomena, but rather extensions of the same behaviour, albeit carried out in different ways. This strong relationship has implications for interpreting research findings. On the positive side, findings on traditional bullying can be generalised to most of those involved in cyberbullying, and can inform the design of interventions. However, insight will remain limited if research continues to examine cyberbullying without considering whether children are also involved in traditional bullying. To determine whether specific risk factors for cyberbullying exist, research must distinguish between children who are only involved in cyberbullying, those only involved in traditional bullying, and the largest group, involved in both traditional and cyberbullying. The low prevalence of cyberbullying and high degree of overlap with traditional bullying requires large samples for research. However, this research is necessary to ultimately determine whether there are specific risk factors for roles in cyberbullying. Of the findings currently available, there are some aspects of cyberbullying that may be considered unique, in particular the frequency and way in which children use technology. To conclude, considering the strong association of traditional and cyberbullying, interventions will only succeed if they target both traditional and cyberbullying. Interventions should include aspects specifically tailored to address cyberbullying, such as teaching children how to use the Internet safely. However, ultimately the most effective interventions must address risk factors associated with all forms of bullying, including improving the school and family environment, raising social skills, and encouraging positive and supportive peer relationships.

References

Alikasifoglu, M., Erginoz, E., Ercan, O., Uysal, O., & Albayrak-Kaymak, D. (2007). Bullying behaviours and psychosocial health: results from a cross-sectional survey among high school students in Istanbul, Turkey. *European Journal of Pediatrics, 166*(12), 1253–1260.

Almeida, A., Correia, I., & Marinho, S. (2009). Moral disengagement, normative beliefs of peer group, and attitudes regarding roles in bullying. *Journal of School Violence, 9*(1), 23–36.

Analitis, F., Velderman, M. K., Ravens-Sieberer, U., Detmar, S., Erhart, M., Herdman, M., Berra, S., Alonso, J., & Rajmil, L. (2009). Being bullied: Associated factors in children and adolescents 8 to 18 years old in 11 European countries. *Pediatrics, 123*(2), 569–577.

Ang, R. P., & Goh, D. H. (2010). Cyberbullying among adolescents: The role of affective and cognitive empathy, and gender. *Child Psychiatry & Human Development, 41*(4), 387–397.

Aricak, T., Siyahhan, S., Uzunhasanoglu, A., Saribeyoglu, S., Ciplak, S., Yilmaz, N., & Memmedov, C. (2008). Cyberbullying among Turkish adolescents. *CyberPsychology & Behavior, 11*(3), 253–261.

Arseneault, L., Bowes, L., & Shakoor, S. (2010). Bullying victimization in youths and mental health problems: "Much ado about nothing"? *Psychological Medicine, 40*(5), 717–729. doi:http://dx.doi.org/10.1017/S0033291709991383

Baldry, A. C. (2003). Bullying in schools and exposure to domestic violence. *Child Abuse & Neglect, 27*(7), 713–732.

Baldry, A. C., & Farrington, D. P. (1998). Parenting influences on bullying and victimization. *Legal and Criminological Psychology, 3*(2), 237–254.

Bandura, A. (1977). *Social learning theory*. Oxford, UK: Prentice-Hall.

Barker, E. D., Arseneault, L., Brendgen, M., Fontaine, N., & Maughan, B. (2008). Joint development of bullying and victimization in adolescence: Relations to delinquency and self-harm. *Journal of the American Academy of Child & Adolescent Psychiatry, 47*(9), 1030–1038.

Bayar, Y., & Ucanok, Z. (2012). School social climate and generalized peer perception in traditional and cyberbullying status. *Educational Sciences: Theory and Practice, 12*(4), 2352–2358.

Bentley, K. M., & Li, A. K. F. (1996). Bully and victim problems in elementary schools and students' beliefs about aggression. *Canadian Journal of School Psychology, 11*(2), 153–165.

Beran, T., & Li, Q. (2008). The relationship between cyberbullying and school bullying. *The Journal of Student Wellbeing, 1*(2), 16–33.

Bollmer, J. M., Milich, R., Harris, M. J., & Maras, M. A. (2005). A friend in need: The role of friendship quality as a protective factor in peer victimization and bullying. *Journal of Interpersonal Violence, 20*(6), 701–712.

Boulton, M. J., Bucci, E., & Hawker, D. D. S. (1999). Swedish and English secondary school pupils' attitudes towards, and conceptions of, bullying: Concurrent links with bully/victim involvement. *Scandinavian Journal of Psychology, 40*(4), 277–284.

Boulton, M. J., Trueman, M., Chau, C., Whitehand, C., & Amatya, K. (1999). Concurrent and longitudinal links between friendship and peer victimization: Implications for befriending interventions. *Journal of Adolescence, 22*(4), 461–466.

Boulton, M. J., & Underwood, K. (1992). Bully/victim problems among middle school children. *British Journal of Educational Psychology, 62*(1), 73–87.

Bowes, L., Arseneault, L., Maughan, B., Taylor, A., Caspi, A., & Moffitt, T. E. (2009). School, neighborhood, and family factors are associated with children's bullying involvement: A nationally representative longitudinal study. *Journal of the American Academy of Child & Adolescent Psychiatry, 48*(5), 545–553.

Brighi, A., Melotti, G., Guarini, A., Genta, M. L., Ortega, R., Mora-Merchán, J., Smith, P. K., & Thompson, F. (2012). Self-esteem and loneliness in relation to cyberbullying in three European countries. In L. Qing, D. Cross & P. K. Smith (Eds.), *Cyberbullying in the Global Playground: Research from International Perspectives* (pp. 32–56). Chichester, UK: Wiley-Blackwell.

Calvete, E., Orue, I., Estévez, A., Villardón, L., & Padilla, P. (2010). Cyberbullying in adolescents: Modalities and aggressors' profile. *Computers in Human Behavior, 26*(5), 1128–1135.

Card, N. A., Stucky, B. D., Sawalani, G. M., & Little, T. D. (2008). Direct and indirect aggression during childhood and adolescence: A meta-analytic review of gender differences, intercorrelations, and relations to maladjustment. *Child Development, 79*(5), 1185–1229.

Carlyle, K. E., & Steinman, K. J. (2007). Demographic differences in the prevalence, co-occurrence, and correlates of adolescent bullying at school. *Journal of School Health, 77*(9), 623–629.

Carney, A. G., & Merrell, K. W. (2001). Bullying in schools: Perspectives on understanding and preventing an international problem. *School Psychology International, 22*(3), 364–382.

Cook, C. R., Williams, K. R., Guerra, N. G., Kim, T. E., & Sadek, S. (2010). Predictors of bullying and victimization in childhood and adolescence: A meta-analytic investigation. *School Psychology Quarterly, 25*(2), 65.

Craig, W. M. (1998). The relationship among bullying, victimization, depression, anxiety, and aggression in elementary school children. *Personality and Individual Differences, 24*(1), 123–130.

Craig, W. M., Harel-Fisch, Y., Fogel-Grinvald, H., Dostaler, S., Hetland, J., Simons-Morton, B., Molcho, M., de Mato, M. G., Overpeck, M., & Due, P. (2009). A cross-national profile of bullying and victimization among adolescents in 40 countries. *International Journal of Public Health, 54*(2), 216–224.

Craig, W. M., Pepler, D., & Atlas, R. (2000). Observations of bullying in the playground and in the classroom. *School Psychology International, 21*(1), 22–36.

Crick, N. R., & Dodge, K. A. (1999). 'Superiority' is in the eye of the beholder: A comment on Sutton, Smith, and Swettenham. *Social Development, 8*(1), 128–131.

Crick, N. R., & Grotpeter, J. K. (1996). Children's treatment by peers: Victims of relational and overt aggression. *Development and Psychopathology, 8*(2), 367–380.

Dehue, F., Bolman, C., & Völlink, T. (2008). Cyberbullying: Youngsters' experiences and parental perception. *CyberPsychology & Behavior, 11*(2), 217–223.

Dehue, F., Bolman, C., Völlink, T., & Pouwelse, M. (2012). Cyberbullying and traditional bullying in relation to adolescents' perception of parenting. *Journal of CyberTherapy and Rehabilitation, 5*, 25–34.

Dilmaç, B. (2009). Psychological needs as a predictor of cyber bullying: A preliminary report on college students. *Educational Sciences: Theory and Practice, 9*(3), 1307–1325.

Dilmaç, B., & Aydoğan, D. (2010). Parental attitudes as a predictor of cyber bullying among primary school children. *International Journal of Psychological and Brain Sciences, 5*(10), 649–653.

Duncan, R.D. (1999). Peer and sibling aggression: An investigation of intra- and extra-familial bullying. *Journal of Interpersonal Violence, 14*(8), 871–886.

Durkin, K., Hunter, S., Levin, K.A., Bergin, D., Heim, D., & Howe, C. (2012). Discriminatory peer aggression among children as a function of minority status and group proportion in school context. *European Journal of Social Psychology, 42*(2), 243–251.

Egan, S.K., & Perry, D.G. (1998). Does low self-regard invite victimization? *Developmental Psychology, 34*(2), 299.

Endresen, I.M., & Olweus, D. (2001). Self-reported empathy in Norwegian adolescents: Sex differences, age trends, and relationship to bullying. In A.C. Bohart & D.J. Stipel (Eds.), *Constructive & destructive behavior: Implications for family, school & society.* Washington, DC: American Psychological Association.

Ensor, R., Marks, A., Jacobs, L., & Hughes, C. (2010). Trajectories of antisocial behaviour towards siblings predict antisocial behaviour towards peers. *Journal of Child Psychology and Psychiatry, 51*(11), 1208–1216.

Eslea, M., & Mukhtar, K. (2000). Bullying and racism among Asian schoolchildren in Britain. *Educational Research, 42*(2), 207–217.

Espelage, D.L., Mebane, S.E., & Swearer, S.M. (2004). Gender differences in bullying: Moving beyond mean level differences. In D.L. Espelage & S.M. Swearer (Eds.), *Bullying in American schools: A social-ecological perspective on prevention and intervention* (pp. 15–35). Mahwah, NJ: Erlbaum.

Estell, D.B., Farmer, T.W., Pearl, R., Van Acker, R., & Rodkin, P.C. (2008). Social status and aggressive and disruptive behavior in girls: Individual, group, and classroom influences. *Journal of School Psychology, 46*(2), 193–212.

Farrington, D.P., & Baldry, A.C. (2010). Individual risk factors for school bullying. *Journal of Aggression, Conflict and Peace Research, 2*(1), 4–16.

Finkelhor, D., Ormrod, R., Turner, H., & Hamby, S.L. (2005). The victimization of children and youth: A comprehensive, national survey. *Child Maltreatment, 10*(1), 5–25.

Frisèn, A., Jonsson, A.K., & Persson, C. (2007). Adolescents' perception of bullying: Who is the victim? Who is the bully? What can be done to stop bullying? *Adolescence, 42*(168), 749–761.

Garner, P.W., & Hinton, T.S. (2010). Emotional display rules and emotion self-regulation: Associations with bullying and victimization in community-based after school programs. *Journal of Community & Applied Social Psychology, 20*(6), 480–496.

Genta, M.L., Smith, P.K., Ortega, R., Brighi, A., Guarini, A., Thompson, F., Tippett, N., Mora-Merchán, J., & Calmaestra, J. (2011). Comparative aspects of cyberbullying in Italy, England, and Spain. In Q. Li, D. Cross & P.K. Smith (Eds.), *Cyberbullying in the Global Playground: Research from International Perspectives* (pp. 15–31). Chichester, UK: Wiley-Blackwell.

Gradinger, P., Strohmeier, D., Schiller, E.M., Stefanek, E., & Spiel, C. (2012). Cyber-victimization and popularity in early adolescence: Stability and predictive associations. *European Journal of Developmental Psychology, 9*(2), 228–243.

Gradinger, P., Strohmeier, D., & Spiel, C. (2009). Traditional bullying and cyberbullying. *Zeitschrift für Psychologie/Journal of Psychology, 217*(4), 205–213.

Griffin, R.S., & Gross, A. M. (2004). Childhood bullying: Current empirical findings and future directions for research. *Aggression and Violent Behavior, 9*(4), 379–400.

Hawker, D.S.J., & Boulton, M.J. (2000). Twenty years' research on peer victimization and psychosocial maladjustment: A meta-analytic review of cross-sectional studies. *The Journal of Child Psychology and Psychiatry, 41*(4), 441–455.

Haynie, D.L., Nansel, T., Eitel, P., Crump, A.D., Saylor, K., Yu, K., & Simons-Morton, B. (2001). Bullies, victims, and bully/victims: Distinct groups of at-risk youth. *The Journal of Early Adolescence, 21*(1), 29–49.

Hinduja, S., & Patchin, J.W. (2008a). *Bullying beyond the schoolyard: Preventing and responding to cyberbullying.* Thousand Oaks, CA: Sage.

Hinduja, S., & Patchin, J.W. (2008b). Cyberbullying: An exploratory analysis of factors related to offending and victimization. *Deviant Behavior, 29*(2), 129–156.

Hodges, E.V.E., Malone, M.J., & Perry, D.G. (1997). Individual risk and social risk as interacting determinants of victimization in the peer group. *Developmental Psychology, 33*(6), 1032–1039.

Huesmann, L.R., & Guerra, N.G. (1997). Children's normative beliefs about aggression and aggressive behavior. *Journal of Personality and Social Psychology, 72*(2), 408–419.

Ingoldsby, E.M., Shaw, D.S., & Garcia, M.M. (2001). Intrafamily conflict in relation to boys' adjustment at school. *Development and Psychopathology, 13*(1), 35–52.

Jankauskiene, R., Kardelis, K., Sukys, S., & Kardeliene, L. (2008). Associations between school bullying and psychosocial factors. *Social Behavior and Personality: An International Journal, 36*(2), 145–162.

Jansen, D., Veenstra, R., Ormel, J., Verhulst, F.C., & Reijneveld, S.A. (2011). Early risk factors for being a bully, victim, or bully/victim in late elementary and early secondary education. The longitudinal TRAILS study. *BMC Public Health, 11*(1), 440–446.

Jansen, P.W., Verlinden, M., Dommisse-van Berkel, A., Mieloo, C., van der Ende, J., Veenstra, R., Verhulst, F.C., Jansen, W., & Tiemeier, H. (2012). Prevalence of bullying and victimization among children in early elementary school: Do family and school neighbourhood socioeconomic status matter? *BMC Public Health, 12*(1), 494.

Jolliffe, D., & Farrington, D.P. (2006). Examining the relationship between low empathy and bullying. *Aggressive Behavior, 32*(6), 540–550.

Juvonen, J., Graham, S., & Schuster, M.A. (2003). Bullying among young adolescents: The strong, the weak, and the troubled. *Pediatrics, 112*(6), 1231–1237.

Juvonen, J., & Gross, E.F. (2008). Extending the school grounds? – Bullying experiences in cyberspace. *Journal of School Health, 78*(9), 496–505.

Kaltiala-Heino, R., Rimpelä, M., Rantanen, P., & Rimpelä, A. (2000). Bullying at school – an indicator of adolescents at risk for mental disorders. *Journal of Adolescence, 23*(6), 661–674.

Kasen, S., Berenson, K., Cohen, P., & Johnson, J.G. (2004). The effects of school climate on changes in aggressive and other behaviors related to bullying. In D.L. Espelage & S.M. Swearer (Eds.), *Bullying in American schools: A social-ecological perspective on prevention and intervention* (pp. 187–210). Mahwah, NJ: Erlbaum.

Katzer, C., Fetchenhauer, D., & Belschak, F. (2009). Cyberbullying: Who are the victims? *Journal of Media Psychology: Theories, Methods, and Applications, 21*(1), 25–36.

Klomek, A.B., Marrocco, F., Kleinman, M., Schonfeld, I.S., & Gould, M.S. (2007). Bullying, depression, and suicidality in adolescents. *Journal of the American Academy of Child & Adolescent Psychiatry, 46*(1), 40–49

Kowalski, R.M., & Limber, S.P. (2007). Electronic bullying among middle school students. *Journal of Adolescent Health, 41*(6), S22-S30.

Kowalski, R.M., & Limber, S.P. (2013). Psychological, physical, and academic correlates of cyberbullying and traditional bullying. *Journal of Adolescent Health, 53*(1), S13-S20.

Ladd, G. W. (1992). Themes and theories: Perspectives on processes in family-peer relationships. In R. D. Parke & G. W. Ladd (Eds.), *Family-peer relationships: Modes of linkage* (pp. 3–34). Hillsdale, NJ: Erlbaum.

Lee, S. S., & Wong, D. S. (2009). School, parents, and peer factors in relation to Hong Kong students' bullying. *International Journal of Adolescence and Youth, 15*(3), 217–233.

Lereya, S. T., Samara, M., & Wolke, D. (2013). Parenting behavior and the risk of becoming a victim and a bully/victim: A meta-analysis study. *Child Abuse & Neglect, 37*(12), 1091–1108.

Lereya, S. T., Winsper, C., Heron, J., Lewis, G., Gunnell, D., Fisher, H. L., & Wolke, D. (2013). Being bullied during childhood and the prospective pathways to self-harm in late adolescence. *Journal of the American Academy of Child & Adolescent Psychiatry, 52*(6), 608–618.

Lereya, S. T., & Wolke, D. (2013). Prenatal family adversity and maternal mental health and vulnerability to peer victimisation at school. *Journal of Child Psychology and Psychiatry, 54*(6), 644–652.

Li, Q. (2006). Cyberbullying in schools: A research of gender differences. *School Psychology International, 27*(2), 157–170.

Li, Q. (2007). New bottle but old wine: A research of cyberbullying in schools. *Computers in Human Behavior, 23*(4), 1777–1791.

Ma, X. (2001). Bullying and being bullied: To what extent are bullies also victims? *American Educational Research Journal, 38*(2), 351–370.

Marini, Z. A., Dane, A. V., Bosacki, S. L., & Cura, Y. L. C. (2006). Direct and indirect bully-victims: Differential psychosocial risk factors associated with adolescents involved in bullying and victimization. *Aggressive Behavior, 32*(6), 551–569.

McConville, D. W., & Cornell, D. G. (2003). Aggressive attitudes predict aggressive behavior in middle school students. *Journal of Emotional and Behavioral Disorders, 11*(3), 179–187.

Mesch, G. S. (2009). Parental mediation, online activities, and cyberbullying. *CyberPsychology & Behavior, 12*(4), 387–393.

Mishna, F., Khoury-Kassabri, M., Gadalla, T., & Daciuk, J. (2012). Risk factors for involvement in cyber bullying: Victims, bullies and bully–victims. *Children and Youth Services Review, 34*(1), 63–70.

Monks, C. P., Ortega-Ruiz, R., & Rodríguez-Hidalgo, A. J. (2008). Peer victimization in multicultural schools in Spain and England. *European Journal of Developmental Psychology, 5*(4), 507–535.

Nansel, T. R., Overpeck, M., Pilla, R. S., Ruan, W. J., Simons-Morton, B., & Scheidt, P. (2001). Bullying behaviors among US youth. *JAMA: The Journal of the American Medical Association, 285*(16), 2094–2100.

Navarro, R., Yubero, S., Larrañaga, E., & Martínez, V. (2012). Children's cyberbullying victimization: Associations with social anxiety and social competence in a Spanish sample. *Child Indicators Research, 5*(2), 281–295.

Olweus, D. (1993). *Bullying at school: What we know and what we can do.* Oxford, UK: Blackwell.

Olweus, D. (1997). Bully/victim problems in school: Facts and intervention. *European Journal of Psychology of Education, 12*(4), 495–510.

Olweus, D. (2012). Cyberbullying: An overrated phenomenon? *European Journal of Developmental Psychology, 9*(5), 520–538.

O'Moore, M., & Hillery, B. (1989). Bullying in Dublin schools. *The Irish Journal of Psychology, 10*(3), 426–441.

O'Moore, M., & Kirkham, C. (2001). Self-esteem and its relationship to bullying behaviour. *Aggressive Behavior, 27*(4), 269–283.

Patchin, J. W., & Hinduja, S. (2006). Bullies move beyond the schoolyard: A preliminary look at cyberbullying. *Youth Violence and Juvenile Justice, 4*(2), 148–169.

Patchin, J. W., & Hinduja, S. (2010). Cyberbullying and self-esteem. *Journal of School Health, 80*(12), 614–621.

Pepler, D., Jiang, D., Craig, W. M., & Connolly, J. (2008). Developmental trajectories of bullying and associated factors. *Child Development, 79*(2), 325–338.

Perren, S., & Alsaker, F. D. (2006). Social behavior and peer relationships of victims, bully-victims, and bullies in kindergarten. *Journal of Child Psychology and Psychiatry, 47*(1), 45–57.

Perren, S., & Hornung, R. (2005). Bullying and delinquency in adolescence: Victims' and perpetrators' family and peer relations. *Swiss Journal of Psychology/Schweizerische Zeitschrift für Psychologie/Revue Suisse de Psychologie, 64*(1), 51.

Raskauskas, J., & Stoltz, A. D. (2007). Involvement in traditional and electronic bullying among adolescents. *Developmental Psychology, 43*(3), 564.

Reijntjes, A., Kamphuis, J. H., Prinzie, P., & Telch, M. J. (2010). Peer victimization and internalizing problems in children: A meta-analysis of longitudinal studies. *Child Abuse & Neglect, 34*(4), 244–252.

Rigby, K. (2005). Why do some children bully at school? The contributions of negative attitudes towards victims and the perceived expectations of friends, parents and teachers. *School Psychology International, 26*(2), 147–161.

Rigby, K. (2007). *Bullying in schools: And what to do about it. Revised and updated.* Camberwell, Victoria: Australian Council for Education Research Press.

Rigby, K., & Slee, P. T. (1991). Bullying among Australian school children: Reported behavior and attitudes toward victims. *The Journal of Social Psychology, 131*(5), 615–627.

Rigby, K., Slee, P. T., & Martin, G. (2007). Implications of inadequate parental bonding and peer victimization for adolescent mental health. *Journal of Adolescence, 30*(5), 801–812.

Rivers, I., & Noret, N. (2010). 'I h8 u': Findings from a five-year study of text and email bullying. *British Educational Research Journal, 36*(4), 643–671.

Rodkin, P. C., Farmer, T. W., Pearl, R., & Van Acker, R. (2006). They're cool: Social status and peer group supports for aggressive boys and girls. *Social Development, 15*(2), 175–204.

Şahin, M. (2012). The relationship between the cyberbullying/cybervictimization and loneliness among adolescents. *Children and Youth Services Review, 34*(4), 834–837.

Salmivalli, C., Kaukiainen, A., Kaistaniemi, L., & Lagerspetz, K. M. J. (1999). Self-evaluated self-esteem, peer-evaluated self-esteem, and defensive egotism as predictors of adolescents' participation in bullying situations. *Personality and Social Psychology Bulletin, 25*(10), 1268–1278.

Salmivalli, C., Lagerspetz, K., Björkqvist, K., Österman, K., & Kaukiainen, A. (1996). Bullying as a group process: Participant roles and their relations to social status within the group. *Aggressive Behavior, 22*(1), 1–15.

Salmivalli, C., & Nieminen, E. (2002). Proactive and reactive aggression among school bullies, victims, and bully-victims. *Aggressive Behavior, 28*(1), 30–44.

Salmivalli, C., & Voeten, M. (2004). Connections between attitudes, group norms, and behaviour in bullying situations. *International Journal of Behavioral Development, 28*(3), 246–258.

Sapouna, M., & Wolke, D. (2013). Resilience to bullying victimization: The role of individual, family and peer characteristics. *Child Abuse & Neglect, 37*(11), 997–1006.

Sawyer, A. L., Bradshaw, C. P., & O'Brennan, L. M. (2008). Examining ethnic, gender, and developmental differences in the way children report being a victim of "bullying" on self-report measures. *Journal of Adolescent Health, 43*(2), 106–114.

Scheithauer, H., Hayer, T., Petermann, F., & Jugert, G. (2006). Physical, verbal, and relational forms of bullying among German students: Age trends, gender differences, and correlates. *Aggressive Behavior, 32*(3), 261–275.

Schultze-Krumbholz, A., & Scheithauer, H. (2009). Social-behavioral correlates of cyberbullying in a German student sample. *Zeitschrift für Psychologie/Journal of Psychology, 217*(4), 224–226.

Schwartz, D., Dodge, K. A., Pettit, G. S., & Bates, J. E. (1997). The early socialization of aggressive victims of bullying. *Child Development, 68*(4), 665–675.

Schwartz, D., Dodge, K. A., Pettit, G. S., & Bates, J. E. (2000). Friendship as a moderating factor in the pathway between early harsh home environment and later victimization in the peer group. *Developmental Psychology, 36*(5), 646.

Seals, D., & Young, J. (2002). Bullying and victimization: Prevalence and relationship to gender, grade level, ethnicity, self-esteem, and depression. *Adolescence, 38*(152), 735–747.

Sengupta, A., & Chaudhuri, A. (2011). Are social networking sites a source of online harassment for teens? Evidence from survey data. *Children and Youth Services Review, 33*(2), 284–290.

Shechtman, Z. (2002). Cognitive and affective empathy in aggressive boys: Implications for counseling. *International Journal for the Advancement of Counselling, 24*(4), 211–222.

Shields, A., & Cicchetti, D. (2001). Parental maltreatment and emotion dysregulation as risk factors for bullying and victimization in middle childhood. *Journal of Clinical Child Psychology, 30*(3), 349–363.

Siann, G., Callaghan, M., Glissov, P., Lockhart, R., & Rawson, L. (1994). Who gets bullied? The effect of school, gender and ethnic group. *Educational Research, 36*(2), 123–134.

Slonje, R., & Smith, P. K. (2008). Cyberbullying: Another main type of bullying? *Scandinavian Journal of Psychology, 49*(2), 147–154.

Smith, P. K., Madsen, K. C., & Moody, J. C. (1999). What causes the age decline in reports of being bullied at school? Towards a developmental analysis of risks of being bullied. *Educational Research, 41*(3), 267–285.

Smith, P. K., Mahdavi, J., Carvalho, M., Fisher, S., Russell, S., & Tippett, N. (2008). Cyberbullying: Its nature and impact in secondary school pupils. *Journal of Child Psychology and Psychiatry, 49*(4), 376–385.

Smith, P. K., & Myron-Wilson, R. (1998). Parenting and school bullying. *Clinical Child Psychology and Psychiatry, 3*(3), 405–417.

Solberg, M. E., & Olweus, D. (2003). Prevalence estimation of school bullying with the Olweus Bully/Victim Questionnaire. *Aggressive Behavior, 29*(3), 239–268.

Solberg, M. E., Olweus, D., & Endresen, I. M. (2007). Bullies and victims at school: Are they the same pupils? *British Journal of Educational Psychology, 77*(2), 441–464.

Sontag, L. M., Clemans, K. H., Graber, J. A., & Lyndon, S. T. (2011). Traditional and cyber aggressors and victims: A comparison of psychosocial characteristics. *Journal of Youth and Adolescence, 40*(4), 392–404.

Sourander, A., Brunstein Klomek, A., Ikonen, M., Lindroos, J., Luntamo, T., Koskelainen, M., Ristkari, T., & Helenius, H. (2010). Psychosocial risk factors associated with cyberbullying among adolescents: A population-based study. *Archives of General Psychiatry, 67*(7), 720.

Stassen Berger, K. (2007). Update on bullying at school: Science forgotten? *Developmental Review, 27*(1), 90–126.

Steffgen, G., König, A., Pfetsch, J., & Melzer, A. (2011). Are cyberbullies less empathic? Adolescents' cyberbullying behavior and empathic responsiveness. *Cyberpsychology, Behavior, and Social Networking, 14*(11), 643–648.

Sticca, F., Ruggieri, S., Alsaker, F., & Perren, S. (2013). Longitudinal risk factors for cyberbullying in adolescence. *Journal of Community & Applied Social Psychology, 23*(1), 52–67.

Sutton, J., Smith, P. K., & Swettenham, J. (1999). Social cognition and bullying: Social inadequacy or skilled manipulation? *British Journal of Developmental Psychology, 17*(3), 435–450.

Sweeting, H., Young, R., West, P., & Der, G. (2006). Peer victimization and depression in early–mid adolescence: A longitudinal study. *British Journal of Educational Psychology, 76*(3), 577–594.

Tippett, N., & Wolke, D. (in press). Socioeconomic status and bullying: A meta-analysis. *American Journal of Public Health.*

Tippett, N., & Wolke, D. (submitted). Aggression between siblings: Associations with the home environment and peer bullying.

Tippett, N., Wolke, D., & Platt, L. (2013). Ethnicity and bullying involvement in a national UK youth sample. *Journal of Adolescence, 36*(4), 639–649.

Tokunaga, R. S. (2010). Following you home from school: A critical review and synthesis of research on cyberbullying victimization. *Computers in Human Behavior, 26*(3), 277–287.

Twyman, K., Saylor, C., Taylor, L. A., & Comeaux, C. (2010). Comparing children and adolescents engaged in cyberbullying to matched peers. *Cyberpsychology, Behavior, and Social Networking, 13*(2), 195–199.

Vandebosch, H., & Van Cleemput, K. (2009). Cyberbullying among youngsters: Profiles of bullies and victims. *New Media & Society, 11*(8), 1349–1371.

Varjas, K., Henrich, C. C., & Meyers, J. (2009). Urban middle school students' perceptions of bullying, cyberbullying, and school safety. *Journal of School Violence, 8*(2), 159–176.

Veenstra, R., Lindenberg, S., Munniksma, A., & Dijkstra, J. K. (2010). The complex relation between bullying, victimization, acceptance, and rejection: Giving special attention to status, affection, and sex differences. *Child Development, 81*(2), 480–486.

Veenstra, R., Lindenberg, S., Oldehinkel, A. J., De Winter, A. F., Verhulst, F. C., & Ormel, J. (2005). Bullying and victimization in elementary schools: A comparison of bullies, victims, bully/victims, and uninvolved preadolescents. *Developmental Psychology, 41*(4), 672.

Volk, A. A., Camilleri, J. A., Dane, A. V., & Marini, Z. A. (2012). Is adolescent bullying an evolutionary adaptation? *Aggressive Behavior, 38*(3), 222–238.

Walrave, M., & Heirman, W. (2011). Cyberbullying: Predicting victimisation and perpetration. *Children & Society, 25*(1), 59–72.

Wang, J., Iannotti, R. J., & Nansel, T. R. (2009). School bullying among adolescents in the United States: Physical, verbal, relational, and cyber. *Journal of Adolescent Health, 45*(4), 368–375.

Warden, D., & Mackinnon, S. (2003). Prosocial children, bullies and victims: An investigation of their sociometric status, empathy and social problem-solving strategies. *British Journal of Developmental Psychology, 21*(3), 367–385.

Whitney, I., & Smith, P. K. (1993). A survey of the nature and extent of bullying in junior/middle and secondary schools. *Educational Research, 35*(1), 3–25.

Wild, L. G., Flisher, A. J., Bhana, A., & Lombard, C. (2004). Associations among adolescent risk behaviours and self-esteem in six domains. *Journal of Child Psychology and Psychiatry, 45*(8), 1454–1467.

Williams, K.R., & Guerra, N.G. (2007). Prevalence and predictors of internet bullying. *Journal of Adolescent Health, 41*(6), S14-S21.

Wolak, J., Mitchell, K. J., & Finkelhor, D. (2007). Does online harassment constitute bullying? An exploration of online harassment by known peers and online-only contacts. *Journal of Adolescent Health, 41*(6), S51-S58.

Wolke, D., & Samara, M. M. (2004). Bullied by siblings: Association with peer victimisation and behaviour problems in Israeli lower secondary school children. *Journal of Child Psychology and Psychiatry, 45*(5), 1015–1029.

Wolke, D., & Stanford, K. (1999). Bullying in school children. In D. Messer & S. Millar (Eds.), *Developmental Psychology* (pp. 341–360). London, UK: Arnold.

Wolke, D., Woods, S., & Samara, M. (2009). Who escapes or remains a victim of bullying in primary school? *British Journal of Developmental Psychology, 27*(4), 835–851.

Wolke, D., Woods, S., Stanford, K., & Schulz, H. (2001). Bullying and victimization of primary school children in England and Germany: Prevalence and school factors. *British Journal of Psychology, 92*(4), 673–696.

Wong, D.S. (2003). *School bullying and responding tactics: A life education approach studies.* Hong Kong: Li Koo Publishing Co., Ltd.

Woods, S., Wolke, D., Nowicki, S., & Hall, L. (2009). Emotion recognition abilities and empathy of victims of bullying. *Child Abuse & Neglect, 33*(5), 307–311.

Ybarra, M.L., Diener-West, M., & Leaf, P.J. (2007). Examining the overlap in Internet harassment and school bullying: Implications for school intervention. *Journal of Adolescent Health, 41*(6), S42-S50.

Ybarra, M.L., & Mitchell, K. J. (2004a). Online aggressor/targets, aggressors, and targets: a comparison of associated youth characteristics. *Journal of Child Psychology and Psychiatry, 45*(7), 1308–1316.

Ybarra, M.L., & Mitchell, K. J. (2004b). Youth engaging in online harassment: Associations with caregiver–child relationships, Internet use, and personal characteristics. *Journal of Adolescence, 27*(3), 319–336.

Ybarra, M.L., Mitchell, K. J., Wolak, J., & Finkelhor, D. (2006). Examining characteristics and associated distress related to Internet harassment: findings from the Second Youth Internet Safety Survey. *Pediatrics, 118*(4), e1169-e1177.

Yoneyama, S., & Rigby, K. (2006). Bully/victim students and classroom climate. *Youth Studies Australia, 25*(3), 34.

4

COMPARING ASSOCIATED HARM WITH TRADITIONAL BULLYING AND CYBERBULLYING

A narrative overview of mental, physical and behavioural negative outcomes

Nicole Gunther,[1] *Ann DeSmet,*[1] *Niels C. L. Jacobs and Ilse De Bourdeaudhuij*

Introduction

The experience of traditional and cyberbullying, for either victim, bully or bully-victim, has been linked to several negative outcomes among youth, such as mental and physical health problems and behavioural problems. Since cyberbullying differs from traditional bullying, for example due to the possibilities for cyberbullies to remain unknown to the victim, and their ability to reach a large audience quickly and for a long time via the Internet, it has been suggested that its effects are more severe than those of traditional bullying (Campbell, 2005). Some studies concluded that cyberbullying victimization was related to more psychosocial harm in comparison with traditional bullying (Schneider, O'Donnell, Stueve, & Coulter, 2012; Sourander, 2010). Additionally, cyberbullying victims reported significantly more social difficulties and higher levels of anxiety and depression than traditional victims (Campbell, Spears, Slee, Butler & Kift, 2012). Besides a difference in the magnitude of problems, cyberbullying victimization may also be related to different types of problems than traditional victimization.

Most prior research on the negative outcomes of traditional and cyberbullying has focused on the traditional roles of the victim, the bully, and those non-involved, whereas bully-victims (i.e. provocative or aggressive victims) and bystanders have been less studied (Mishna, Khoury-Kassabri, Gadalla, & Daciuk, 2012). Several studies stressed the importance of examining bullying in a broader social context by not viewing participant behaviour in peer victimization as fixed role categories but rather as influenced by circumstances (Bastiaensens et al., 2014; DeSmet et al., 2012; DeSmet, Veldeman et al., 2014; Espelage, Green, & Polanin, 2012; Espelage & Swearer, 2003; Gini, Albiero, Benelli, & Altoè, 2007, 2008; Salmivalli & Voeten, 2004), and by acknowledging that the incident has an impact on youngsters' lives that stretches beyond the outcomes for bullies and victims (Gini, Pozzoli, Borghi, & Franzoni, 2008; Rivers & Smith, 1994; Rivers, Poteat, Noret, & Ashurst, 2009; Rivers & Noret, 2010; Salmivalli, Lagerspetz, Björkqvist, Österman, & Kaukiainen, 1996; Salmivalli, 2010). Furthermore, most findings stem from cross-sectional data, thus complicating conclusions on causality (Gini & Pozzoli, 2009; Kowalski, Giumetti, Schroeder, & Lattaner, 2014; Reijntjes, Kamphuis, Prinzie, & Telch, 2010). In recent years, however, an increase is seen in the number of studies directly comparing outcomes of traditional bullying with cyberbullying, providing new potential insights in the severity and uniqueness of the harm related to cyberbullying in comparison to traditional bullying forms. A review of outcomes differentially related to cyberbullying and traditional bullying assessed in a broad social context, and summarizing both cross-sectional and longitudinal findings is therefore timely and warranted to help advance both research and prevention and intervention efforts in the field of traditional and cyberbullying.

The aim of this chapter is to provide a narrative overview of negative outcomes of (cyber)bullies, traditional and (cyber) victims, (cyber)bully-victims and online bystanders, and on similarities and differences between negative outcomes of traditional bullying and cyberbullying.

Method

Search strategy

A systematic literature search in PubMed, CINAHL, Web of Science, and PsycInfo databases was conducted for peer-reviewed articles published between the beginning of January 2000 and the end of June 2013. The search was conducted with the following keywords: ((cyber OR online OR internet OR digital) OR (offline OR traditional OR school OR peer) AND (bullying OR harassment OR victimization)) AND ((psychosomatic OR sleep OR pain OR headache OR health OR Quality of life) OR ((harm OR distress OR consequence OR outcome) AND (emotional OR behavioural OR behavioural OR psychosocial OR personality OR depression OR suicide OR substance abuse OR academic OR 'school performance')) AND (child* OR adolescent*))[2]. Additionally, Google Scholar was used with the same keywords, and our professional network was used to find articles on cyberbullying.

Selection criteria

Inclusion criteria were peer-reviewed articles – in English – on traditional bullying, cyberbullying, or both. The studies had to be conducted among children or adolescents and had to focus on mental and/or physical health and/or behaviour. Studies had to present mental and/or physical health and/or behavioural factors as either harm resulting from bullying involvement, or as risk factors for involvement in bullying incidents.

Exclusion criteria were studies that discussed health in (young) adults not related to bullying, that only investigated aspects of bullying other than health (e.g., prevalence, interventions not targeting health), that investigated forms of aggression other than bullying (e.g., dating violence, domestic violence, abuse, incest) or that investigated health problems related to Internet use other than bullying (e.g., Internet addiction, gaming). This selection process is shown in Figure 4.1.

Data extraction

For traditional and cyberbullying, this chapter provides a narrative overview of original research articles. Fifty-nine articles were included and entered into a database documenting sampling method, sample size, age of participants, independent variables, dependent variables, theoretical framework and results. Mental health (as dependent or independent variable) contains, for example, psychological distress, depression, suicidal ideation, self-esteem, anxiety, loneliness, or stress. Physical health contains general (self-perceived) health, psychosomatic complaints (e.g., sleeping disorders, stomach aches, and headaches), and health-reducing conditions (e.g., obesity). Behaviour contains, for example, self-harm, hyperactivity, drug and

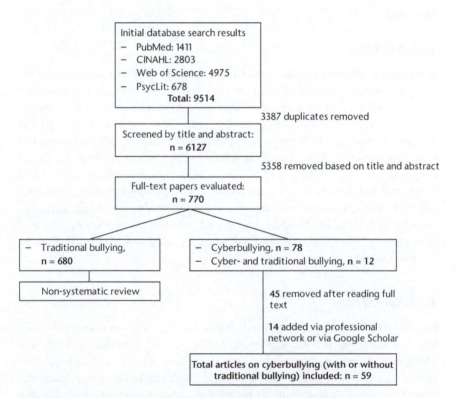

FIGURE 4.1 Flowchart of literature search and selection process.

alcohol use, or conduct problems. Findings from these articles were synthesized by type of outcome related to bullying involvement.

Results

In this part, negative outcomes[3] of traditional and cyberbullying on mental and physical health and behaviour are described. In each category, the outcomes for victims, bullies, bully-victims and bystanders are outlined separately. First, these negative outcomes are discussed for (participant roles in) traditional bullying. Second, these negative outcomes are also outlined for cyberbullying. Moreover, the influence of possible moderators, mediators and different forms of cyberbullying on the negative outcomes is discussed. Studies are included that focus exclusively on the negative outcomes of traditional bullying and cyberbullying respectively. Third, studies are summarized that directly compare how outcomes differ between traditional bullying and cyberbullying.

Traditional bullying

Mental health

Numerous cross-sectional and longitudinal studies have shown that, compared to all other participant roles including bully-victims, (Menesini, Modena & Tani, 2009), *victimized children* displayed significantly higher levels of depression, anxiety and loneliness, had lower levels of self-esteem (see e.g. Hawker & Boulton, 2000), poorer quality of life (Wilkins-Shurmer et al., 2003; Frisén & Bjarnelind, 2010), and more psychotic symptoms (Schreier et al., 2009; Campbell & Morrison, 2007; Lataster et al., 2006). A meta-analytic review of cross-sectional association between traditional victimization and psychosocial maladjustment provided clear evidence that traditional victimization was the most strongly related to symptoms of depression and the least strongly with anxiety (Hawker & Boulton, 2000).

In cross-sectional studies, being a *bully* has also been associated with depression (Kaltiala-Heino, Rimpelä, Martunnen, Rimpela & Rantanen, 1999; Kim, Koh, & Leventhal, 2005; Brunstein Klomek, Marrocco, Kleinman, Schonfeld & Gould, 2007; Saluja et al., 2004; Slee, 1995). Some studies reported that bullies suffer from anxiety and depressive symptoms just as much as, or even more than victims (Forero, McLellan, Rissel, & Bauman, 1999; Kaltiala-Heino, Rimpelä, Rantanen & Rimpelä, 2000). However, other research did not find an association between bullying perpetration and depression or psychosomatic symptoms (Fekkes, Pijpers, Verloove-Vanhorick, 2004). Some researchers found that bullies have low self-esteem (O'Moore, 2000), while others found that bullies do not have low self-esteem (Olweus, 1997). There is also substantial evidence from longitudinal studies that bullying behaviour can be seen as an indicator of risk for various psychological problems in adolescence: for example, Kaltiala-Heino et al. (2000)

found that involvement in bullying perpetration was associated with an increased risk for two or more co-occurring mental disorders (e.g., depression and anxiety).

Cross-sectional and longitudinal studies revealed that *bully-victims* displayed more depressive symptoms and anxiety than any other subgroup involved in bullying (Nansel, Craig, Overpeck, Saluja, & Ruan, 2004; Kaltiala-Heino et al., 2000; Menesini et al., 2009). Bully-victims also had an increased risk of future psychiatric problems (Kumpulainen & Räsänen, 2000).

Being a *bystander* of bullying was associated with increased mental health problems as well, even after controlling for past bully and victim experiences (Rivers et al., 2009). Furthermore, bystanders were slightly more at risk of thinking about ending their lives, compared to youth who had not witnessed bullying (i.e., they were assumed to experience a degree of co-victimization that makes them vulnerable to psychological distress (Rivers & Noret, 2010)).

Physical health

Victimized children displayed physical problems such as obesity (for a review, see Midei & Matthews, 2011) and psychosomatic complaints (for a meta-analysis, see Gini & Pozzoli, 2009). Likewise, longitudinal research showed that *bullies* and *bully-victims* were also more at risk for excessive psychosomatic symptoms (Kaltiala-Heino et al., 2000).

Behaviour

Compared to their non-victimized peers, *victimized* children displayed more aggression (Arseneault et al., 2006; Craig, 1998) and suicidal behaviours (Kaltiala-Heino et al., 1999; Brunstein Klomek et al., 2007). Furthermore, peer victimization was associated with higher levels of engagement in problem behaviours (Lester, Cross & Shaw, 2012) and lower academic achievement scores, absenteeism and school avoidance (e.g., Glew, Fan, Katon, Rivara & Kernic, 2005; Juvonen, Nishina & Graham, 2000; Kochenderfer & Ladd, 1996; Card & Hodges, 2008).

Longitudinal studies showed that *bullies*, when compared to victims and bully-victims, reported more externalising behavioural problems, such as aggression and frequent alcohol and drug use (e.g., Nansel, et al., 2004; Kaltiala-Heino et al., 2000; Menesini et al., 2009). Other longitudinal studies indicated that bullies were significantly more likely than others to exhibit antisocial and violent behaviour during adolescence and later adulthood (for a review, see Rigby, 2003), and being a bully predicted later criminality (Sourander et al., 2007). In a review, Brunstein Klomek, Sourander and Gould (2010) concluded that bullying others was a risk factor for later suicidal tendencies, especially when there was comorbid psychopathology. This relation was also found by other researchers (Kaltiala-Heino et al., 1999; Kim et al., 2005; Brunstein Klomek et al., 2007; Saluja et al., 2004; Slee, 1995). Other research also showed that bullying others was associated with academic problems and social adjustment problems (Estell, Farmer, Irvin, Crowther, Akos & Boudah, 2009).

Cross-sectional and longitudinal studies showed that *bully-victims* displayed more psychosocial adjustment problems, eating disorders and externalising symptoms (e.g., conduct problems, aggressiveness, attention deficit, problems in peer relationships and hyperactivity disorders) and school adjustment problems than any other subgroup involved in bullying (Nansel et al. 2004; Kaltiala-Heino et al., 2000; Menesini et al., 2009; Schwartz, 2000; O'Brennan, Bradshaw, & Sawyer, 2009; Skrzypiec, Slee, Askell-Wiliams, & Lawson, 2012). Bully-victims also have an increased risk of anti-social behaviour and having a criminal record as adults (Haynie, Nansel, Eitel, Crump, Saylor, Yu & Simons-Morton, 2001; Kumpulainen & Räsänen, 2000; Perren & Hornung, 2005). Being a *bystander of bullying* predicted an increased risk for substance abuse, even after controlling for past bully and victim experiences (Rivers, Poteat, Noret and Ashurst, 2009).

Conclusion

There is substantial evidence from longitudinal studies that not only victims, but also bullies, bully-victims and bystanders of traditional bullying are vulnerable to a host of negative outcomes that may not only have short-term, but also long-term negative effects for children's and adolescents' mental health (Sourander et al., 2007; Machmutow, Perren, Sticca, & Alsaker, 2012; Zwierzynska, Wolke, & Lereya, 2013). In general, being a victim is often related to internalising problems: depressive symptoms are amongst the most prominent negative consequences of peer victimization (Hawker & Boulton, 2000). Being a bully is often associated with externalising problems such as delinquency and aggressive behaviour, and being a bully-victim is associated with both externalising and internalising problems, showing that bully-victims are the most vulnerable group of traditional bullying. Even being a bystander is associated with increased risks for mental health and behavioural problems. However, previous longitudinal studies have revealed that the association between having psychological problems and peer victimization can be bidirectional, suggesting that psychological problems can also predict increases in peer victimization over time. For example, two large meta-analyses of longitudinal studies examining prospective linkages between peer victimization on the one side, and internalising or externalising problems on the other, concluded that these problems function as both antecedents and consequences of peer victimization (Reijntjes, Kamphuis, Prinzie, & Telch, 2010; Reijntjes, Kamphuis, Prinzie, Boelen, van der Schoot, & Telch, 2011). This bidirectional relationship was also found for the relationship between victimization and low self-esteem (Card & Hodges, 2008). These bidirectional relations may explain why peer victimization is highly stable across time and context. Consequently, certain psychological, health and behavioural factors could not only be an outcome of victimization but could also be a risk factor increasing victimization.

Cyberbullying

Mental health

For *victims of cyberbullying*, several cross-sectional studies demonstrated an association between the degree of cyber victimization and feelings of anxiety (Bauman, Toomey, & Walker, 2013; Campbell, Spears, Slee, Butler, & Kift, 2012; Goebert, Else, Matsu, Chung-Do, & Chang, 2011; Helwig-Larsen, Schütt, & Larsen, 2012; Lam & Li, 2013; Mitchell, Ybarra, & Finkelhor, 2007; Wang, Nansel, & Iannotti, 2011). One cross-sectional study, however, did not find a significant higher risk for cyber victims experiencing anxiety compared to youngsters who were not cyber victimized (Goebert et al., 2011). In this study, only older adolescents were included, while the other studies also included younger adolescents (i.e., distress of cyber victimization is the highest among younger adolescents (Campbell et al., 2012)). Findings from a longitudinal study showed significant associations between anxiety at baseline and cyber victimization two years later, but not when adjusted for other environmental factors (Yang et al., 2013). Similarly, social anxiety was found to predict cyber victimization, but not vice versa (van den Eijnden, Vermulst, van Rooij, Scholte, & van de Mheen, 2014). This suggests that (social) anxiety is an antecedent of cyber victimization rather than a consequence.

Cyber victimization, compared to non-involved children and cyberbullies, appeared to be related to lower levels of self-esteem, even after controlling for age, gender and race (Patchin & Hinduja, 2010). Self-esteem may, as anxiety, be a predictor of cyber victimization rather than an outcome, as longitudinal data showed that lower self-esteem at baseline was associated with cyber victimization at follow-up (Yang et al., 2013).

Several studies demonstrated that being the victim of cyberbullying is related to significantly higher odds of experiencing depressive symptoms compared to those who were not cyber victimized (Goebert et al., 2011; Helwig-Larsen et al., 2012; Lam & Li, 2013; Mitchell et al., 2007; Wang et al., 2011). Moreover, frequent cyber victims reported higher levels of depression than frequent cyberbullies. They also reported higher depression levels than occasional victims (Wang et al., 2011). However, one cross-sectional study could not replicate the results of cyber victims showing higher levels of depression after controlling for other forms of relational victimization (Dempsey, Sulkowski, Nichols, & Storch, 2009). In a longitudinal study using a 6-month follow-up time, Gámez-Guadix et al. (2013) found a bidirectional relationship between cyber victimization and depressive symptoms: cyber victimization increased depressive symptoms, which in turn increased the risk of being cyberbullied. This finding applied even for adolescents having experienced infrequent (i.e., less than one or two incidents) cyber victimization (Gámez-Guadix et al., 2013). Another study found that cyber victimization was a significant predictor of depression (Lam & Li, 2013) only for girls and not for boys (Bauman et al., 2013).

In another longitudinal study, with a 3-month follow-up time, no confirmation was found for clear internalising patterns (e.g., anxiety, depression, low self-esteem) for cyber victims. Only for girls did higher levels of cyber victimization predict higher depression at follow-up (Schultze-Krumbholz, Jäkel, Schultze, & Scheithauer, 2012).

Cyberbullies often experienced depression as well. Occasional cyberbullies experienced similar levels of depressive symptoms as occasional cyber victims, but frequent cyberbullies experienced no higher levels of depressive symptoms than occasional cyberbullies (Wang et al., 2011). Although one study reported that depressive symptoms, despite being correlated with cyberbullying, did not significantly predict perpetration of cyberbullying (Perren, Dooley, Shaw, & Cross, 2010), a longitudinal study found that depressive symptoms and anxiety were stable predictors of cyberbullying perpetration (Yang et al., 2013). This result was also found for cyberbullies and cyber bully-victims (Chang et al., 2013). However, cyberbullying predicted depressive symptoms to a lesser extent than victimization (Chang et al., 2013). Furthermore, one study found that cyberbullies reported lower levels of self-esteem compared to non-involved youth, even after controlling for age, gender and race (Patchin & Hinduja, 2010). Low self-esteem was considered a predictor of cyber perpetration in a longitudinal study (Yang et al., 2013), while other research only found lower self-esteem for pure cyberbullies compared to non-involved youth (Chang et al., 2013).

In particular, cyber *bully-victims* reported feeling more depressed, anxious and stressed compared with non-involved youth (Campbell et al., 2012; Sourander, 2010) and other participant roles in cyberbullying (Chang et al., 2013; Gámez-Guadix et al., 2013).

Physical health

Research showed that several participant roles in cyberbullying experienced physical health problems. *Victims* had a two- to threefold increased risk for psychosomatic problems and self-reported the worst health (Sourander, 2010). Not only victims, but also bullies and bully-victims were at significantly higher risk for a variety of psychosomatic problems (e.g., sleep problems, headaches, stomach aches) than those not involved in cyberbullying. Bully-victims reported the most psychosomatic problems (Beckman, Hagquist, & Hellström, 2012; Sourander, 2010) and reported suffering the same problems as victims and bullies (Sourander, 2010). Furthermore, when looking at self-perceived general health, a significant association was found for all participant roles in cyberbullying, which remained significant after controlling for traditional victimization involvement.

Behaviour

The effects of cyberbullying victimization are also related to adolescents' behaviour. In a study by Helwig-Larsen et al. (2012) *victims*, compared to non-victimized children, were more likely to display problem behaviours such as antisocial behaviour. In other studies, victims were three times more likely (Goebert et al., 2011), and obese victims were five times more likely (DeSmet, Deforche, Hublet, Tanghe, & De Bourdeaudhuij, 2014), to consider suicide than those non-victimized by cyberbullying. Also Hinduja and Patchin (2010) found higher rates of suicidal thoughts and attempts; however, the cyberbullying experience was assumed not to cause suicidal ideation by itself but to further contribute to stressful life events and problems already experienced by these youngsters. Being a cyber victim, in this study, was also positively related to self-harm (e.g., cutting, burning, deliberately hurting yourself).

Additionally, cyber victims were two times more likely to report substance abuse (Mitchell et al., 2007) and were 2.5 times more likely to engage in binge drinking, smoking or using marijuana than youngsters who were not cyber-victimized (Goebert et al., 2011). Another study, however, did not find a significant association between cyber victimization and alcohol or other substance abuse (Helwig-Larsen et al., 2012). A longitudinal study showed that cyber victimization did not increase the risk of substance abuse, but substance abuse predicted an increase in cyberbullying victimization at follow-up, suggesting that substance abuse is a predictor of cyberbullying victimization rather than a consequence (Gámez-Guadix et al., 2013).

Furthermore, in one study, cyber victimization was found to be significantly, but not very strongly, related to ADHD symptoms (Helwig-Larsen et al., 2012). However, another (longitudinal) study did not find a significant relation between ADHD symptoms at age 10 and cyber victimization – or cyberbullying – at age 12 (Yang et al., 2013). Cyber victims more often reported lower performance at school (i.e., grades) than youth not involved in cyberbullying. Students with lower school performance and lower school attachment were more likely to be cyberbullied than A-students (Schneider, O'Donnell, Stueve, & Coulter, 2012). Moreover, lower performance among victims of cyberbullying was significantly associated with truancy and poor concentration (Beran & Li, 2007). Other researchers, however, did not find a significant association between victimization and school truancy (Katzer, Fetchenhauer, & Belschak, 2009).

Cyberbullies reported more suicidal ideation and more suicidal attempts than those non-involved in cyberbullying, but less than cyber victims (Hinduja & Patchin, 2010). Furthermore, compared to children not involved in cyberbullying, cyberbullies were up to five times more likely to consume alcohol weekly, and three times more likely to be regular smokers (Sourander, 2010). Additionally, cyberbullies appeared to smoke and drink significantly more than youth not involved in any form of bullying (Vieno, Gini, & Santinello, 2011).

Cyber bully-victims were more likely to perform poorly at school and reported lower school attachment than cyber victims (Chang et al., 2013). They also had a higher risk for smoking and drinking than youth not involved in any form of bullying. Cyber bully-victims were six times more likely to use alcohol every week, seven times more likely to be drunk more than once per week, and three times more likely to be weekly or daily smokers. These figures were comparable or higher to those of cyberbullies but much higher than those of cyber victims (Sourander, 2010; Vieno et al., 2011).

Moderators and mediators of negative outcomes

From earlier research it is known that not all adolescents who experience cyberbullying report negative outcomes (e.g., Hinduja & Patchin, 2007). In recent studies, several moderators and mediators in the relationship between victimization and negative outcomes have been investigated. For example, one study reported that cyber victimization was a significant predictor of depression only for girls (Bauman et al., 2013). A longitudinal study by Machmutow et al. (2012) showed that seeking support from peers and family emerged as a highly adaptive coping strategy in the relation between cyber victimization and depressive symptoms. Others, however, reported that peer support did not protect against depressive feelings (Aoyama, Saxon, & Fearon, 2011). Helpless reactions seemed to aggravate the negative impact of cyber victimization (Machmutow et al., 2012), and also emotion-focused coping appeared not to be effective in reducing depressive feelings associated with cyberbullying victimization (Völlink, Bolman, Dehue, & Jacobs, 2013).

A longitudinal study suggested that the relationship between cyber victimization and anxiety may be explained by environmental factors, such as stressful life events, cyber perpetration, family situation, social life, gender, or poor academic achievement (Yang et al., 2013). The relationship between cyber victimization and problem behaviours was found to be fully mediated by the strain youngsters experienced from various stressful life events (Hinduja & Patchin, 2007). Several mediators were also reported in the relationship between cyber victimization and suicide, such as the level of depressive symptoms (only among girls) (Bauman et al., 2013), substance abuse and violent behaviour (Litwiller & Brausch, 2013). In the study by Hay and Meldrum the relation between victimization on the one hand and self-harm (e.g., cutting, burning, deliberately hurting yourself) and suicidal ideation on the other was partially mediated by negative emotions (anxiety, depression and low self-esteem) and partially moderated by highly authoritative parenting and high self-control (Hay & Meldrum, 2010).

Negative outcomes and different forms of cyberbullying

Recently, studies have started to investigate differences between negative outcomes of different forms of cyberbullying. In one study, computer-based cyber victimization significantly predicted negative mental health outcomes, such as depressive symptoms, anxiety and low self-esteem, while phone-based cyber victimization did not (Fredstrom, Adams, & Gilman, 2011). Furthermore, less prevalent forms of cyberbullying such as cyber stalking, denigration, outing and trickery, exclusion and impersonation were considered as more emotionally distressing by victims than other forms of cyberbullying (Staude-Müller, Hansen, & Voss, 2012). One study compared several forms of cyberbullying and traditional bullying. Picture and video clip forms are perceived as worse, email, instant messaging, website and chat room forms are perceived as similar and phone call and text message forms are perceived as less severe than traditional bullying (Smith, Mahdavi, Carvalho, Fisher, Russell & Tippett, 2008).

Conclusion

Most studies on cyberbullying focused on the negative outcomes related to victimization. The cross-sectional studies in this review suggest that cyber victimization is associated with several serious negative outcomes such as anxiety, depression, low self-esteem, suicidal ideation, substance abuse and psychosomatic problems. Yet, it is still unclear if these negative outcomes are consequences of cyber victimization or, rather, predict increases in victimization over time. The few longitudinal studies available showed a bidirectional relation between victimization and psychosocial harm such as depression, or indicated that some negative 'outcomes' were in fact antecedents of cyber victimization (e.g., anxiety, low self-esteem, substance abuse) or of cyber perpetration (e.g., ADHD), rather than consequences of cyberbullying involvement. However, more longitudinal studies are direly needed to increase our understanding of how cyberbullying experiences affect negative health or behavioural outcomes over time.

It was apparent that bullies experience negative mental, physical and behavioural outcomes as well. Bully/victims especially appeared to be at risk for negative health outcomes and are most in need for help, as they experienced both problems related to victimization and those related to perpetration. When studying health outcomes related to cyberbullying, this review's findings indicate that in order to guide future anti-cyberbullying interventions, more research is needed that also takes into account health outcomes for cyberbullies.

Both individual characteristics (e.g., gender, coping styles) and incident characteristics (e.g., the form, number of incidents the person experienced) appeared to influence the relation between involvement in cyberbullying and negative health outcomes. In light of the above-mentioned negative impact of cyberbullying on mental and physical health and behaviour, it is important that future (longitudinal) research examines more potential mediating and moderating processes that might influence the relationship between cyberbullying and negative outcomes. This knowledge can be used to develop and sustain effective prevention and intervention programs to reduce cyberbullying experiences and their associated harm.

Comparing negative outcomes between traditional bullying and cyberbullying

It is a common notion in the developmental literature that the number of risks a youngster is exposed to, rather than a single risk factor, is most predictive of psychological outcomes. This is in line with the multiple victimization framework (Rutter, 1987), and suggests that the co-occurrence of traditional and cyberbullying results in additional negative outcomes for victims. The question arises whether cyberbullying leads to negative outcomes that are similar in nature and severity to those resulting from traditional bullying. If outcomes are similar and/ or comparable in nature and severity, this may suggest that health promoting interventions for youth involved in traditional bullying can also be used for youth involved in cyberbullying. Several studies directly comparing cyber victims to victims of traditional bullying have used a sufficiently large sample of both cyber- and traditional victims, allowing for the singling out of the individual relation of each type of victimization with negative outcomes.

Studies comparing cyber victims to victims of traditional bullying on the negative outcomes related to mental health, such as depressive symptoms, stress and anxiety, concurred in their findings: the relationship between victimization and these negative outcomes was indeed strongest for the combined victim group (cyber and traditional victimization) (Campbell et al., 2012; Gradinger, Strohmeier, & Spiel, 2009; Raskauskas, 2010; Schneider et al., 2012). Victims who were bullied both offline and online were more likely to suffer from psychological problems than adolescents not involved, followed by pure cyber victims, and finally pure traditional victims (Campbell et al., 2012; Gradinger et al., 2009; Raskauskas, 2010; Schneider et al., 2012). An exception to this was low self-esteem, where the association was stronger for traditional victimization than for cyber victimization (Chang et al., 2013). Several studies demonstrated that being the victim of cyberbullying was related to significantly higher odds of experiencing depressive symptoms compared to traditional victims (Campbell et al., 2012) and those not victimized by either traditional or cyber bullying (Mitchell et al., 2007). Another study reported different results, showing that those who were victimized reported significantly higher anxiety and depression levels than the non-victim group, but these levels did not differ significantly between victims of traditional bullying or cyberbullying, or of both forms. A similar finding was noted for bullies (Sontag, Clemans, Graber, & Lyndon, 2011).

A cross-sectional study by Beckman, Hagquist and Hellström (2012) comparing cyber victims and traditional victims on psychosomatic problems indicated that traditional bullying involvement and cyberbullying involvement were associated with a similar degree of psychosomatic problems. Cyber bullies, however, experienced as many psychosomatic problems as victims, while traditional bullies experienced fewer psychosomatic problems than traditional victims. The risk of psychosomatic problems for victims or bullies involved in both types of bullying (traditional and cyberbullying) did not appear higher than when they were victims or bullies of only one form of bullying (Beckman et al., 2012).

When examining studies controlling for traditional forms of victimization, one study showed that online victimization was significantly related to high substance use, even after adjusting for these victims' involvement in traditional victimization (Mitchell et al., 2007). Furthermore, as mentioned earlier, bully-victims of cyberbullying showed the greatest behavioural problems, such as aggression (Gradinger et al., 2009) and suicidal ideation (Bonanno & Hymel, 2013), also after correction for their involvement in traditional bullying. In a recent large-scale study of adolescents, Låftman, Modin and Östberg (2013) found that cyber victimization was associated with poorer physical health, even when controlling for traditional bullying. Most cross-sectional studies have shown that cyber victimization remained a significant predictor for several mental health outcomes above and beyond the influence of traditional victimization (Bonanno & Hymel, 2013; Campbell et al., 2012; Dempsey et al., 2009; Fredstrom et al., 2011; Juvonen & Gross, 2008; Machmutow et al., 2012; Perren et al., 2010; Wang et al., 2011), although two studies concluded the opposite. For example, Mitchell et al. (2007) concluded that, after adjusting for traditional victimization, life adversity and demographic factors, online victimization was no longer significantly related to depressive symptoms (Mitchell et al., 2007). This finding was also confirmed for depression in another study (Dempsey et al., 2009), but here cyber victimization did significantly explain social anxiety, even after controlling for traditional victimization. Similarly, a cross-sectional study of Olweus (2012) came to the tentative conclusion that when a youngster is exposed to both traditional and cyberbullying, the additional impact of cyber victimization on poor self-esteem may be negligible (Olweus, 2012). Olweus's finding, however, only related to one type of psychosocial outcome (i.e., poor self-esteem), which several studies also found to be poorly related to cyberbullying.

A possible reason for the contradictory findings on the role of cyberbullying in negative health outcomes between the above mentioned studies is, as suggested by Olweus (2012), that cyber victimization is experienced differently by pure cyber victims than by victims of both traditional bullying and cyber bullying. For pure cyber victims, the association with negative mental health outcomes is strong, and often stronger than the association for pure traditional victims. For victims who are experiencing both traditional and cyber victimization, it may be the traditional victimization that has the highest impact. This may explain why some studies that use traditional victimization as a confounder do not find a significant relation of cyber victimization with mental health, while the few studies using large enough samples to separate the effects for pure cyber victims and combined traditional and cyber victims do find associations between cyber victimization and negative outcomes. To assess whether this could serve as an explanation, more large-scale studies are needed.

Since the above mentioned studies are all cross-sectional, it cannot be determined whether victims experienced more mental health problems as a result of victimization or whether adolescents with depressive, anxiety and stress symptoms were more likely to be online and/or offline. When studying these reciprocal relationships between cyberbullying and, for example, mental health problems, it is again crucial to concurrently examine the mental health antecedents and consequences of traditional bullying and cyberbullying. Only a few longitudinal studies exist that can shed more light onto the longitudinal change in psychosocial well-being following cyber victimization. These longitudinal studies indicated that cyber victimization is predictive of an increase in later depressive symptoms (Gámez-Guadix et al., 2013; Machmutow et al., 2012; Schultze-Krumbholz et al., 2012) and one study confirmed this prediction existed over and beyond traditional victimization in adolescents (Machmutow et al., 2012). One 3-year follow-up study concluded that loneliness and social anxiety predicted an increase in later cyber victimization, rather than the reverse. However, for traditional victimization, the results did indicate a bidirectional relationship (van den Eijnden et al., 2014). Another longitudinal study did find bidirectional relations between cyber victimization and depression (Gámez-Guadix et al., 2013). Possibly, different types of mental health problems increase a youngster's vulnerability to traditional victimization more than to cyber victimization. This requires further validation in future longitudinal studies, as it may imply that different target groups and psychosocial warning signals should be identified for cyberbullying than for traditional bullying prevention programs.

Research concurrently looking into traditional and cyber victimization reported some mediators and moderators in the relation between either traditional and/or cyberbullying and health outcomes. Both traditional and cyberbullying victimization were found to be related to self-harm (cutting, burning, deliberately hurting yourself) and suicidal ideation. However, this relation was partially mediated by negative emotions (stronger for traditional than for cyber victimization) and partially moderated by social circumstances and self-control. Further, the moderating role of authoritative parenting was significant for the relation between cyberbullying and suicidal ideation, but not for self-harm. In traditional bullying, parenting moderated for both self-harm and suicidal ideation (Hay & Meldrum, 2010).

In sum, although traditional and cyber victimization are related, the majority of research evidence suggests that cyber victimization appears to have its own unique contribution to these negative psychological outcomes. However, some studies did not find that the negative outcomes of cyberbullying go above and beyond the negative outcomes of traditional bullying. The initial conclusion should therefore be interpreted with caution. In addition to the unique contribution of cyberbullying to the negative outcomes, cyberbullying seemed to have a larger impact than traditional bullying on mental health outcomes. This seemingly more severe impact of cyberbullying (Campbell, 2005; Campbell et al., 2012) may come from the larger breadth of the potential audience, the potential for perpetrator anonymity, for perpetrators' ability to access victims 24 hours per day, and the permanency of written words/images (Dredge, Gleeson, & de la Piedad Garcia, 2014). Victims of both forms of bullying suffered the most, and possibly, when by both forms of bullying, the experience of traditional bullying weighs heavier than that of cyberbullying for some outcomes (i.e., self-esteem), while this may be the reverse for other outcomes (i.e., depression, suicidal ideation). This last hypothesis warrants further research.

Discussion

Research to date has demonstrated that cyber victimization and cyberbullying are related to serious negative outcomes, such as depression, anxiety, low self-esteem, substance use and suicidal behaviour. In addition, most previous studies suggest that cyber victimization is associated with types of negative outcomes that are similar to those documented for traditional victimization. However, it is hard to draw definite conclusions about this matter, due to several methodological differences (e.g., sample sizes, measures, methods of analysis) between cross-sectional studies finding an association or no association between cyber victimization and types of negative outcomes. Furthermore, studies addressing the longitudinal change in negative outcomes following cyber victimization (controlling for traditional victimization) are scarce and sometimes contradicted results from cross-sectional studies.

Notably, of studies that have compared participant roles in cyberbullying, bully-victims experienced the most adverse outcomes, especially with regard to suicidal ideation, and in some cases depression. These results suggest that this group of adolescents may require extra support from health care professionals and educators. However, more work is needed to increase our understanding of this potentially vulnerable group.

Most, but not all, of the studies concurrently looking into traditional and cyber victimization showed that the experience of combined victims of traditional and cyberbullying appears to be more strongly related to mental health problems than the experience for pure cyber victims or pure traditional victims. However, when looking at pure cyber victims or pure traditional victims, the association between cyber victimization and mental health problems was found to be stronger in most studies.

It also remains unclear whether cyber victimization exhibits its own unique contribution to several negative outcomes. Most, but not all, studies indicate that cyber victimization does contribute uniquely to negative outcomes. According to some researchers this contribution was the highest in depression and suicidal ideation. The contribution of cyber victimization to low self-esteem and anxiety seems more contested. Specifically for self-esteem, it has been suggested that when adding traditional victimization as a confounder, the additional impact of cyber victimization seems negligible (Olweus, 2012). Further investigation into this line of inquiry is important and may have implications for cyberbullying interventions.

In addition, more complex studies should be conducted to analyse potential moderator and/or mediator effects, such as the influence of coping strategies, gender, social support and parenting on the relation between negative outcomes, cyberbullying and cyber victimization. These types of studies can pinpoint which youngsters involved in bullying are at greatest risk of showing difficulties across the broad spectrum of mental and physical health and behavioural problems, and can help better target the interventions. Some suggestions include investigating moderating effects of coping strategies on the impact of cyber victimization on depressive symptoms, using longitudinal studies, to assess the differential impact of victimization through different types of technology, and to have more qualitative input through diary report on how electronic victimization takes place (Sandstrom, Cillessen, & Eisenhower, 2003).

The exploration of potential differences in negative outcomes between cyberbullying and traditional bullying struggles with a number of methodological issues. First, there is a high degree of overlap between involvement in cyberbullying and involvement in traditional bullying, and only a few individuals experience only cyberbullying (e.g., Juvonen & Gross, 2008; Perren & Gutzwiller-Helfenfinger, 2012). Second, there is a plethora of bullying types, which makes it almost impossible to assess the whole range and perform a systematic comparison. Third, cyberbullying has been defined in several ways, and these differences create additional difficulties in comparing cyberbullying and traditional bullying. Lastly, the aspects believed to distinguish cyberbullying from traditional bullying are hard to implement in a standard cyberbullying and traditional bullying scale in such a way that makes systematic comparisons possible. Sticca and Perren (2013) suggest that these issues call for a tool allowing for the assessment of the severity of different forms of bullying, and to compare them systematically. Moreover, this tool should be able to account simultaneously for a number of aspects that may influence the severity of the bullying experience, such as the medium (traditional vs. cyber) used to bully, the publicity, and the bully's anonymity.

To conclude, in this chapter several questions were raised, such as: 'does cyberbullying relate to more severe outcomes than traditional bullying?' and 'does cyberbullying relate to similar types of negative outcomes than traditional bullying?' To provide definite answers to these and many other questions raised in this chapter, more studies with larger samples that allow for the singling out of (combined) participant roles are direly needed, as well as longitudinal studies (controlling for traditional victimization) that examine the reciprocal relationship between cyber victimization and negative outcomes, studies looking into mediating and moderating variables and studies using valid instruments that allow systematic comparisons. However, despite the relevance of knowing which type of negative outcome relates to which type of bullying and to which severity level, the study findings described above suggest a strong need to address both forms of bullying simultaneously in future interventions. These interventions may be most effective, as suggested by several researchers (e.g., Olweus, 2012), for several reasons. First, the high overlap between these types of bullying may make a distinction relevant only for a small group of youngsters. Second, the youngsters victimized by both forms suffer the most. And third, previous research has indicated that targeting only one form of bullying causes an increase in another type of bullying (Elledge et al., 2013).

Notes

1 Shared first authorship.
2 An asterisk indicates a wildcard symbol, by which any word starting with child or adolescent will qualify for the search, including child, children, adolescent, adolescents . . .

3 The term 'outcomes' was used to refer to psychological, physical and behavioural phe-nomena that are traditionally thought to result from victimization or perpetration/ victimization in bullying. However, it should be noted that most studies on bullying in this review were cross-sectional (i.e., variables are correlated), and therefore, causal claims cannot always be made.

References

Aoyama, I., Saxon, T. F., & Fearon, D. D. (2011). Internalizing problems among cyber-bullying victims and moderator effects of friendship quality. *Multicultural Education & Technology Journal, 5*(2), 92–105. doi:10.1108/17504971111142637

Arseneault, L., Bowes, L., & Shakoor, S. (2010). Bullying victimization in youths and men-tal health problems: 'much ado about nothing'? *Psychological Medicine, 40*(5), 717–729. doi:10.1017/S0033291709991383

Bastiaensens, S., Vandebosch, H., Poels, K., Van Cleemput, K., DeSmet, A., & De Bourde-audhuij, I. (2014). Cyberbullying on social network sites. An experimental study into bystanders' behavioural intentions to help the victim or reinforce the bully. *Computers in Human Behavior, 31*, 259–271. doi:10.1016/j.chb.2013.10.036

Bauman, S., Toomey, R. B., & Walker, J. L. (2013). Associations among bullying, cyber-bullying, and suicide in high school students. *Journal of Adolescence, 36*(2), 341–350. doi:10.1016/j.adolescence.2012.12.001

Beckman, L., Hagquist, C., & Hellström, L. (2012). Does the association with psychoso-matic health problems differ between cyberbullying and traditional bullying? *Emotional and Behavioural Difficulties, 17*(3–4), 421–434. doi:10.1080/13632752.2012.704228

Beran, T. & Li, Q. (2007). The relationship between cyberbullying and school bullying. *The Journal of Student Wellbeing, 1*(2), 15–33.

Bonanno, R. A., & Hymel, S. (2013). Cyber bullying and internalizing difficulties: above and beyond the impact of traditional forms of bullying. *Journal of Youth and Adolescence, 42*(5), 685–697. doi:10.1007/s10964-013-9937-1

Brunstein Klomek, A., Marrocco, F., Kleinman, M., Schonfeld, I. S., & Gould, M. S. (2007). Bullying, depression, and suicidality in adolescents. *American Academy of Child and Adolescent Psychiatry, 46*(1), 40–49. doi:10.1097/01.chi.0000242237.84925.18

Brunstein Klomek, A., Sourander, A, & Gould, M. (2010). The association of suicide and bullying in childhood to young adulthood: a review of cross-sectional and longitudinal research findings. *Canadian Journal of Psychiatry, 55*(5), 282–288.

Campbell, M. A. (2005). Cyber bullying: an old problem in a new guise? *Australian Journal of Guidance and Counselling, 15*(1), 68–76. doi:10.1375/ajgc.15.1.68

Campbell, M. L., & Morrison, A. P. (2007). The relationship between bullying, psychotic-like experiences and appraisals in 14–16-year olds. *Behavior Research and Therapy, 45*(7), 1579–1591. doi:10.1016/j.brat.2006.11.009

Campbell, M., Spears, B., Slee, P., Butler, D., & Kift, S. (2012). Victims' perceptions of tra-ditional and cyberbullying and the psychosocial correlates of their victimization. *Emo-tional and Behavioral Difficulties, 17*(3–4), 389–401. doi:10.1080/13632752.2012.704316

Card, N. A. & Hodges, E. V. E. (2008). Peer victimization among schoolchildren: correla-tions, causes, consequences, and considerations in assessment and intervention. *School Psychology Quarterly, 23*(4), 451–461. doi:10.1037/a0012769

Chang, F.-C., Lee, C.-M., Chiu, C. H., Hsi, W.-Y., Huang, T.-F., & Pan, Y.-C. (2013). Relationships among cyberbullying, school bullying, and mental health in Taiwanese adolescents. *Journal of School Health, 83*(6), 454–462. doi:10.1111/josh.12050

Craig, W. M. (1998). The relationship among bullying, victimization, depression, anxiety, and aggression in elementary school children. *Personality and Individual Differences, 24*(1), 123–130. doi:10.1016/S0191-8869(97)00145-1

Dempsey, A. G., Sulkowski, M. L., Nichols, R., & Storch, E. A. (2009). Differences between peer victimization in cyber and physical settings and associated phycosocial adjustment in early adolescence. *Psychology in the Schools, 46*(10), 962–972. doi:10.1002/pits.20437

DeSmet, A., Bastiaensens, S., Van Cleemput, K., Poels, K., Vandebosch, H., & De Bourdeaudhuij, I. (2012). Mobilizing bystanders of cyberbullying: an exploratory study into behavioural determinants of defending the victim. *Annual Review of Cybertherapy and Telemedicine, 181*, 58–63. doi:10.3233/978-1-61499-121-2-58.

DeSmet, A., Deforche, B., Hublet, A., Tanghe, A., & De Bourdeaudhuij, I. (2014). Traditional and cyberbullying victimization as correlates of psychosocial distress and barriers to a healthy lifestyle among severely obese adolescents – a matched case-control study on prevalence and results from a cross-sectional study. *BMC Public Health, 14*, 224–236. doi:10.1186/1471-2458-14-224

DeSmet, A., Veldeman, C., Poels, K., Bastiaensens, S., Van Cleemput, K., Vandebosch, H., & De Bourdeaudhuij, I. (2014). Determinants of self-reported bystander behavior in cyberbullying incidents amongst adolescents. *Cyberpsychology Behavior and Social Networking, 17*(4), 207–215. doi:10.1089/cyber.2013.0027

Dredge, R., Gleeson, J. F. M., & de la Piedad Garcia, X. (2014). Risk factors associated with impact severity of cyberbullying victimization: a qualitative study of adolescent online social networking. *Cyberpsychology, Behavior and Social Networking, 17*(5), 287–291. doi:10.1089/cyber.2013.0541

Elledge, L. C., Williford, A., Boulton, A. J., DePaolis, K. J., Little, T. D., & Salmivalli, C. (2013). Individual and contextual predictors of cyberbullying: the influence of children's provictim attitudes and teachers' ability to intervene. *Journal of Youth and Adolescence, 42*(5), 698–710. doi:10.1007/s10964-013-9920-x

Espelage, D., Green, H., & Polanin, J. (2012). Willingness to intervene in bullying episodes among middle school students: individual and peer-group influences. *Journal of Early Adolescence, 32*(6), 776–801. doi:10.1177/0272431611423017

Espelage, D. L. & Swearer, S. M. (2003). Research on school bullying and victimization: what have we learned and where do we go from here? *School Psychology Review, 32*(3), 365–383.

Estell, D. B., Farmer, T. W., Irvin, M. J., Crowther, A., Akos, P., & Boudah, D. J. (2009). Students with exceptionalities and the peer group context of bullying and victimization in late elementary school. *Journal of Child and Family Studies, 18*(2), 136–150. doi:10.1007/s10826-008-9214-1

Fekkes, M., Pijpers, F. I. M., Verloove-Vanhorick, S. P. (2004). Bullying behavior and associations with psychosomatic complaints and depression in victims. *The Journal of Pediatrics, 144*(1), 17–22. doi:10.1016/j.jpeds.2003.09.025

Forero, R., McLellan, L., Rissel, C., & Bauman, A. (1999). Bullying behaviour and psychosocial health among school students in New South Wales, Australia: cross sectional survey. *British Medical Journal, 319*(7206), 344–348.

Fredstrom, B. K., Adams, R. E., & Gilman, R. (2011). Electronic and school-based victimization: unique contexts for adjustment difficulties during adolescence. *Journal of Youth and Adolescence, 40*(4), 405–415. doi:10.1007/s10964-010-9569-7

Frisén, A., & Bjarnelind, S. (2010). Health-related quality of life and bullying in adolescence. *Acta Paediatrica, 99*(4), 597–603. doi:10.1111/j.1651-2227.2009.01664.x

Gámez-Guadix, M., Orue, I., Smith, P. K., & Calvete, E. (2013). Longitudinal and recipro-cal relations of cyberbullying with depression, substance use, and problematic inter-net use among adolescents. *Journal of Adolescent Health, 53*(4), 446–452. doi:10.1016/j.jadohealth.2013.03.030

Gini, G., Albiero, P., Benelli, B., & Altoè, G. (2007). Does empathy predict adolescents' bul-lying and defending behavior? *Aggressive Behavior, 33*(5), 467–476. doi:10.1002/ab.20204

Gini, G., Albiero, P., Benelli, B., & Altoè, G. (2008). Determinants of adolescents' active defending and passive bystanding behavior in bullying. *Journal of Adolescence, 31*(1), 93–105. doi:10.1016/j.adolescence.2007.05.002

Gini, G., & Pozzoli, T. (2009). Association between bullying and psychosomatic problems: a meta-analysis. *Pediatrics, 123*(3), 1059–1065. doi:10.1542/peds.2008-1215

Gini, G., Pozzoli, T., Borghi, F., & Franzoni, L. (2008). The role of bystanders in students' perception of bullying and sense of safety. *Journal of School Psychology, 46*(6), 617–638. doi:10.1016/j.jsp.2008.02.001

Glew, G. M., Fan, M. Y., Katon, W., Rivara, F. P., & Kernic, M. A. (2005). Bullying, psycho-social adjustment, and academic performance in elementary school. *Archives of Pediat-rics & Adolescent Medicine, 159*(11), 1026–1031. doi:10.1001/archpedi.159.11.1026

Goebert, D., Else, I., Matsu, C., Chung-Do, J., & Chang, J. Y. (2011). The impact of cyber-bullying on substance use and mental health in a multiethnic sample. *Maternal and Child Health Journal, 15*(8), 1282–1286. doi:10.1007/s10995-010-0672-x

Gradinger, P., Strohmeier, D., & Spiel, C. (2009). Traditional bullying and cyberbullying. Identification of risk groups for adjustment problems. *Zeitschrift für Psychologie/Journal of Psychology, 217*(4), 205–213. doi:10.1027/0044-3409.217.4.205

Hawker, D. S. J., & Boulton, M. J. (2000). Twenty years' research on peer victimization and psychosocial maladjustment: a meta-analytic review of cross-sectional studies. *Journal of Child Psychology and Psychiatry, 41*(4), 441–455. doi:10.1111/1469-7610.00629

Hay, C. & Meldrum, R. (2010). Bullying victimization and adolescent self-harm: testing hypotheses from general strain theory. *Journal of Youth and Adolescence, 39*(5), 446–459. doi:10.1007/s10964-009-9502-0

Haynie, D. L., Nansel, T., Eitel, P., Crump, A. D., Saylor, K., Yu, K., & Simons-Morton, B. (2001). Bullies, victims, and bully/victims: distinct groups of at-risk youth. *The Journal of early Adolescence, 21*(1), 29–49. doi:10.1177/0272431601021001002

Helwig-Larsen, K., Schütt, N., & Larsen, H. B. (2012). Predictors and protective factors for adolescent internet victimization: results from a 2008 nationwide Danish youth survey. *Acta Paediatrica, 101*(5), 533–539. doi:10.1111/j.1651-2227.2011.02587.x

Hinduja, S. & Patchin, J. W. (2007). Offline consequences of online victimization: school violence and delinquency. *Journal of School Violence, 6*(3), 89–112. doi:10.1300/J202v06n03_06

Hinduja, S. & Patchin, J. W. (2010). Bullying, cyberbullying, and suicide. *Archives of Suicide Research, 14*(3), 206–221. doi:10.1080/13811118.2010.494133.

Juvonen, J. & Gross, E. F. (2008). Extending the school grounds? – Bullying experiences in cyberspace. *Journal of School Health, 78*(9), 496–505. doi:10.1111/j.1746-1561.2008.00335.x

Juvonen, J., Nishina, A., & Graham, S. (2000). Peer harassment, psychological adjustment, and school functioning in early adolescence. *Journal of Educational Psychology, 92*(2), 349–359. doi:10.1037/0022-0663.92.2.349

Kaltiala-Heino, R., Rimpelä, M., Martunnen, M., Rimpelä, A., & Rantanen, P. (1999). Bullying, depression, and suicidal ideation in Finnish adolescents: School survey. *British Medical Journal, 319*(7206), 348–351. doi:10.1136/bmj.319.7206.348

Kaltiala-Heino, R., Rimpelä, M., Rantanen, P., & Rimpelä, A. (2000). Bullying at school–an indicator of adolescents at risk for mental disorders. *Journal of Adolescence, 23*(6), 661–674. doi:10.1006/jado.2000.0351

Katzer, C., Fetchenhauer, D., & Belschak, F. (2009). Cyberbullying: who are the victims? A comparison of victimization in internet chatrooms and victimization in school. *Journal of Media Psychology: Theories, Methods, and Applications, 21*(1), 25–36. doi:10.1027/1864-1105.21.1.25

Kim, Y. S., Koh, Y. J., & Leventhal, B. (2005). School bullying and suicidal risk in Korean middle school students. *Pediatrics, 115*(2), 357–363. doi:10.1542/peds.2004-0902

Kochenderfer, B. J., & Ladd, G. W. (1996). Peer victimization: cause or consequence of school maladjustment? *Child Development, 67*(4), 1305–1317. doi:10.1111/j.1467-8624.1996.tb01797.x

Kowalski, R. M., Giumetti, G. W., Schroeder, A. N., & Lattaner, M. R. (2014). Bullying in the digital age: a critical review and meta-analysis of cyberbullying research among youth. *Psychological Bulletin, 140*(4), 1073–1137. doi:10.1037/a0035618

Kumpulainen, K., & Räsänen, E. (2000). Children involved in bullying at elementary school age: Their psychiatric symptoms and deviance in adolescence. An epidemiological sample. *Child Abuse & Neglect, 24*(12), 1567–1577. doi:10.1016/S0145-2134(00)00210-6

Låftman, S. B., Modin, B., & Östberg, V. (2013). Cyberbullying and subjective health: A large-scale study of students in Stockholm, Sweden. *Children and Youth Services Review, 35*(1), 112–119. doi:10.1016/j.childyouth.2012.10.020

Lam, L. T. & Li, Y. (2013). The validation of the E-Victimization Scale (E-VS) and the E-Bullying Scale (E-BS) for adolescents. *Computers in Human Behavior, 29*(1), 3–7. doi:10.1016/j.chb.2012.06.021

Lataster, T., van Os, J., Drukker, M., Henquet, C., Feron, F., Gunther, N., Myin-Germeys, I. (2006). Childhood victimization and development expression of non-clinical delusional ideation and hallucinatory experiences: victimization and non-clinical psychotic experiences. *Social Psychiatry and Psychiatric Epidemiology, 41*(6), 423–428. doi:10.1007/s00127-006-0060-4

Lester, L., Cross, D. & Shaw, T. (2012). Problem behaviours, traditional bullying and cyberbullying among adolescents: longitudinal analyses. *Emotional and Behavioural Difficulties, 17*(3–4), 435–447. doi:10.1080/13632752.2012.704313

Litwiller, B. J. & Brausch, A. M. (2013). Cyber bullying and physical bullying in adolescent suicide: the role of violent behavior and substance use. *Journal of Youth and Adolescence, 42*(5), 675–684. doi:10.1007/s10964-013-9925-5.

Machmutow, K., Perren, S., Sticca, F., & Alsaker, F. D. (2012). Peer victimization and depressive symptoms: can specific coping strategies buffer the negative impact of cybervictimization? *Emotional and Behavioural Difficulties, 17*(3–4), 403–420. doi:10.10 80/13632752.2012.704310

Menesini, E., Modena, M., & Tani, F. (2009). Bullying and victimization in adolescence: concurrent and stable roles and psychological health symptoms. *The Journal of Genetic Psychology: Research and Theory on Human Development, 170*(2), 115–134. doi:10.3200/GNTP.170.2.115-134

Midei, A. J., & Matthews, K. A. (2011). Interpersonal violence in childhood as a risk factor for obesity: a systematic review of the literature and proposed pathways. *Obesity Review, 12*(5), e159-e172. doi:10.1111/j.1467-789X.2010.00823.x

Mishna, F., Khoury-Kassabri, M., Gadalla, T., & Daciuk, J. (2012). Risk factors for involvement in cyber bullying: victims, bullies and bully-victims. *Children and Youth Services Review, 34*(1), 63–70. doi:10.1016/j.childyouth.2011.08.032

Mitchell, K. J., Ybarra, M. L., & Finkelhor, D. (2007). The relative importance of online victimization in understanding depression, delinquency, and substance abuse. *Child Maltreatment, 12*(4), 314–324. doi:10.1177/1077559507305996

Nansel, T., Craig, W., Overpeck, M., Saluja, G. & Ruan, W. (2004). Cross-national consistency in the relationship between bullying behaviors and psychosocial adjustment.

Archives of Pediatrics & Adolescent Medicine, 158(8), 730–736. doi:10.1001/archpedi. 158.8.730

O'Brennan, L. M., Bradshaw, C. P., & Sawyer, A. L. (2009). Examining developmental differences in the social-emotional problems among frequent bullies, victims, and bully/victims. *Psychology in the Schools, 46*(2), 100–115. doi:10.1002/pits.20357

Olweus, D. (1997). Bully/victim problems in school: knowledge base and an effective intervention programme. *The Irish Journal of Psychology, 18*(2), 170–190. doi:10.1080/0 3033910.1997.10558138

Olweus, D. (2012). Cyber bullying: an overrated phenomenon? *European Journal of Developmental Psychology, 9*(5), 520–538. doi:10.1080/17405629.2012.682358

O'Moore, M. (2000). Critical issues for teacher training to counter bullying and victimization in Ireland. *Aggressive Behavior, 26*(1), 99–111. doi:10.1002/(SICI)1098-2337(2000) 26:1<99::AID-AB8>3.0.CO;2-W

Patchin, J. W. & Hinduja, S. (2010). Cyberbullying and self-Esteem. *Journal of School Health, 80*(12), 614–621. doi:10.1111/j.1746-1561.2010.00548.x

Perren, S., Dooley, J., Shaw, T., & Cross, D. (2010). Bullying in school and cyberspace: associations with depressive symptoms in Swiss and Australian adolescents. *Child and Adolescent Psychiatry and Mental Health, 4*(28), 28–38. doi:10.1186/1753-2000-4-28

Perren, S., & Gutzwiller-Helfenfinger, E. (2012). Cyberbullying and traditional bullying in adolescence: differential roles of moral disengagement, moral emotions, and moral values. *European Journal of Developmental Psychology, 9*(2), S195–209. doi:10.1080/17405 629.2011.643168

Perren, S., & Hornung, R. (2005). Bullying and delinquency in adolescence; victims' and perpetrators' family and peer relations. *Swiss Journal of Psychology, 64*(1), 51–64. doi:10. 1024/1421-0185.64.1.51

Raskauskas, J. (2010). Text-Bullying: Associations with traditional bullying and depression among New Zealand adolescents. *Journal of School Violence, 9*(1), 74–97. doi:10.1080/ 15388220903185605

Reijntjes, A., Kamphuis, J. H., Prinzie, P., Boelen, P. A., van der Schoot, M., & Telch, M. J. (2011). Prospective linkages between peer victimization and externalizing problems in children: a meta-analysis. *Aggressive Behavior, 37*(3), 215–222. doi:10.1002/ab.20374

Reijntjes, A., Kamphuis, J. H., Prinzie, P., & Telch, M. J. (2010). Peer victimization and internalizing problems in children: a meta-analysis of longitudinal studies. *Child Abuse & Neglect, 34*(4), 244–252. doi:10.1016/j.chiabu.2009.07.00

Rigby, K. (2003). Consequences of bullying in schools. *The Canadian Journal of Psychiatry, 48*(9), 583–590.

Rivers, I. & Noret, N. (2010). Participant roles in bullying behavior and their association with thoughts of ending one's life. *The Journal of Crisis Intervention and Suicide Prevention, 31*(3), 143–148. doi:10.1027/0227-5910/a000020

Rivers, I., Poteat, V. P., Noret, N., & Ashurst, N. (2009). Observing bullying at school: the mental health implications of witness status. *School Psychology Quarterly, 24*(4), 211–223. doi:10.1037/a0018164

Rivers, I. & Smith, P. K. (1994). Types of bullying behaviour and their correlates. *Aggressive Behavior, 20*(5), 359–368. doi:10.1002/1098-2337(1994)20:5<359::AID-AB2480200 503>3.0.CO;2-J

Rutter, M. (1987). Psychosocial resilience and protective mechanisms. *American Journal of Orthopsychiatry, 57*, 316–331.

Salmivalli, C. (2010). Bullying and the peer group: a review. *Aggression and Violent Behavior, 15*(2), 112–120. doi:10.1016/j.avb.2009.08.007

Salmivalli, C., Lagerspetz, K., Björkqvist, K., Österman, K., & Kaukiainen, A. (1996). Bullying as a group process: Participant roles and their relations to social status within the group.

Aggressive Behavior, 22(1), 1–15. doi:10.1002/(SICI)1098-2337(1996)22:1<1::AID-AB1> 3.0.CO;2-T

Salmivalli, C. & Voeten, M. (2004). Connections between attitudes, group norms, and behaviour in bullying situations. *International Journal of Behavioral Development, 28*(3), 246–258. doi:10.1080/01650250344000488

Sandstrom, M., Cillessen, A., & Eisenhower, A. (2003). Children's appraisal of peer rejection experiences: Impact on social and emotional adjustment. *Social Development, 12*(4), 530–550. doi:10.1111/1467-9507.00247

Saluja, G., Iachan, R., Scheidt, P. C., Overpeck, M. D., Sun, W., & Giedd, J. N. (2004). Prevalence of and risk factors for depressive symptoms among young adolescents. *Archives of Pediatrics & Adolescent Medicine, 158*(8), 760–765. doi:10.1001/archpedi.158.8.760

Schneider, S. K., O'Donnell, L., Stueve, A., & Coulter, R. W. S. (2012). Cyberbullying, school bullying, and psychological distress: a regional census of high school students. *American Journal of Public Health, 102*(1), 171–177. doi:10.2105/AJPH.2011.300308

Schreier, A., Wolke, D., Thomas, K., Horwood, J., Hollis, C., Gunnell, D., Lewis, G., Thompson, A., Zammit, S., Duffy, L., Salvi, G., & Harrison, G. (2009). Prospective study of peer victimization in childhood and psychotic symptoms in a nonclinical population at age 12 years. *Archives of General Psychiatry, 66*(5), 527–536. doi:10.1001/archgenpsychiatry.2009.23

Schultze-Krumbholz, A., Jäkel, A., Schultze, J., & Scheithauer, H. (2012). Emotional and behavioural problems in the context of cyberbullying: a longitudinal study among German adolescents. *Emotional and Behavioural Difficulties, 17*(3–4), 329–345. doi:10.1080/13632752.2012.704317

Schwartz, D. (2000). Subtypes of victims and aggressors in children's peer groups. *Journal of Abnormal Child Psychology, 28*(2), 181–192. doi:10.1023/A:1005174831561

Skrzypiec, G., Slee, P. T., Askell-Wiliams, H., & Lawson, M. J. (2012). Associations between types of involvement in bullying, friendships and mental health status. Special issue: Bullying and cyberbullying: emotional and behavioural correlates. *Emotional and Behavioural Difficulties, 17*(3–4), 259–272. doi:10.1080/13632752.2012.704312

Slee, P. T. (1995). Peer victimization and its relationship to depression among Australian primary school students. *Personality and Individual Differences, 18*(1), 57–62. doi:10.1016/0191-8869(94)00114-8

Smith, P. K., Mahdavi, J., Carvalho, M., Fisher, S., Russell, S., & Tippett, N. (2008). Cyberbullying: its nature and impact in secondary school pupils. *Journal of Child Psychology and Psychiatry, 49*(4), 376–385. doi:10.1111/j.1469-7610.2007.01846.x

Sontag, L. M., Clemans, K. H., Graber, J. A., & Lyndon, S. T. (2011). Traditional and Cyber Aggressors and victims: a comparison of psychosocial characteristics. *Journal of Youth and Adolescence, 40*(4), 392–404. doi:10.1007/s10964-010-9575-9

Sourander, A. (2010). Psychosocial risk factors associated with cyberbullying among adolescents: A population-based study. *Archives of General Psychiatry, 67*(7), 720–728. doi:10.1001/archgenpsychiatry.2010.79.

Sourander, A., Jensen, P., Rönning, J. A., Elonheimo, H., Niemelä, S, Helenius, H., Kumpulainen, K., Piha, J., Tamminen, T., Moilanen, I., & Almqvist, F. (2007). Childhood bullies and victims and their risk of criminality in late adolescence. The Finnish from a boy to a man study. *Archives of Pediatrics & Adolescent Medicine, 161*(6), 546–552. doi:10.1001/archpedi.161.6.546

Staude-Müller, F., Hansen, B., & Voss, M. (2012). How stressful is online victimization? Effects of victim's personality and properties of the incident. *European Journal of Developmental Psychology, 9*(2), 260–274. doi:10.1080/17405629.2011.643170

Sticca, F., & Perren, S. (2013). Is cyberbullying worse than traditional bullying? Examining the differential roles of medium, publicity and anonymity for the perceived severity of bullying. *Journal of Youth and Adolescence, 42*(5), 739–750. doi:10.1007/s10964-012-9867-3

van den Eijnden, R., Vermulst, A., van Rooij, A. J., Scholte, R., & van de Mheen, D. (2014). The bidirectional relationships between online victimization and psychosocial problems in adolescents: A comparison with real-life victimization. *Journal of Youth and Adolescence, 43*(5), 790–802. doi:10.1007/s10964-013-0003-9

Vieno, A., Gini, G., & Santinello, M. (2011). Different forms of bullying and their association to smoking and drinking behavior in Italian adolescents. *Journal of School Health, 81*(7), 393–399. doi:10.1111/j.1746-1561.2011.00607.x

Völlink, T., Bolman, C., Dehue, F., & Jacobs, N. (2013). Coping with cyberbullying: differences between victims, bully-victims and children not involved in bullying. *Journal of Community & Applied Social Psychology, 23*(1), 7–24. doi:10.1002/casp.2142

Wang, J., Nansel, T. R., & Iannotti, R. J. (2011). Cyber and traditional bullying: differential association with depression. *Journal of Adolescent Health, 48*(4), 415–417. doi:10.1016/j.jadohealth.2010.07.012.

Wilkins-Shurmer, A., O'Callaghan, M. J., Najman, J. M., Bor, W., Williams, G. M., & Anderson, M. J. (2003). Association of bullying with adolescent health-related quality of life. *Journal of Paediatrics and Child Health, 39*(6), 436–441. doi:10.1046/j.1440-1754.2003.00184.x

Yang, S.-J., Stewart, R., Kim, J.-M., Kim, S.-W., Shin, I.-S., Dewey, M. E. et al. (2013). Differences in predictors of traditional and cyber-bullying: a 2-year longitudinal study in Korean school children. *Eur Child Adolesc Psychiatry, 22*(5), 309–318. doi:10.1007/s00787-012-0374-6

Zwierzynska, K., Wolke, D., & Lereya, T. (2013). Peer victimization in childhood and internalizing problems in adolescence: A prospective longitudinal study. *Journal of Abnormal Child Psychology, 41*(2), 309–323.

PART II

ICT based intervention programs against cyberbullying

5

LEARNING HOW TO COPE WITH CYBERBULLYING IN THE VIRTUAL WORLD

Lessons from FearNot!

Maria Sapouna, Sibylle Enz, Margaritis Samaras and Dieter Wolke

Introduction

Despite the fact that there is clear and consistent evidence that cyberbullying is related to a number of negative life outcomes including psychosomatic problems, declining academic performance and increasing alcohol use, there is not much evidence on how it can be best prevented. A recent Campbell systematic review identified only four short-term interventions that were designed to deal specifically with cyberbullying (Mishna, Saini, & Solomon, 2009). However, it is not uncommon for interventions dealing with traditional bullying to be extended to address cyberbullying, too (Slonje, Smith, & Frisen, 2013). One such programme that was primarily designed to target traditional bullying but has proven as effective in reducing cyberbullying is the Finnish anti-bullying programme KiVa (Slonje, Smith, & Frisen, 2013). Salmivalli, Kärnä, & Poskiparta, 2011). KiVa is a multi-component anti-bullying programme that is designed to change the power dynamics in the classroom that often contribute to bullying. The programme, which comprises school lessons, the KiVa computer game, an online website for parents and a virtual mailbox that students can use to disclose their victimisation, has been found to reduce bullying by approximately 15 per cent (Salmivalli, Kärnä, & Poskiparta, 2011).

One approach to combatting cyberbullying is to teach children and young people effective ways of dealing with the problem. Evidence from the traditional bullying literature suggests that telling someone can be effective in averting further victimisation (Slonje, Smith, & Frisen, 2013). In the context of cyberbullying, most studies find that few students seek support from their family, teachers and friends (Dehue, Bolman, & Völlink, 2008; Slonje, Smith, & Frisen, 2013). Students seem to prefer to cope with bullying by resorting to technological solutions, such as blocking email addresses and/or Internet profiles, and/or changing phone numbers (Aricak et al., 2008; Smith et al., 2008). Finally, some students may choose confrontational ways of responding to the problem, for example by telling the bully to stop or fighting back (Dehue et al., 2008).

In this chapter we propose a new approach to teaching children and adolescents how to cope with cyberbullying based on the trial of the virtual learning intervention FearNot! (Fun with Empathic Agents to Reach Novel Outcomes in Teaching), which was designed to address traditional forms of bullying. FearNot! is a novel virtual environment that was designed on the premise that children can learn how to cope with bullying more effectively if they get the opportunity to role-play different coping strategies in an immersive virtual world (Enz et al., 2008a, b; Wright, 2006). In the following part of this chapter, we will briefly describe the FearNot! virtual learning environment and summarise the main results from the evaluation of the programme. Drawing on these results, we will next try to identify the components of the programme that made it work and that should be adopted by researchers who might want to develop similar interventions to address cyberbullying. In the final part of this chapter, we will highlight some important challenges that intervention designers might face in trying to develop virtual learning interventions for cyberybullying, drawing on our experiences of evaluating FearNot!. The chapter will conclude with an overall comment on the usefulness of taking an immersive role-play approach to dealing with cyberbullying.

The FearNot! intervention – learning experientially

The FearNot! intervention was developed as a novel approach to teaching children how to effectively avert traditional bullying victimisation based on the proven educational benefits of role-play as a form of experiential learning. Experiential learning is defined as the process which transforms experience into knowledge that students should acquire (Kolb & Kolb, 2005: 194). According to this educational theory, learning materializes in a process where the individual is involved in an event (*concrete experience*), which he then analyzes (*reflective observation*), and, after readjusting his former knowledge to the new experience (*abstract conceptualization*), he tests his theory by verifying it (*active experimentation*), (Mughal & Zafar, 2011: 29). Generally, models of experiential learning include not only experience and reflection but also application (Clark, Threeton, & Ewing, 2010: 54). And this is the reason why experiential learning thrives as it takes the form of "a total learning environment philosophy that takes into account both content and context", in which students participate actively, use their emotional intelligence, and socially interact, and so provoke the emergence of affective learning (Hawtrey, 2007: 144).

Experiential learning is widely used both in primary and secondary education, in the form of various teaching techniques, such as problem-based learning, concept mapping, decision-making roles in simulations of real situations (Truscott, Rustogi, & Young, 2000: 60), and every kind of role playing games or simulation, where a learner can ask, experimenting, investigating, solving problems, assuming responsibility and being creative (Estes, 2004: 142). Although this particular form of learning is highly efficient, it presupposes that the student, beyond his desire to learn, recognizes the fact that learning should not only be practical and personal, but also based on real experience, and that it should be an informal and continuous process, incompatible with formal events, such as final examinations (Hawtrey, 2007: 144). Experiential learning aids the development of students' meta-cognitive abilities and reinforces their capability to use new concepts to enhance everyday activities (Boggs, Mickel, & Holtom, 2007: 833). They can discover their field of interest and direct themselves towards a new way of learning. Through these activities and due to their active participation in the process of learning, students can understand human relationships and control their way of thinking and feeling. In other words, students are motivated to learn, to live in a class of social and intellectual equality, where every individual action leads to a therapeutic situation for the class in as a whole (Jarvis, 2004: 172).

Role-play, as a form of experiential learning, has proven to be a particularly effective tool for dealing with social and emotional difficulties in school, as it allows students to take over someone else's role, including their thoughts, feelings and behaviour, and, ultimately, to empathise with other people's experiences and change their own way of thinking (Davis, 1996). In social contexts, role-play is particularly effective, as it offers children and adolescents the opportunity to get immediate feedback on how they deal with difficult situations and emotions (Enz et al., 2008a, b). By acting out new roles, new attitudes and behaviours develop within the role-player and are differentially reinforced through immediate feedback in a supportive and positive atmosphere. In order to be effective, role-play needs to be immersive in the sense that the learner is able to relinquish their own identity and completely take over their assigned identity (Enz et al., 2008).

However, role-play is not very easy to apply in a standard educational context. First, role-play is a rather time-consuming and staff-intensive educational tool which often clashes with the curriculum-driven reality of the classroom. Second, because role-play is traditionally administered as a group activity, it can expose victims to the rest of the class and thus cause more trauma or stigmatisation, or it might exacerbate pre-existing conflictual relationships between students. Most importantly, traditional role-play does not provide a safe environment in which victims of bullying can openly express themselves without fear of retaliation or ridicule, as most likely the perpetrators of bullying and their assistants will be present.

The approach presented in this chapter suggests avoiding the negative implications of role-play as an educational tool by transferring it to a safe virtual environment in which students interact and get immediate feedback from cartoon characters. This approach is seen as particularly effective in dealing with sensitive issues that often involve the whole class, such as traditional bullying and cyberbullying. In fact, victims of bullying may be hesitant to take part in traditional role-play activities in class out of fear that their vulnerabilities and lack of effective coping might be discovered and exploited by other students even more. In contrast, in a virtual role-play situation, victims can work on their own without any fear of being identified as victims.

An example of such a virtual role-play intervention designed to address the problem of face-to-face school bullying was FearNot!. This computer game comprised the sole component of an anti-bullying intervention for primary school students aged 8 to 11. Two versions of the game were developed to reflect gender differences in the way primary school children bully; one for boys where a male cartoon character, John, was being physically and verbally bullied and one for girls where a female cartoon character, named Frances, was being socially excluded and verbally bullied. FearNot! was developed for use in the UK and Germany with slightly different storyboards created for each country to account for differences in the educational systems and to make the characters more believable. For example, the cartoon characters were wearing school uniforms only in the UK version of the game. Particular attention was also paid to ensure any insulting language used in the software game was realistic and expressed the conventions used in each of the two countries.

When playing this game, children watched a number of bullying incidents that occurred between animated characters in a virtual school. At the end of each episode, the victimised cartoon character would appear on the screen asking the student player for advice on what to do to stop being bullied in the future. This appeal for help put the student player in the position of an off-stage "invisible friend" to the victimised cartoon character. After each request for help, an open-text dialogue box would open where the student player could type in any advice they could think of that they wanted to offer to the cartoon victim. Usually, students suggested that the victim cartoon character tell someone else that they are being bullied, make a new friend or find the courage to stand up for themselves. In FearNot! cartoon characters were modelled in such a way so that they could understand the advice given by each child and enact it in the next episode of the game. If, for example, a student advised the victim cartoon character to make a new friend, in the next episode they would see the victim character asking one of their virtual classmates to hang out with them. When the student player suggested a strategy that is known in the literature to be effective they would witness firsthand how that strategy worked for the victimised cartoon character in the virtual world of FearNot!. For example, in the case of making a new friend the victimised cartoon character would carry out that strategy successfully, avoiding being bullied, at least temporarily, before the next learning session, where they would have to try out another coping strategy. Where the student player suggested a strategy that is known in the literature to be ineffective, at least in some cases, such as fighting back, the student player would again witness firsthand how that strategy did not work for the victim cartoon character and gave the bully more ammunition to continue bullying.

However, it is worth noting here that to make the game believable, not every suggestion that was offered by a student was enacted by the cartoon character. First of all, inappropriate coping strategies such as "kill the bully" were immediately blocked out from the computer system. Also, the victim cartoon character would not always feel emotionally and physically powerful enough to stand up to the cartoon character(s) that bullied him/her. In those cases, the virtual victim would admit to the student player that they do not feel ready to do what has been suggested, exactly as it may happen in real life where victims may need to build up their coping competence first before they can effectively stand up to their bullies. Figure 5.1 shows a screenshot of the English version of FearNot! depicting a bullying episode between John (the victim) and Luke (the bully).

The FearNot! computer game was evaluated in 2007 with the participation of a total of 27 primary schools from the UK (Warwick, Coventry and Hertfordshire) and Germany (Bavaria, Hesse) rendering a final sample of 942 students who completed all assessments throughout the evaluation period, 455 in the intervention group and 487 in the waiting control group. Although initially it was planned to randomise schools to the two experimental conditions of intervention and waiting control group, this did not prove possible, because some schools' computer equipment was too old and outdated to run such sophisticated software. Eventually, and to ensure the smooth implementation of the intervention, it was decided that the

FIGURE 5.1 The Fearnot! evaluation

Source: Sapouna et al., (2010). Virtual learning intervention to reduce bullying victimization in primary school: A controlled trial. *Journal of Child Psychology and Psychiatry, 51(*1), 104–112. Reproduced by permission of John Wiley and Sons.

schools with the highest-performing computer equipment would be assigned to the intervention group (n = 13, total number of eligible students = 555) and the schools with the lowest-performing computer equipment that did not meet the technical requirements of FearNot! were allocated to the control group (n = 15, total number of eligible students = 623). Baseline data were collected in November 2007. All participants in the intervention and control groups were given a brief awareness-raising session on the type of behaviours that are defined as bullying before they were asked to fill in the baseline questionnaires. The same questionnaires were filled in one (post-test 1) and four weeks (post-test 2) after the intervention had finished. Questionnaires took no longer than an hour to complete and were available in English and German, and were back and forward translated. Among the final sample of 942 children who took part in the study, 494 (52.4 per cent) were male and 448 (47.6 per cent) were female. UK pupils (n = 514) were older than German pupils (n = 422) (9.36 vs. 8.34; t = 28.71; p < .001, missing data for 6 pupils).

The intervention group children were asked to use the FearNot! software once a week for approximately 30 minutes, for a total of three consecutive weeks. The game was programmed to stop after approximately 30 minutes had passed. Children were asked to use the same computer throughout the period of the intervention so that they could pick up the story where they had left it. Children were supervised by their teachers, who had received clear instructions on how to deliver the intervention and were also provided with an intervention manual. Teachers were allowed to help any children facing comprehension problems but they were discouraged from providing help with coping strategies unless children were struggling to find advice for the victim (this happened rarely). The control group participated in the pre- and post-tests and in between followed the normal curriculum. After the evaluation had finished, the waiting control group children were given the opportunity to use the computer game in their classes but their use of the software was not evaluated.

Demographic data was collected on participants' gender, age, number of siblings and living arrangements (i.e. with whom they lived at home). The main individual-level outcome was victimisation (experienced and escaped). Children were asked to indicate how often they had experienced either direct or relational victimisation over the last month. Direct victimisation included being hit/beaten up, having things stolen, being threatened/blackmailed, being called nasty names and having nasty tricks played on them. Relational victimisation included being left out of games, having children telling them they don't want to be their friend anymore and having nasty lies or rumours spread about them. Children were classified as victims if they had experienced direct and/or relational bullying "more than 4 times" or "at least once a week" in the last month. Children were categorized as escaped victims if they reported being directly and/or relationally bullied at baseline, but had experienced neither form of bullying at the first (T1 escaped victim) or the second follow-up (T2 escaped victim).

The intervention was expected to work mainly by increasing students' knowledge about which coping strategies are (mostly) effective and which are not. To assess students' level of coping knowledge a new questionnaire was developed by the evaluation team (Watson et al., 2010). The questionnaire used storyboards showing children being bullied at school to elicit students' suggestions on what the victimised character in the story should do to avert further victimisation. Students could choose between 13 options that reflected the most common coping strategies identified in the literature. Each of these 13 options was given a numerical weighting that represented the likelihood of their being effective in real life. These weightings are provided in Table 5.1 below. For the purposes of scoring the CSK questionnaire, the weighting of all selected strategies were added together and then divided by the total number of strategies selected to ensure the number of strategies selected did not bias the results.

To assess the effect that the computer game might have on students who were not being bullied at school or were bullying others (i.e. whether it was more likely to turn outsiders into defenders), a peer nomination item (adapted from Schäfer & Korn 2004; Salmivalli et al., 1996, respectively) asked the children to name up to six classmates who tell bullies to stop bullying others.

Finally, computer log files of users' inputs recorded the total amount of time each child interacted with the software (in seconds), the total number of episodes that enacted bullying incidents and the total number of interaction episodes (i.e. during which children were able to type in advice) for each child across the three sessions. With this information, we were able to test whether better outcomes were achieved for those children who interacted longer and more actively with the software. For more details of the methodology of the study see Sapouna et al. (2010) and Watson et al. (2010).

TABLE 5.1 Coping strategy weightings

Coping strategy	Weighting (out of 10)
Start Crying	1
Run away (from the bully)	2
Stay away (from school)	0
Tell (the victim's own) parents	7
Avoid (the bully)	0
Call (the bully) names	4
Tell (the victim's own) friends	8
Ignore (the bully)	4
Tell (the victim's own) teacher	8
Ask (the bully) to stop	6
Laugh it off	6
Fight (the bully)	5
Blame (the victim's own) self	0

Did FearNot! work and why?

As we were not able to randomise, it was important to check that there were no significant baseline differences between the intervention and the control group in terms of measured characteristics. Our analyses indicated that participants in the intervention and control groups were comparable at baseline in terms of gender, age, living arrangements and family composition. In addition, intervention and control classes were similar with respect to size and socioeconomic status. There were fewer victims among the intervention group children compared with controls at baseline but the difference was not statistically significant. Both groups also reported similar rates of bullying perpetration. Comparisons between the two countries showed that UK and German children experienced similar rates of victimisation (28.6 per cent vs. 23.6 per cent; $\chi^2_1 = 2.82$; $p = .09$). However, there was a significantly higher number of bullies among UK children than German children (20.3 per cent vs. 3.7 per cent; $\chi^2_1 = 54.47$; $p < .001$).

As only 83.4 per cent of the initial eligible sample completed all assessments and, therefore, were analyzed for the purposes of this study, we investigated whether non-responders differed in some significant way from responders. The children who missed follow-up 1 were similar to completers in terms of gender, age, living arrangements, family composition and baseline victimisation. However, the children who were lost at follow-up 2 were significantly less likely than responders to be living with their mothers (90.6 per cent vs. 98 per cent; $\chi^2_1 = 13.68$; $p < .001$) and younger (8.68 vs. 8.91; $t = 2.41$; $p = .02$) at baseline.

Having established that intervention students were experiencing similar levels of bullying victimisation as control group students, the main outcome of interest was whether baseline victims (i.e. those children who reported being victims of bullying at the baseline assessment) managed to escape bullying victimisation one and four weeks after the intervention. Indeed, that proved to be the case, with baseline victims in the intervention group being significantly more likely, compared to baseline victims in the control group, to be classified as escaped victims (i.e. non-victim at follow-up 1 but victim at baseline) one week after the intervention was completed (adjusted RR = 1.41, 95% CI: 1.02–1.81; n = 230). More specifically, out of 106 baseline victims in the intervention group, 53 (50 per cent) managed to escape victimisation at follow-up 1, compared to 44 out of 124 (35.5 per cent) baseline victims in the control group. To provide some support for the cause–effect relationship of the intervention to this outcome, we investigated whether children who interacted longer or more actively with the software achieved better outcomes. Indeed, it was found that children who took part in a greater number of interaction episodes with the FearNot! characters were more likely to escape victimisation at follow-up 1 (adjusted OR, 1.09; 95% CI: 1.003–1.18). However, a dose–response relationship was not found for total time of interaction with the software and total number of episodes watched. This means that what really mattered was the amount of active interaction children had with the characters and not simply how much time they spent playing with the software or watching episodes. Although results of the FearNot! intervention were positive when victimisation status was re-assessed one week after the intervention was completed, this significant treatment effect was lost when victimisation status was assessed again four weeks after the intervention.

In summary, the evaluation of FearNot! found that the intervention had a positive but short-term effect whereby victims who received the intervention were less likely to self-report being a victim of bullying one week after the intervention was completed. At the same time, we did not find any evidence that playing with FearNot! made children more likely to bully others (Sapouna et al., 2010). Hence, the software did not appear to generate any adverse consequences.

These results paint a rather optimistic picture about the use of virtual role-play educational technologies in the fight against bullying. But why did FearNot! actually work? First, there was evidence that FearNot! increased students' knowledge about which strategies are effective and which are not (Vannini et al., 2011). However, this increase was only found among the German sample. This difference between the two ethnic samples may be due to the fact that English children were found to have a better knowledge of effective coping strategies to begin with, so potentially there was very little room for improvement. These differences between the two samples in coping strategy knowledge may reflect differences in the levels of general awareness of the problem in the two countries (Watson et al., 2010; Vannini et al., 2011). Bullying appears to be recognised as a problem more in the UK than in Germany (Wolke et al., 2001) and, therefore, it is possible that children in the UK might have already received some awareness lessons about how to cope with bullying prior to the FearNot! intervention. Indeed, Watson et al., (2010) found that children from the UK score significantly higher on both relational (t[896.61] 8.66, $p < .001$) and physical (t[892.67] 7.87, $p < .001$) CSK scales than the German sample, with medium effect sizes for both (relational CSK: $d = .58$; and physical CSK: $d = .53$). Since German students were significantly younger than UK students, it is likely that the country effect also masks an age effect (Watson et al., 2010).

Another important finding that potentially explains how the computer game worked was that, at least in Germany, students who were previously outsiders were more likely to be identified by their peers as being active defenders of victims following the intervention (Vannini et al., 2011). However, the same effect was not found among the UK sample. Vannini et al. (2011) have suggested that perhaps within the UK sample there is a ceiling effect considering that only two German schools compared to 16 UK schools were implementing an anti-bullying policy prior to the start of the intervention.

Developing a successful virtual role-play intervention to tackle cyberbullying

As the results of the above evaluation demonstrate, FearNot! was met with some success and in particular it seemed to help some students escape the role of the victim at least temporarily. The computer intervention seemed to be particularly effective for those students who interacted actively with the software, providing a good number of coping suggestions to the victimised cartoon characters. FearNot! potentially worked because it helped students, especially those in Germany who did not know a lot about bullying, to learn effective coping strategies through the role-play. FearNot! also seemed to heighten empathy for victims, especially among non-involved bystanders, who were more likely to act as defenders of victims, at least in Germany. These results, although not conclusive at this stage, point to the significant potential of using this form of learning technology to fight against other forms of bullying such as cyberbullying. With this in mind, we outline below some of the elements of FearNot! that made it successful and should be replicated in future uses of this same methodology to reduce cyberybullying.

Believability

Believability of the story and the characters are very important considerations when designing a virtual role-play intervention similar to the one described here to ensure that the students can develop an empathic relationship with the game characters. If the computer game lacks believability, players will most likely disengage and fail to see the relevance of the game to their own experiences. To ensure that both character design and story content were meaningful to the target group, students and teachers were involved throughout the project in the development of story content and the design of characters. This ensured that the game characters' way of interacting with each other was similar enough to the interactions students would have in the real world. These initial usability studies with the target group revealed that students preferred cartoon-like characters (Zoll et al., 2006). Indeed, studies have found that near-realistic characters can pose a problem for the believability of the characters, a paradox that has been previously named the "uncanny valley" (Mori, 2005). Preliminary evaluations of various prototypes of the software indicated that the majority of children found the characters to be believable and, subsequently, they were able to empathise with the victimised character and feel sorry for them (Hall & Woods, 2005).

Expressivity

Bullying is a social problem among students that implies a wide variety of risks to the victims' social adaptation and emotional well-being. If a virtual role-play game aims at believably depicting the problem of bullying in schools, virtual characters enacting these bullying episodes need to be able to express themselves emotionally. This is important if the learner is to understand the internal states of victims of bullying behaviour (cognitive empathy) and also if the learner is to be affected by the emotions that they perceive in the victim (affective empathy). The emotional expressivity of character actions is reflected in gestures and facial expressions, and in the tone of voice of the character.

Emergent narrative

The aim of FearNot! was to engage learners emotionally with the situation of victims of bullying in schools. But how can this emotional engagement be fostered apart from how the characters look and behave? As has been outlined above, the FearNot! player had a certain control over the events by interacting with the victimised character and thus influencing – to a certain degree – its decisions in the bullying episodes to come. However, this influence was only partial, since the characters acted autonomously in creating the story. This highly flexible real-time storytelling approach that has previously been termed "emergent narrative" (Aylett, 1999) results in a highly believable experience for the learner. In contrast to a script-based approach, the learner is provided with a complex and engaging virtual space inhabited with intelligent agents that accept or do not accept his/her suggestions, just like in real life. On the one hand, the autonomy of the characters is creating a believable and realistic story about bullying; on the other hand, handing over control solely to autonomous characters and their interactions with one another and the learner poses some risk: how can one prevent the characters and their autonomously unfolding behaviour to oppose or hinder the educational goals, that is, how can one ensure, even though the control of what happens next in the story lies with the characters and their decisions made in real-time, a believable, meaningful and appropriate (in the sense of the educational goal) learning experience for the learner? It is important for future projects following this approach to find the right balance between believability and immersion as prerequisites of learning and the need for a specific learning outcome to emerge.

Challenges

There are undoubtedly, however, also some challenges in implementing this kind of virtual role-play approach to tackling cyberbullying. First of all, this is a computer-based intervention and as such it relies on schools having sufficiently robust computers to ensure the software can run without regularly crashing. Technical problems can affect not only the learner experience but also the extent to which teachers continue to buy into the intervention. Indeed, in Germany where school computers were not as good, teachers reported having a lot of problems implementing the intervention robustly, and that often caused them to have negative views about the software (Sapouna et al., 2010). Due to the fact that software developers usually do not have access to the school computers during software development they are not aware of the technical limitations attached to these machines. For example, primary schools tend to purchase lower specification computers because they simply do not need highly powerful machines to meet their basic requirements (e.g. regarding graphic cards, processors, RAM, etc.). Another issue is caused by large variability among the technical equipment, as well as management of administration rights, between different primary schools. This means that educational software for use in primary school classrooms needs to be very flexible and stable in order to run on many different systems. In sum, it is recommended that software developers not only undertake a thorough survey of the equipment available in the schools they are aiming at, but also use machines for their development work that are comparable to those available to schools. In schools where teachers are not very experienced in the use of computers, extra work and training will need to take place to ensure teachers are comfortable with using this approach and see the benefits of it in terms of creating a better and more effective learning experience for the learner. Interventions are unlikely to work unless they can be successfully implemented without placing too much burden on those responsible for delivery and sufficient motivational work takes places at the start of the programme to ensure buy-in from all relevant stakeholder groups (e.g. teachers, head principals, parents; Rohrbach, D'Onofrio, Backer, & Montgomery, 1996).

However well a virtual role-play approach is implemented in schools, it is also important to ensure that it is not the only intervention component offered. All forms of bullying, including cyberbullying, are quite stable behavioural patterns that develop over a long period of time, and thus it would be naive to think that they could change by playing a computer game for 90 minutes in total. Therefore, it is important that such an approach is incorporated within a whole-school system approach that intervenes at various aspects of children's lives with the participation of the whole school community and parents.

Conclusion

On the whole, the results from the evaluation of the FearNot! anti-bullying intervention provide initial support for the use of virtual role-play programmes to tackle cyberbullying at schools. The positive effects of incorporating computer-based learning tools in anti-bullying interventions have been highlighted in a recent systematic review of anti-bullying programmes that found the biggest reductions in bullying victimisation to have been produced by interventions with a computer-based learning element (Farrington & Ttofi, 2009). These findings are encouraging in light of the growing use of computers in education and the development of new anti-bullying interventions that rely on virtual learning environments such as the KiVa Programme in Finland (Salmivalli, Kärnä, & Poskiparta, 2009) and the Pestkoppenstoppen Programme in the Netherlands (Jacobs, Völlink, Deue, & Lechner, 2014). This type of virtual role-playing games can help children learn how to respond in similar situations in real life and, as this evaluation has shown, they can be particularly effective as an intervention (and possibly prevention) tool to equip victims with the necessary skills to deal with bullying effectively, especially if incorporated within a whole-school anti-bullying policy and rigorously implemented. To achieve the best possible results, we have suggested that any new virtual learning programmes for victims of cyberbullying be designed in such a way that characters are believable, expressive and relatively autonomous in the sense that they do not follow a pre-scripted narrative. More research is also needed to establish whether such approaches work better when implemented in the class environment or can work equally as well or better when used by students at home. As our own results have indicated, it is unlikely that this kind of approach will be similarly effective for all students who might be experiencing bullying; therefore, future evaluations should attempt to examine in more detail who is more likely to be receptive to this kind of intervention.

References

Aricak, T., Siyahhan, S., Uzunhasanoglu, A., Saribeyoglu, S., Ciplak, S., Yilmaz, N., & Memmedov, C. (2008). Cyberbullying among Turkish Adolescents. *Cyberpsychology & Behavior, 11*(3), 253-261.

Aylett, R. (1999). Narrative in Virtual Environments - Towards Emergent Narrative. From: AAAI Technical Report FS-99-01.

Boggs, J. G., Mickel, A. E., & Holtom, B. C. (2007). Experiential learning through interactive drama: An alternative to student role plays. *Journal of Management Education, 31*, (6), 832–858. doi:10.1177/1052562906294952

Clark, R. W., Threeton, M. D., & Ewing, J. C. (2010). The potential of experiential learning models and practices in career and technical education and career and technical teacher education. *Journal of Career and Technical Education, 25*(2), 46–62.

Davis, M. H. (1996). *Empathy: A social psychological approach*. Madison, WI: Westview Press.

Dehue, F., Bolman, C., & Völlink, T. (2008). Cyberbullying: youngsters' experiences and parental perception. *Cyberpsychology & Behavior: The Impact of the Internet, Multimedia and Virtual Reality on Behavior and Society, 11*(2), 217–23.

Enz, S., Zoll, C., Vannini, N., Schneider, W., Hall, L., Paiva, A., & Aylett, R. (2008a). Emotional learning in primary schools: FearNot! an anti-bullying intervention based on virtual role play with intelligent synthetic characters. *Electronic Journal of e-Learning, 6*(2), 111–11.

Enz, S., Zoll, C., Vannini, N., Watson, S., Aylett, A., Hall, L., Paiva, A., Wolke, D., Dautenhahn, K., Andre, E. and Rizzo, P. (2008b). Virtual Role-Play in the Classroom. Experiences with FearNot! In P. Cunningham & M. Cunningham (Eds.). *Collaboration and the Knowledge Economy*. Amsterdam: IOS Press.

Estes, C. A. (2004). Promoting student-centered learning in experiential education. *Journal of Experiential Education, 27*(2), 141–160.

Farrington, D. P., & Ttofi, M. M. (2009). Reducing school bullying: Evidence based implications for policy. *Crime and Justice, 38*(1), 281–345.

Hall, L., & Woods, S. (2005). Empathic interaction with synthetic characters: the importance of similarity. In C. Ghaoui (Ed.), *Encyclopaedia of Human Computer Interaction*. Hershey PA: Idea Group Reference.

Hawtrey, K. (2007). Using experiential learning techniques. *The Journal of Economic Education, 38*(2), 143–152. doi:10.3200/JECE.38.2.143-152.

Jacobs, J. N. C., Völlink, T., Dehue, F. & Lechner, L. (2014). Online Pestkoppenstoppen: systematic and theory-based development of a web-based tailored intervention for adolescent cyberbully victims to combat and prevent cyberbullying. *BMC Public Health, 14*, 396. doi:10.1186/1471-2458-14-396

Jarvis, Peter (2004). *Adult Education and Lifelong Learning: Theory and Practice*. London and New York: RoutledgeFalmer.

Kolb, A. Y. & Kolb, D. A. (2005). Learning styles and learning spaces: Enhancing experiential learning in higher education. *Academy of Management Learning & Education, 4*(2), 193–212.

Mishna, F., Saini, M., & Solomon, S. (2009). Ongoing and online: Children and youth's perceptions of cyber bullying. *Children and Youth Services Review, 31*(12), 1222-1228.

Mori, M. (2005). On the Uncanny Valley. Proceedings of the Humanoids-2005 workshop: Views of the Uncanny Valley. Tsukuba, Japan.

Mughal, F. & Zafar, A. (2011). Experiential learning from a constructivist perspective: Reconceptualizing the Kolbian Cycle, *International Journal of Learning and Development*, *1*(2), 27–37. doi:http://dx.doi.org/10.5296/ijld.v1i2.1179

Rohrbach, L. A., D'Onofrio, C. N., Backer, T. E., & Montgomery, S. B. (1996). Diffusion of school-based substance abuse prevention programs. *American Behavioral Scientist, 39*, 919–934.

Salmivalli, C., Kärnä, A. and Poskiparta, E. (2009). From peer putdowns to peer support: A theoretical model and how it translated into a national anti-bullying program. In S. Shimerson, S. Swearer & D. Espelage (Eds.), The *Handbook of School Bullying: An International Perspective.* Mahwah, NJ: Lawrence Erlbaum.

Salmivalli, C., Kärnä, A., & Poskiparta, E. (2010). Development, evaluation, and diffusion of a national anti-bullying program, KiVa. In B. Doll, W. Pfohl, & J. Yoon (Eds.), *Handbook of Youth Prevention Science* (pp. 238–252). New York: Routledge.

Salmivalli, C., Lagerspetz, K., Björkqvist, K., Osterman, K., & Kaukiainen, A. (1996). Bullying as a group process: Participant roles and their relations to social status within the group. *Aggressive Behavior, 22*, 1–15.

Sapouna, M., Wolke, D., Vannini, N., Watson, S., Woods, S., Schneider, W., Enz, S., Hall, L., Paiva, A., Andre, E., Dautenhahn, K. & Aylett, R. (2010). Virtual learning intervention to reduce bullying victimization in primary school: A controlled trial. *Journal of Child Psychology and Psychiatry, 51*(1), 104–112. doi:10.1111/j.1469-7610.2009.02137.x

Schäfer, M. & Korn, S. (2004). Bullying als Gruppenphänomen. *Zeitschrift für Entwicklungspsychologie und Pädagogische Psychologie, 36*(1), 19–29.

Slonje, R., Smith, P. K. and Frisen, A. (2013). The nature of cyberbullying and strategies for prevention. *Computers in Human Behaviour.* doi:10.1016/j.chb.2012.05.024

Smith, P. K., Mahdavi, J., Carvalho, M., Fisher, S., Russell, S., & Tippett, N. (2008). Cyberbullying: its nature and impact in secondary school pupils. *Journal of Child Psychology and Psychiatry, and Allied Disciplines, 49*(4), 376–85. doi:10.1111/j.1469-7610.2007.01846.x

Truscott, M. H., Rustogi, H. & Young, C. B. (2000). Enhancing the macroeconomics course: an experiential learning approach. *The Journal of Economic Education, 31*(1), 60–65. doi:10.1080/00220480009596762

Vannini, N., Enz, S., Sapouna, M., Wolke, D., Watson, S., Woods, S. Dautenhahn, K. Hall, L. Paiva, A., André, E., Aylett, R. & Schneider, W. (2011). "FearNot!" A computer-based anti-bullying-program designed to foster peer intervention. *European Journal of Psychology of Education, 26*(1), 21–44.

Watson, S., Vannini, N., Woods, S. Dautenhahn, K., Sapouna, M., Enz, S., Schneider, W., Wolke, D., Hall, P., Paiva, A., Andre, E. & Aylett, R. (2010). Inter-cultural differences in response to a computer based anti-bullying intervention. *Educational Research, 52*(1), 61–80. doi:10.1080/00131881003588261

Wolke, D., Woods, S., Stanford, K., & Schulz, H. (2001). Bullying and victimization of primary school children in England and Germany: Prevalence and school factors. *British Journal of Psychology, 92*, 673–696.

Zoll, C., Enz, S., Schaub, H., Aylett, R., & Paiva, A. (2006). Fighting Bullying with the Help of Autonomous Agents in a Virtual School Environment. Proceedings of the 7th International Conference on Cognitive Modelling (ICCM-2006).

6

THE DEVELOPMENT OF A SERIOUS GAME ON CYBERBULLYING

A concept test

Katrien Van Cleemput, Heide Vandebosch,
Karolien Poels, Sara Bastiaensens, Ann DeSmet
and Ilse De Bourdeaudhuij

Introduction

This chapter discusses the development process and concept test of a digital serious game to combat cyberbullying in the first and second grade of secondary schools in Flanders (Belgium). The term 'serious game' is used to describe 'any form of interactive computer-based game software for one or multiple players to be used on any platform and that has been developed with the intention to be more than entertainment' (Ritterfeld, Cody, & Vorderer, 2009, p. 6). Other terms have been used for serious games referring to specific goals: games for health, persuasive games, social impact games, etc. It is often argued that serious games are theoretically well suited for learning and behaviour change among young people: 1) games are intrinsically motivating; they are 'fun' (Baranowski, Buday, Thompson, & Baranowski, 2008; Prensky, 2007; Ritterfeld et al., 2009); 2) games have the potential to incorporate processes that are important for learning and behaviour change: immediate feedback, scaffolding, practice, reward structures, etc. (Baranowski et al., 2008; Shegog, 2010; Whitton, 2012); and (3) games already have young people's attention; they provide a good 'fit' with the target group (Prensky, 2007). Empirical studies, moreover, have shown that serious games can indeed be effective for learning and for behaviour change (for reviews see: Connolly, Boyle, MacArthur, Hainey, & Boyle, 2012; Kharrazi, Shirong Lu, Gharghabi, & Coleman, 2012).

The serious game on cyberbullying that is discussed in this chapter is created in the context of an interdisciplinary project, called "Friendly ATTAC" (ATTAC = Adaptive Technological Tools Against Cyberbullying). The game is still in an early phase of development. This chapter will provide an overview of the formative research that was conducted in the past two years, and present the results of a first concept test in which the background story, the first graphics, and the main game characters were presented to the target group.

Cyberbullying prevention

Cyberbullying appeared on the public (and research) agenda for the first time in 2005 in Flanders, but also worldwide. Since then, it has continued to be considered an important problem by principals, teachers, and students of Flemish schools, as well as by the larger public (Steffgen, Vandebosch, Völlink, & Dehue, 2010; Vandebosch, Beirens, D'Haese, Wegge, & Pabian, 2012; Vandebosch & Van Cleemput, 2008, 2009). Internationally recognized scientific studies have investigated different aspects of cyberbullying (e.g. frequency, profiles of bullies and victims, impact on well-being, etc.) and their findings have consolidated societal concerns (e.g., Notar, Padgett, & Roden, 2013; Tokunaga, 2010; Wingate, Minney, & Guadagno, 2012).

To tackle this form of bullying, a multi-faceted approach is required in which schools (students, staff, parents), (cyber)police, software providers, e-safety organizations, media sources, policy-makers, and researchers cooperate (Cross, Li, Smith, & Monks, 2012; Diamanduros, Downs, & Jenkins, 2008; Mishna, Cook, Saini, Wu, & MacFadden, 2009; Pearce, Cross, Monks, Waters, & Falconer, 2011; Slonje, Smith, & Frisén, 2013; Steffgen et al., 2010). Prevention is an important facet of this approach. However, there is a distinct lack of prevention programs and materials to increase knowledge, change attitudes, and ultimately change behaviour in Flanders. Those that exist lack a theoretical and evidence-based approach, or only aim to increase awareness. One theoretically sound and evidence-based research project for Flanders on bullying exists (Stevens, De Bourdeaudhuij, & Van Oost, 2000). However, it does not include cyberbullying. Therefore, the aim of the Friendly ATTAC project is to take the first step in the development of a theoretically sound and evidence-based prevention programme on cyberbullying.

Formative research

The theoretical planning model that is used in this project is the "Intervention Mapping approach" (Bartholomew et al., 2011). The intervention mapping protocol (IM) describes a series of steps that programme planners can follow to create theory- and evidence-informed intervention programmes, in order to maximise the effectiveness of their programmes. Intervention mapping has been used to develop serious games in the past on, for example, healthy nutrition, physical activity promotion, and sex education (Baranowski et al., 2011; Brown et al., 2012; Shegog et al., 2001).

In the first step of IM, a stakeholder group was established that involves societal (educational policy makers, mental health promotion organisations, educators, youth organisations) and technological stakeholders. This group was asked to discuss the progress, development, and expert views on the project biannually. Also, focus groups with youngsters, educational stakeholders, and cyberbullying and health intervention experts were organised to map current initiatives and to get better insight into the expectations of each of these groups. Next, a needs assessment of cyberbullying was performed, based on the PRECEDE model (Green & Kreuter, 2005). This model draws the researchers' attention to different aspects of a phenomenon: in this case, the quality of life and health problems related to involvement in cyberbullying, behavioural factors (i.e., the forms of cyberbullying, victims' coping behaviour, bystanders' reactions) and environmental factors (e.g., the school, technological affordances of online services), and their respective personal determinants (e.g., social skills, knowledge, attitude).

Based on the discussions with the stakeholders, the focus groups, and the needs assessment results, it was decided to aim the intervention at 12- to 14-year-olds. In Flanders, this is the period when cyberbullying reaches its peak. As the youngsters emphasised in the focus groups that they would like to play a game on cyberbullying in a safe environment, a single-player game was chosen, and it was decided that the game should be played in the school context.

In the second step of intervention mapping, the focus is shifted from describing and explaining the detrimental behaviour toward describing the behavioural changes that should be made in order to minimise negative mental health consequences. In choosing these behaviours, it is important to prioritise behavioural changes that are most beneficial for positive mental health outcomes (Bartholomew, Parcel, Kok, Gottlieb, & Fernandez, 2011). The serious game will, first of all, focus on the behaviour of the bystanders of cyberbullying. Adolescents are typically most often confronted with cyberbullying as bystanders and not necessarily victims or bullies. Intervention programs (primarily) aiming at changing bystanders' behaviour, moreover, prove to be effective in reducing the bullying (Polanin, Espelage, & Pigott, 2012; Salmivalli, Kärnä, & Poskiparta, 2011). In order to describe the behavioural outcomes (i.e., the desired behaviour) for bystanders, additional research was required. Thus, focus groups were conducted among 12- to 15-year-olds (N = 61) (DeSmet et al., 2014) to explore the behavioural determinants of bystander behaviour in cyberbullying. The findings of these focus groups were validated in a survey that was conducted among students in Flemish schools (N = 1,750).

Based on these results and the results of recent studies on bystander behaviour (see e.g. Barlińska, Szuster, & Winiewski, 2013; Freis & Gurung, 2013; Kowalski, Schroeder, & Smith, 2013; Macháčková, Dedkova, Sevcikova, & Cerna, 2013; Pöyhönen, Juvonen, & Salmivalli, 2012), behavioural outcomes could be described and broken down into smaller behavioural steps called "performance objectives". The end product of the second step in the intervention mapping protocol consists of matrices in which these performance objectives are crossed with their determinants (e.g., knowledge, skills and self-efficacy, attitudes and outcomes and perceived social norms) to form change objectives. In Table 6.1 an example is provided of a matrix for the performance objective 'Always comfort the victim'. The column headings represent the determinants, and the change objectives can be found in the cells.

In the third step of intervention mapping, theory-informed intervention methods for behaviour change are selected. Basic methods for behaviour change are, for instance, active learning (Elaboration Likelihood Model, Social Cognitive Theory) and modelling (Social Cognitive Theory) (Bartholomew et al., 2011). These theories

TABLE 6.1 Example of matrix for performance objective 'Always comfort the victim', determinants and change objectives

Performance objective	Knowledge	Self-efficacy	Outcome expectancies	Perceived social norms
Always comfort the victim	Recognize that by comforting the victim, you are making the victim feel better	Express confidence in being able to comfort or provide advice to the victim	Expect that by comforting the victim, they will feel better	Recognize that your friends expect you to comfort or provide advice to the victim
	Describe ways to comfort a victim that is in line with your personality			

are translated into practical applications, in our case as features/mechanisms of a digital serious game. In the following sections, the use of a background narrative in the game, as one specific method for behaviour change, will be discussed.

Creation of the materials

Step four of the intervention mapping protocol consists of the creation of the programme materials. The development of the game is an iterative process in which phases of implementation and evaluation are alternated. The remainder of this chapter will be devoted to a description of the concept test of the background narrative whilst also describing the playable and non-playable characters, their graphical representations, and their specific role within the game. The elements that are more specifically related to video game experience, for example game controls, feedback mechanisms (Boyle, Connolly, Hainey, & Boyle, 2012; Ryan et al., 2006), will be tested in a later phase of the project.

In this phase of intervention mapping, creative professionals (story writer, game designer, graphic designer, etc.) are involved in the process. The materials are created through a back-and-forth movement between the program planners and the creative professionals. The program planners let the creative professionals do their work, but periodically check if the change objectives are addressed using an appropriate method (Bartholomew et al., 2011).

Four professional story writers were asked to write a short proposal for a story. The story writers were briefed about the phenomenon of cyberbullying, and about the performance objectives. A choice was made based on several criteria: is the story not too childish or too tragic?; is the story appealing to both sexes?; are there possibilities to include cyberbullying situations in the story?; etc. After a specific story was selected, several meetings were held between the story writer and the research team to develop the story further. The final story is displayed in Box 6.1.

BOX 6.1   THE MESSENGER

It is the year 2044 and Barbara West, a famous research journalist, dies when she tries to reveal the identity of a mysterious cyber terrorist who calls himself "The Messenger". She leaves behind a suitcase containing six objects that could lead to the evil terrorist. Her courageous son, Rafa, wants to travel through time in a time machine that was built by his father, the genius Professor West, and save her. However, because of a fault in the machine, he does not get sent two years back in time, but instead he arrives thirty years back in time, to 2014. When the time machine turns out to be broken, it looks like Rafa is stuck in the past. Then he recognises something from a picture in Barbara's suitcase: a school building. Rafa realises that, in 2014, "The Messenger" is only a teenager. He decides to infiltrate the school building and look for the five remaining trails that could lead to "The Messenger". If he can stop "The Messenger" in the past, he might be able to save his mother. Rafa suspects everyone, and when he starts his search he is confronted with a web of intrigue and cyberbullying. Soon it becomes clear that "The Messenger" is some-one who was involved in the bullying. To change the future he needs to get more insight into the cyberbullying and change "The Messenger". (Uytendhouwen, 2013)

Narratives in health communication

The two main theories that inform us about the role of a story or "narrative" in health communication are Transportation Theory and the Extended Elaboration Likelihood Model (see Busselle & Bilandzic, 2009; Green, Brock, & Kaufman, 2004; Green & Brock, 2000; Moyer-Guse, 2008; Slater & Rouner, 2002). A good narrative allows the participant to get "transported", "engaged", "immersed" or "engrossed" in the story (Moyer-Guse, 2008). The most commonly used term, "transportation", is defined as "a convergent process, where all mental systems and capacities become focused on events occurring in the narrative" (Green & Brock, 2000).

Narrative engagement has two important outcomes: higher narrative engagement is associated with higher enjoyment of media content (Busselle & Bilandzic, 2009), and narrative engagement can lead to a change in beliefs and attitudes (Green & Brock, 2000, 2013; Moyer-Guse, 2008; Slater & Rouner, 2002). With regard to change in beliefs and attitudes, Transportation Theory states that participants that are more engaged in a story show more story-consistent beliefs and opinions, because they are less likely to look for counter-arguments to the beliefs and opinions that are expressed in the story (Green et al., 2004; Green & Brock, 2000).

For programme planners, it is important to know what dimensions narrative engagement consists of, and how optimal circumstances for reaching narrative engagement can be created.

Green and Brock (2000) distinguished three dimensions of transportation:

- emotional reactions (being curious about how the story ends, feeling the emotions along with the characters);
- mental imagery (being able to picture the events taking place and having a vivid image of the characters);
- loss of access to real-world information (losing sense of time, not being distracted by the events occurring in the room).

Buselle and Bilandzic (2009) elaborated on this work and created a comprehensive process model of narrative engagement including insights from transportation theory, but also from the literature on the related concepts of identification (Cohen, 2001), presence (Lee, 2004), and flow (Csikszentmihalyi, 1997). They constructed a "narrative engagement scale" consisting of four components:

- narrative understanding (the story is not difficult to understand);
- attentional focus (not being distracted);
- narrative presence (sensation of being in the story);
- emotional engagement (feeling for and with the characters).

The concept of narrative transportation was later integrated in the Extended Elaboration Likelihood Model (E-ELM). The E-ELM is a version of the Elaboration Likelihood Model (Cacioppo & Petty, 1984) that was adapted to explain why and how entertainment education can be effective (Slater & Rouner, 2002). According to this model, transportation (or absorption) is positively predicted by story line appeal, quality of production, unobtrusiveness of persuasive subtext and homophily (which will be discussed below in the section on the characters) (Slater & Rouner, 2002).

With regard to the quality of the production, Green, Brock and Kaufman (2004) also emphasised the importance of "craftsmanship" for transportation, asserting that "poorly constructed narratives do not help readers enter the story world" (p 320). As mentioned above, the story in our game (Box 6.1) was developed by a professional story writer and has a typical narrative structure (Baranowski et al., 2008; Sood, Menard, & Witte, 2004). The story consists of a protagonist (Rafa = the player), an antagonist (The Messenger, a terrorist who killed Rafa's mother), internal conflict (Rafa has to remain friendly with the other characters, but at the same time needs to find which of these characters is The Messenger), and external conflict (several characters try to thwart Rafa in his objectives). Throughout the story, Rafa goes through a shift from hesitance to confidence in reacting to cyberbullying. The plot also contains a love triangle. Referring to the discussion above, the following topics will be investigated in the concept test:

TABLE 6.2 Topics for investigating the narrative

Story line appeal	E-ELM
Quality of production	E-ELM
Story	Transportation theory/ E-ELM
Graphics	E-ELM
Unobtrusiveness of persuasive subtext	E-ELM
Narrative immersion/transportation	
Narrative understanding	Narrative engagement scale
Emotional reactions	Transportation theory/narrative engagement scale
Mental imagery	Transportation theory/narrative engagement scale
Loss of access to real world information	Transportation theory/narrative engagement scale

Involvement with characters

The characters are connected to the story, yet they fulfil a crucial role in both media enjoyment and the persuasive power of media content. In the field of media studies, "identification" with characters is considered a key factor in explaining media enjoyment (Cohen, 2001; Hoffner & Buchanan, 2005). People like watching television shows and movies because they start to share the feelings of the character (affective), share the perspective of the character (cognitive), internalise and share the goals of the character, and, ultimately, get absorbed in the characters (self-awareness is lost) (Cohen, 2001). This process is very closely related to transportation (although the focus is explicitly on the characters), and according to the Extended Elaboration Likelihood model for Entertainment-Education (Slater & Rouner, 2002), identification with characters will also reduce counterarguing. According to Cohen (2001), identification can be used consciously to persuade by making the source of the message attractive, rather than the message itself. Thus, the participant can be involved with the characters in the game in many different ways.

In video games, it is expected that a player will identify with the playable character (in our case Rafa). In this sense, the avatar that will be used to represent Rafa needs to be chosen carefully. Research has noted (Van Looy, Courtois, De Vocht, & De Marez, 2012) that "avatar identification" has three subcomponents: similarity identification (seeing resemblance between the self and the character), wishful identification (wanting to have the same characteristics as the character), and embodied presence (feelings of acting through the character). The avatar for Rafa will be adaptable in the game. The players will be able to choose between a female or male Rafa and they will be able to alter physical attributes.

Besides playable characters, other, pre-programmed or "non-playable" characters will also play a role in the game. These other characters, "satellite characters" in the Entertainment-Education literature (Sabido, 2004), can be used as role models. A core theory in Entertainment-Education is Bandura's Social Cognitive Theory (SCT) (Bandura, 2004). According to this theory, people do not only learn through direct experiences, but also through the power of social modelling. Social modelling implies that a person learns by observing the successes and mistakes of others. In our game, some of the non-playable characters will serve as positive role models. In order for social modelling to occur, it is imperative that these role models are actively and decisively chosen. Positive role models are usually created to be culturally admired characters. Thus, through a process of "wishful" identification, the participant is likely to adopt the role model's beliefs, attitudes, and, ultimately, their behaviour (Hoffner & Buchanan, 2005). Furthermore, role models should look and feel familiar to the participant. Viewing an individual similar to themselves change his or her life for the better raises a participant's sense of self-efficacy, which is an important predictor of behaviour (Bandura, 2004). The following topics will be investigated in the concept test:

TABLE 6.3 Topics for investigating the characters

Similarity	
Visual representation of the character	E-ELM
Background characteristics of the character (e.g. interests)	SCT, identification
Wishful identification	SCT
Adaptivity	identification

Method

In December of 2013 and January of 2014, twelve focus group interviews were conducted among 63 students from the first and second year of secondary education in Flanders (12- to 14-year-olds). In each selected school, four to six boys and four to six girls were randomly selected from the students that had received active parental consent to participate in the study. The respondents were informed of the goals of the study and the ways in which the data would be handled before they were asked to give their consent to participate in the study.

In the focus group interviews, the students were shown a five-minute introductory clip (images and voice) of the narrative, and a video of the tutorial level. For Rafa's character, six possible avatars were presented and the respondents were asked which avatar they would like to use for playing Rafa, and how they would like to personalize it. Finally, the role of the non-playing characters was described to the students, and again six possible avatars for each of the characters were presented. The questionnaire that was used during the interviews was based on the topics mentioned in Tables 6.2 and 6.3. The interviews were transcribed and analysed using Nvivo 10. A thematic analysis (Gomm, 2004) was performed starting from the topics that were presented Tables 6.2 and 6.3.

Results

Story line appeal and quality of production

In general, the respondents found the story appealing. They described it as 'exciting' and 'adventurous', and they were curious about the story's ending. Story elements that were especially appreciated were the assault (that killed the journalist), the time travelling, and the 'detective style'. There was, however, a difference between the first graders (12- to 13-year-olds) and the second graders (13- to 14-year-olds). While the groups of first graders reacted very enthusiastically, in the groups with second graders several students were more critical. They found the story a bit cliché and predictable and suggested adding some surprising elements.

The respondents agreed that the quality of the images was good, but that they should be presented in a more attractive way and preferably in animated form. Moreover, the story should be told by a professional voice actor. The students had interesting suggestions for improving the quality of the clip. Some of these suggestions (e.g., tell the story from Rafa's perspective, add colour accents, and add background music and noises) are fairly easy to change. Others, for example using animation or visual effects, are less feasible within the scope of this project.

TABLE 6.4 Quality of production

	Positive	*Negative*	*Suggestions*
Story	Well-constructed, Exciting, adventurous	Too cliché, too predictable	Add surprising elements (e.g. unexpected identity of The Messenger)
Images	Not too many images Nice images Dark, but fits with story	Too few images Too much grey	More images Show visual representation of 'The Messenger' Moving images/visual effects Show action (e.g. assault) Add colour accents (e.g. time machine)
Narrator	Slow and clear	Too slow Intonation too flat Too formal	Hire a professional voice actor Tell the story from Rafa's perspective (instead of third person perspective) Use multiple voices (dialogs)
Other			Add music Add background noises (explosion, etc.)

Unobtrusiveness of persuasive subtext

With regard to the persuasive subtext of the story, the students were asked whether they had noticed the association between the story and cyberbullying behaviour. The most obvious link for the respondents was that between the hacker in the story ('The Messenger') and cyberbullying behaviour. Most of the respondents comprehended that something in The Messenger's past needs to be changed so that he never becomes The Messenger and Rafa's mother is never killed. Several respondents, however, did have some difficulty with the transition from the 'harder' violence in the introductory clip (assaults, explosions) to the 'softer' nature of cyberbullying at school. A girl from the second year, for instance, said: "yeah, but this Messenger controls the entire world in 2044, but it is not like you can rule the world by cyberbullying. You can make people nauseous by bullying. If you are bullied you feel bad, but it is not like you can suddenly control the electricity or something like that".

Narrative immersion

In order for a reader to get immersed in a story, he or she needs to understand the story line. In our focus groups we asked the respondents three control questions to check whether they understood the story line: 'When does the story take place?', 'Who is Barbara?' and 'What is Rafa's task at the end of the story?'. These control questions were answered correctly in all groups. However, throughout the conversations, it became clear that several aspects were not clear to all respondents, e.g. why only Rafa goes back in time, what Rafa's age is and whether The Messenger knows that Rafa went back in time or not. In the final version of the introduction clip, these aspects will need to be clarified.

A second important aspect of narrative immersion is emotional reactions to a story. The two story aspects that the respondents reacted to emotionally were the death of Rafa's mother and the idea of Rafa being stuck in the past. Several respondents indicated that they found it difficult to become emotionally engaged in the story because the pace of the clip was too slow. With regard to graphics, several respondents indicated that they were affected by the representation of the future as a dark and gloomy place. Respondents from all groups were curious about the story's ending.

Finally, with regard to mental imagery, the respondents agreed that the images helped them to picture the events in their mind. Using moving images, showing the characters more explicitly in the clip, and telling the story from Rafa's perspective would, however, make this process easier. While the groups of second graders were more critical to the story line than the first graders, they did seem to have reached a higher level of mental imagery as they started to suggest additional plots for the story (e.g. complicated love triangles, possible endings, etc.).

It was expected that the fourth aspect of narrative immersion, loss of access to real world information, would be difficult to achieve in the setting in which this concept test took place (during school, in a group setting . . .). The respondents indeed seemed to be easily distracted by other students in the room and by other elements (background noises, school materials . . .).

Involvement with characters

Playable character: Rafa

We showed the respondents six possible visual representations for Rafa that were drawn from a character database. The girls could choose among six female avatars, the boys among six male avatars. Both boys and girls thought that the characters looked more like 17- to 18-year-olds than like people of their own age. For the girl characters, this was especially related to the large breast sizes and the mature faces. The male characters were too muscled (especially the arms) and had too much facial hair growth for people of their age. Also with regard to the clothing, the respondents agreed that the characters were not dressed like themselves. Specific aspects that they regarded as old-fashioned were the boot-cut trousers, which should be replaced by skinny jeans, and the shoes, which should be replaced by fashionable sneakers.

The players were asked whether they would like to be able to adapt Rafa's appearance. The respondents liked the idea of choosing between different avatars for Rafa and personalizing it with different hair colours, skin colours, etc. Several respondents suggested that additional possibilities for personalization (e.g. handbags, tattoos, jewellery) should be earned throughout the game. In two groups, students suggested that it should be possible to change the name 'Rafa' to a self-chosen name/one's own name.

Overall, the respondents liked the character of Rafa. They thought he/she was a cool and adventurous character ('he/she has guts'). The girls liked that Rafa was not a 'girly' girl, but an adventurous and 'tough' girl.

Non-playable characters

Four non-playable characters were discussed with the respondents. These characters were Febe, Emma, Lars and Kasper.[1] For each of these characters, a short description by the respondents (see Table 6.5) and six possible visual representations were presented.

With regard to the visual representations of the background characters, the respondents again indicated that the characters looked too old to represent people of their age and that their clothes were old-fashioned.

The character 'Febe' was created to serve as a positive role model in the game. The respondents liked the idea that she freely expresses her opinion of the cyberbullying incidents. They imagined her to be kind, trustworthy, funny, smart, energetic, and that she is someone who takes initiative, a bit of a daredevil. A boy in the second year of preparatory vocational education indicated that he liked that

TABLE 6.5 Description of four non-playable characters

Febe	*Febe is the first student that Rafa gets to know when he arrives in The Messenger's school. She and Rafa become friends. Febe always expresses her own opinion with regard to the cyberbullying. She also encourages Rafa to reflect about the cyberbullying instances.*
Emma	*Emma is the prettiest girl at school. She writes for the school blog. Emma is friends with Lars and Kasper (they are both in love with her)*
Lars	*Lars is big and strong. He is older than the other students, because he had to retake his year. Lars sometimes cyberbullies other students. He is in love with Emma.*
Kasper	*Kasper is a skinny and silent boy. He loves science fiction and has a thing for computers. He is secretly in love with Emma and he becomes a victim of cyberbullying in the game.*

Febe is *"less princessy than the girls in other videogames"*. When asked whether they would accept Febe's advice, the respondents indicated that she should earn their trust first, and that it would depend on the advice ". . . *for example, my parents often tell me to stop using Facebook or Twitter. If she would say that, I wouldn't listen, because I don't listen to my parents about that either" (girl, second year preparatory education)*. Febe was considered a realistic character. The respondents indicated that they believed that someone like that exists, and some even spontaneously started naming people they know whom Febe reminded them of.

'Kasper' is one of the characters in the game who is cyberbullied. The majority of the respondents pictured him as a nice, shy, smart person, who is a bit of loner. One respondent described him as *"someone you don't hate, but would not normally hang out with" (girl, second grade vocational education)*. Kasper also reminded the respondents of people they know in real life. The students from the second grade had a somewhat different view on Kasper. They suggested that he would be some-one who seems shy and a bit of a loner at first, but who turns out be really cool in the end (has a cool hobby nobody knows about, and becomes more empow-ered as the game continues). Kasper was most often suspected for growing up to become The Messenger.

'Lars' is a cyberbully in the game. The respondents think of him as someone who is tough and who easily becomes jealous, is not good at school, likes to fight, and hangs out with bad friends. In most of the groups, Lars was considered a real-istic character. One group of girls (first year, general education) thought he was realistic, but could not be someone from their close social environment.

'Emma', finally, is a girl who forms the love interest of both Kasper and Lars. While Emma was intended as a nice, smart girl who was popular among the class members in the game, the respondents interpreted her character as a 'mean girl'. They described her as a person who acts dominant towards the girls ('bossy', 'feels better than other people') and promiscuous towards the boys ('draws the boys' atten-tion, 'overreacts'). The phrase 'Prettiest girl in school' especially seemed to evoke this type of reaction. Also, in several groups the respondents found that 'being the prettiest girl in school' conflicted with 'writing for the school blog'. Emma, as they described her, was also considered a realistic character by the respondents. Again the students started naming other students in the school who resembled Emma.

Conclusion

The concept test provided the researchers with a lot of information on how to improve the current materials, and on what needs to be taken into account when developing new program materials. In order to reach a higher level of narrative engagement with the background story, two main aspects should be taken into account. First, in its final form, the background story cannot be too predictable (i.e. too obvious who The Messenger is) and too cliché (i.e. too stereotypical characters). The researchers should explore how different story endings can be integrated in the game.

Next, the concept tests confirmed Green, Brock and Kaufman's (2004) statement that craftsmanship is important when developing a health intervention. It was clear that the elements that were created by professionals (i.e. the story and the images), were more appreciated by the students than the elements that were created by non-professionals (assemblage of images, voice-over). The quality of the final clip should be at an acceptable level for the target group.

With regard to involvement with the characters, most of the character profiles were considered realistic by the students. The students also provided useful suggestions on how to complete the character profiles. The visual representations of the characters, on the other hand, need to be reconsidered by the researchers. The older look of the characters and the old-fashioned clothes impeded the respondents from feeling similar to the characters.

The development of a serious game is an iterative process. The next iteration, in which the game mechanics and user interface are prototyped and implemented, has already started. The integration of narratives and game mechanics has been a considered a difficult challenge by many (educational) game designers (Amory, 2007; see e.g. Dickey, 2006; Lee, Park, & Jin, 2006). While narratives can contribute to both game enjoyment and behaviour change, as was argued above, the interactive nature of games can be difficult to reconcile with the (often) linear structure of stories: 'The challenge to designers is how to tell a story and still permit the player to affect or possibly change the story, depending on choices made throughout the game' (Dickey, 2006, p. 73). In order to overcome this challenge, game designers can use different strategies (e.g letting the story branch off depending on the player's choices and letting the players choose the order in which they access different components of the story) and narrative devices (cut scenes, flash backs, cliff-hangers, etc.) (Dickey, 2006).

Before changes will be made to the current intervention materials, the researchers will have to clearly map their implications. For instance, if certain parts of the story are omitted, modelling as a method could be deleted, and an alternative should be found.

The process evaluation will continue throughout the development process. As soon as a sufficient amount of intervention materials are available, a controlled lab test will be held to test positive effects and possible side effects on the behavioral determinants of cyberbullying that were mapped in formative research.

Note

1 Due to the time constraints posed by the schools, in most of the groups only two or three characters were discussed. The order of the topic list was changed before each conversation in order to collect data on all characters.

References

Amory, A. (2007). Game object model version II: A theoretical framework for educational game development. *Educational Technology Research and Development, 55,* 51–77. doi:10.1007/s11423

Bandura, A. (2004). Social cognitive theory for personal and social change by enabling media. In Singhal, Michael J. Cody, Everett M. Rogers, & Miguel Sabido (Eds.), *Entertainment-education and social change. history, research, and practice* (pp. 75–96). New York/Oxon: Routledge.

Baranowski, T., Baranowski, J., Thompson, D., Buday, R., Jago, R., Griffith, M. J., & Watson, K. B. (2011). Video game play, child diet, and physical activity behavior change: A randomized clinical trial. *American Journal of Preventive Medicine, 40*(1), 33–38. doi:10.1016/j.amepre.2010.09.029

Baranowski, T., Buday, R., Thompson, D. I., & Baranowski, J. (2008). Playing for real: Video games and stories for health-related behavior change. *American Journal of Preventive Medicine, 34*(1), 74–82.e10.

Barlińska, J., Szuster, A., & Winiewski, M. (2013). Cyberbullying among adolescent bystanders: Role of the communication medium, form of violence, and empathy. *Journal of Community & Applied Social Psychology, 23*(1), 37–51. doi:10.1002/casp.2137

Bartholomew, L. K., Parcel, G. S., Kok, G., Gottlieb, N. H., & Fernandez, M. E. (2011). *Planning health promotion programs. An Intervention Mapping approach* (Third ed.). San Francisco: Jossey-Bass.

Boyle, E. A., Connolly, T. M., Hainey, T., & Boyle, J. M. (2012). Engagement in digital entertainment games: A systematic review. *Computers in Human Behavior, 28*(3), 771–780. doi:10.1016/j.chb.2011.11.020

Brown, K., Newby, K., Bayley, J., Puja, J., Becky, J., & Baxter, A. (2012). *Development and evaluation of a serious game for relationships and sex education using Intervention Mapping. PREPARE (Positive Relationships: Eliminating Pressure and Sexual Coercion in Adolescent Relationships)* (HIEC Project Evaluation Report) (p. 112). Coventry: Coventry University.

Busselle, R., & Bilandzic, H. (2009). Measuring narrative engagement. *Media Psychology, 12*(4), 321–347. doi:10.1080/15213260903287259

Cacioppo, J. T., & Petty, R. E. (1984). The elaboration likelihood model of persuasion. *Advances in Consumer Research, 11*(1), 673–675.

Cohen, J. (2001). Defining identification: A theoretical look at the identification of audiences with media characters. *Mass Communication and Society, 4*(3), 245–264. doi:10.1207/S15327825MCS0403_01

Connolly, T. M., Boyle, E. A., MacArthur, E., Hainey, T., & Boyle, J. M. (2012). A systematic literature review of empirical evidence on computer games and serious games. *Computers & Education, 59*(2), 661–686. doi:10.1016/j.compedu.2012.03.004

Cross, D., Li, Q., Smith, P. K., & Monks, H. (2012). Understanding and preventing cyberbullying. Where have we been and where should we be going? In Q. Li, D. Cross, & P. K. Smith (Eds.), *Cyberbullying in the global playground. Research from international perspectives* (pp. 287–305). West Sussex: Wiley-Blackwell.

Csikszentmihalyi, M. (1997). *Finding flow: The psychology of engagement with everyday life.* New York: Basic Books.

DeSmet, A., Veldeman, C., Poels, K., Bastiaensens, S., Van Cleemput, K., Vandebosch, H., & De Bourdeaudhuij, I. (2014). Determinants of self-reported bystander behavior in cyberbullying incidents amongst adolescents. *Cyberpsychology, Behavior, and Social Networking, 17* (4), 207–215. doi:10.1089/cyber.2013.0027

Diamanduros, T., Downs, E., & Jenkins, S. J. (2008). The role of school psychologists in the assessment, prevention, and intervention of cyberbullying. *Psychology in the Schools, 45*(8), 693–704.

Dickey, M. D. (2006). Game design narrative for learning: appropriating adventure game design narrative devices and techniques for the design of interactive learning environments. *Educational Technology Research and Development, 54* (3), 245–263.

Freis, S. D., & Gurung, R. A. R. (2013). A Facebook analysis of helping behavior in online bullying. *Psychology of Popular Media Culture, 2*(1), 11–19. doi:10.1037/a0030239

Gomm, R. (2004). *Social Research Methodology. A Critical Introduction.* New York: Macmillan.

Green, L., & Kreuter, M. W. (2005). *Health program planning: An educational and ecological approach* (4th ed.). Mountain View, CA: Mayfield.

Green, M. C., & Brock, T. C. (2000). The role of transportation in the persuasiveness of public narratives. *Journal of Personality and Social Psychology, 79*(5), 701–721. doi:10.1037//0022-3514.79.5.701

Green, M. C., & Brock, T. C. (2013). In the mind's eye. Transportation-imagery model of narrative persuasion. In M. C., Green, J. J., Strange & T. C. Brock (Eds.), *Narrative impact. Social and cognitive foundations* (pp. 315–341). New York/Hove: Psychology Press.

Green, M. C., Brock, T. C., & Kaufman, G. F. (2004). Understanding media enjoyment: The role of transportation into narrative worlds. *Communication Theory (10503293), 14*(4), 311–327.

Hoffner, C., & Buchanan, M. (2005). Young adults' wishful identification with television characters: The role of perceived similarity and character attributes. *Media Psychology, 7*(4), 325–351. doi:10.1207/S1532785XMEP0704_2

Kharrazi, H., Shirong Lu, A., Gharghabi, F., & Coleman, W. (2012). A scoping review of health game research: Past, present, and future. *Games for Health Journal, 1*(2), 153–164.

Kowalski, R. M., Schroeder, A. N., & Smith, C. A. (2013). Bystanders and their willingness to intervene in cyber bullying situations. In R. Hanewald (Ed.), *From cyber bullying to cyber safety: Issues and approaches in educational contexts* (pp. 77–100). New York: Nova Science Publishers.

Lee, K. M. (2004). Presence, explicated. *Communication Theory, 14*(1), 27–50. doi:10.1111/j.1468-2885.2004.tb00302.x

Lee, K. M., Park, N., & Jin, S.-A. (2006). Narrative and interactivity in computer games. In P. Vorderer & J. Bryant (Eds.), *Playing video games: Motives, responses, and consequences* (pp. 259–274). Mahwah, NJ: Lawrence.

Macháčková, H., Dedkova, L., Sevcikova, A., & Cerna, A. (2013). Bystanders' support of cyberbullied schoolmates. *Journal of Community & Applied Social Psychology, 23*(1), 25–36. doi:10.1002/casp.2135

Mishna, F., Cook, C., Saini, M., Wu, M.-J., & MacFadden, R. (2009). Interventions for children, youth, and parents to prevent and reduce cyber abuse. *Campbell Systematic Reviews, (2)*, 1–54.

Moyer-Guse, E. (2008). Toward a theory of entertainment persuasion: Explaining the persuasive effects of entertainment-education messages. *Communication Theory, 18*(3), 407–425.

Notar, C.E., Padgett, S., & Roden, J. (2013). Cyberbullying: A review of the literature. *Universal Journal of Educational Research, 1*(1), 1–9. doi:10.13189/ujer.2013.010101

Pearce, N., Cross, D., Monks, H., Waters, S., & Falconer, S. (2011). Current evidence of best practice in whole-school bullying intervention and its potential to inform cyberbullying interventions. *Australian Journal of Guidance and Counselling, 21*(1), 1–21.

Polanin, J.R., Espelage, D.L., & Pigott, T.D. (2012). A meta-analysis of school-based bullying prevention programs' effects on bystander intervention behavior. *School Psychology Review, 41*(1), 47–65.

Pöyhönen, V., Juvonen, J., & Salmivalli, C. (2012). Standing up for the victim, siding with the bully or standing by? Bystander responses in bullying situations. *Social Development, 21*(4), 722–741. doi:10.1111/j.1467-9507.2012.00662.x

Prensky, M. (2007). *Digital Game-Based Learning.* St. Paul: Paragon House.

Ritterfeld, U., Cody, M., & Vorderer, P. (2009). Introduction. In *Serious games. Mechanisms and effects* (pp. 3–9). New York/Oxon: Routledge.

Ryan, R.M., Rigby, C.S., & Przybylski, A. (2006). The motivational pull of video games: A self-determination theory approach. *Motivation and Emotion, 30*(4), 344–360. doi:10.1007/s11031-006-9051-8

Sabido, M. (2004). The origins of entertainment-education. In A. Singhal, M. Cody, E. M. Rogers, & M. Sabido (Eds.), *Entertainment-education and social change* (pp. 61–74). New York and London: Routledge.

Salmivalli, C., Kärnä, A., & Poskiparta, E. (2011). Counteracting bullying in Finland: The KiVa program and its effects on different forms of being bullied. *International Journal of Behavioral Development, 35*(5), 405–411. doi:10.1177/0165025411407457

Shegog, R. (2010). Application of behavioral theory in computer game design for health behavior change. In J. Cannon-Bowers & C. Bowers (Eds.), *Serious game design and development. Technologies for training and learning* (pp. 196–232). Hershey: Information Science Reference.

Shegog, R., Bartholomew, L.K., Parcel, G.S., Sockrider, M.M., Masse, L., & Abramson, S.L. (2001). Impact of a computer-assisted education program on factors related to asthma self-management behavior. *Journal of the American Medical Informatics Association: JAMIA, 8*(1), 49–61.

Slater, M.D., & Rouner, D. (2002). Entertainment-education and elaboration likelihood: Understanding the processing of narrative persuasion. *Communication Theory, 12*(2), 173–191.

Slonje, R., Smith, P.K., & Frisén, A. (2013). The nature of cyberbullying, and strategies for prevention. *Computers in Human Behavior, 29*(1), 26–32. doi:10.1016/j.chb.2012.05.024

Sood, S., Menard, T., & Witte, K. (2004). The theory behind entertainment-education. In A. Singhal, M. Cody, E. M. Rogers, & M. Sabido (Eds.), *Entertainment-education and social change* (pp. 117–149). New York and London: Routledge.

Steffgen, G., Vandebosch, H., Völlink, T., & Dehue, F. (2010). Cyberbullying in the Benelux-Countries: First findings and ways to address the problem. In J. A. Mora-Merchán & T. Jäger (Eds.), *Cyberbullying: A cross-national comparison* (pp. 35–54). Landau: Verlag Empirische Pädagogik.

Stevens, V., De Bourdeaudhuij, I., & Van Oost, P. (2000). Bullying in Flemish schools: An evaluation of anti-bullying intervention in primary and secondary schools. *British Journal of Educational Psychology, 70*(2), 195–210. doi:10.1348/000709900158056

Tokunaga, R. S. (2010). Following you home from school: A critical review and synthesis of research on cyberbullying victimization. *Computers in Human Behavior, 26*(3), 277–287.

Uytdenhouwen (2013). https://www.linkedin.com/pub/bart-uytdenhouwen/5/b35/271

Van Looy, J., Courtois, C., De Vocht, M., & De Marez, L. (2012). Player identification in online games: Validation of a scale for measuring identification in MMOGs. *Media Psychology, 15*(2), 197–221. doi:10.1080/15213269.2012.674917

Vandebosch, H., Beirens, L., D'Haese, W., Wegge, D., & Pabian, S. (2012). Police actions with regard to cyberbullying: the Belgian case./Acciones policiales relacionadas con cyberbullying: el caso belga. *Psicothema, 24*(4), 646–652.

Vandebosch, H., & Van Cleemput, K. (2008). Defining cyberbullying: A qualitative research into the perceptions of youngsters. *CyberPsychology & Behavior, 11*(4), 499–503.

Vandebosch, H., & Van Cleemput, K. (2009). Cyberbullying among youngsters: profiles of bullies and victims. *New Media & Society, 11*(8), 1349–1371.

Whitton, N. (2012). Good game design is good learning design. In N. Whitton & A. Moseley (Eds.), *Using Games to Enhance Learning and Teaching. A Beginner's Guide* (pp. 9–20). New York and London: Routledge.

Wingate, V. S., Minney, J. A., & Guadagno, R. E. (2012). Sticks and stones may break your bones, but words will always hurt you: A review of cyberbullying. *Social Influence, 8*(2–3), 87–106. doi:10.1080/15534510.2012.730491

7

ONLINE PESTKOPPENSTOPPEN [STOP THE BULLY ONLINE]

The systematic development of a web-based tailored intervention for adolescent cyberbully victims to prevent cyberbullying[1]

Niels C. L. Jacobs, Francine Dehue, Trijntje Völlink and Lilian Lechner

Introduction

The growing popularity of social media (e.g., Facebook, Twitter) and instant messenger services (e.g., IMchat, Twitter) do not always lead to positive experiences (Gross, 2004). Cyberbullying is defined as a repeated aggressive and intentional act, carried out by a group or an individual, using electronic forms of contact. This act is directed towards a victim who cannot easily defend him or herself (Smith et al., 2008). Between 20% and 40% of the adolescents worldwide report being a cyberbully victim (Tokunaga, 2010). Research has indicated that cyber victimisation is associated with serious internalising difficulties such as depression (Perren, Dooley, Shaw, & Cross, 2010; Ybarra & Mitchell, 2004), anxiety (Campbell, Spears, Slee, Butler, & Kift, 2012), emotional distress (Ybarra & Mitchell, 2004), and suicidality (Hinduja & Patchin, 2010; Schneider, O'Donnell, Stueve, & Coulter, 2012). Cyberbully victims also more often have experienced drugs, alcohol, physical, or sexual abuse, have displayed delinquent and aggressive behaviour, have problems at school and have dropped out of school (Beran & Li, 2005, 2007; Katzer, Fetchenhauer, & Belschak, 2009; Lewinsohn, Hops, Roberts, & Seeley, 1993; Mitchell, Ybarra, & Finkelhor, 2007; Raskauskas & Stoltz, 2007; Ybarra, Mitchell, Wolak, & Finkelhor, 2006; Ybarra, 2004). Additionally, there appears to be a positive relation between engaging in cyber aggression and adolescents reporting more loneliness, lower global self-worth, having fewer mutual friendships and receiving lower ratings of social acceptance and popularity by peers (Schoffstall & Cohen, 2011). Cyberbullies as well as cyberbully-victims (i.e., both victim and bully) have worse subjective health than those who are not involved (Låftman, Modin, & Östberg, 2013), and victims of both traditional and cyberbullying (i.e., (cyber)bully victims) are four times more likely to experience depressive symptoms and five times more likely to attempt suicide when compared to non-victims (Schneider et al., 2012).

Unfortunately, intervention programmes that deal specifically with cyberbullying are scarce (Slonje, Smith, & Frisén, 2013). Moreover, students perceive that methods used in traditional bullying incidents are not equally effective in cyberbullying incidents (Paul, Smith, & Blumberg, 2012). Therefore, there is an urgent need for effective cyberbullying interventions. Ideally, these interventions should:

- Do more than increase awareness of potential threats of the Internet by offering victims intensive intervention strategies on the basis of individual needs of the student (Snakenborg, Van Acker, & Gable, 2011);
- Offer health education and teach emotional self-management competencies (Patchin & Hinduja, 2011);
- Increase victims' knowledge of reactive (e.g., deleting, blocking and ignoring messages), preventive (e.g., increased awareness and security), and effective strategies and resources that enable victims to cope with the experienced stress and negative emotions (Tenenbaum, Varjas, Meyers, & Parris, 2011);
- Aim at reducing traditional bullying as well (Olweus, 2012), because victims are often involved in both forms of bullying (Casas, Del Rey, & Ortega-Ruiz, 2013; Hemphill et al., 2012; Hinduja & Patchin, 2008);
- Include training in empathy, Internet etiquette, and healthy Internet behaviour (Ang & Goh, 2010; Barlińska, Szuster, & Winiewski, 2013).

Moreover, cyberbully victims often are unwilling to talk to a parent (Ybarra, Diener-West, & Leaf, 2007), teacher (Slonje et al., 2013; Smith et al., 2008) or other adults (Ahlfors, 2010). They spend a lot of time online (Lenhart, Purcell, Smith, & Zickuhr, 2010), prefer to get anonymous help (M. Webb, Burns, & Collin, 2008), and report a need for information and help through the Internet (Havas, de Nooijer, Crutzen, & Feron, 2011). Therefore, the best method to deliver cyberbullying interventions would be via the Internet. Furthermore, web-based interventions can be used whenever and wherever the individual prefers (Oenema, Brug, Dijkstra, Weerdt, & Vries, 2008), can reach a lot of people in a relatively cheap way (Cobiac, Vos, & Barendregt, 2009), and have the possibility to use tailoring (De Vries & Brug, 1999), which appears to be a successful health promotion technique (Krebs, Prochaska, & Rossi, 2010; Noar, Benac, & Harris, 2007).

To increase the effectiveness of such an intervention, a planned, systematic, and theory-based approach is needed (Brug, Oenema, Kroeze, & Raat, 2005). Contrastingly, the interventions that currently exist are often based on practical beliefs or common sense approaches, without a basis in theory or research results (Snakenborg et al., 2011). A theoretically sound and evidence-based intervention should provide a description of what works, under what circumstances and for whom (Smith, Salmivalli, & Cowie, 2012), with a thorough insight into the relevant determinants of behavioural change, the theoretical methods to change these determinants, and how the theoretical methods are translated into practical intervention strategies (Michie, Johnston, Francis, Hardeman, & Eccles, 2008; Webb, Joseph, Yardley, & Michie, 2010). In order to meet the need for theoretically sound and evidence-based interventions, and based on theory and recommenda-tions from the literature, we have developed an intervention containing three web-based and computer tailored pieces of advices for cyberbully victims: *Online Pestkoppenstoppen* (Stop online bullies). This paper will focus on the systemati-cally and theory-based development of the intervention, using the Intervention Mapping (IM) protocol (Bartholomew, Parcel, Kok, Gottlieb, & Fernández, 2011). Effects of the intervention will be described elsewhere.

Method

IM is a protocol consisting of six steps that can be used as an iterative process for theory and evidence-based development of health promotion interventions (Bar-tholomew et al., 2011). The six steps include: (1) conducting a needs assessment of the problem, the study population and forming a logic model of the health problem based on the PRECEDE model (Green & Kreuter, 2005); (2) defining what programme participants have to do in terms of performance objectives, and combining these performance objectives with relevant determinants into change objectives; (3) translating change objectives into practical strategies by selecting theory-based intervention methods; (4) developing, selecting, testing, and produc-ing intervention components in which all strategies are integrated; (5) planning for adoption and implementation of the programme; and, (6) anticipating the pro-cess and effect evaluation of the programme. In this paper we describe how we used each step of the IM protocol to develop the intervention, focusing on the first four steps. We refer to traditional bullying as bullying, to cyberbullying and tra-ditional bullying as (cyber)bullying, and to cyberbully victims and bully-victims as cyberbully victims. When a further distinction is needed, it will be provided.

Results

Step 1: Needs assessment

The target group for this intervention are adolescents (12–15 years old) from the secondary continued vocational education who are just starting to attend sec-ondary school, because: (1) cyberbullying appears to occur more frequently in lower levels of secondary education (Van der Vegt, den Blanken, & Jepma, 2007; Wade & Beran, 2011; Walrave & Heirman, 2011); (2) in this period of develop-ment the interaction with peers is highly valued and new social networks are formed (Gavin & Furman, 1989); and (3) adolescents have an open mind and are eager to learn new skills which enable them to learn how to cope more effectively with problems such as the negative effects of cyberbullying (Faber, Verkerk, van Aken, Lissenburg, & Geerlings, 2006).

   According to the Transactional Model (Lazarus & Folkman, 1987), coping is the cognitive and behavioural effort employed to reduce, master or tolerate inter-nal and external demands resulting from stressful events. In traditional bullying, victims either use more emotion focused (Craig, Pepler, & Blais, 2007; Kowalski, Limber, & Agatston, 2008) and passive coping strategies (e.g., crying, expressing emotions) (Bijttebier & Vertommen, 1998; Kristensen & Smith, 2003; Mahady Wilton, Craig, & Pepler, 2000), or they use emotion focused and aggressive coping strategies (e.g., venting their anger, fighting back). Similarly, cyberbully victims report using aggressive and passive coping strategies (Dooley, Shaw, & Cross, 2012) (e.g., bullying the bully, deleting messages or pretending to ignore the bullying [Dehue, Bolman, & Völlink, 2008]). Others react to cyberbullying by not retaliating and reacting submissively (Aricak et al., 2008), acting helpless, avoiding the situation (Riebel, Jäger, & Fischer, 2009), doing nothing and displaying avoidant behaviour (Perren et al., 2012). Some pretend to ignore the bullying, while others actually ignore it (Dehue et al., 2008). Additionally, adolescents coping with cyberbullying are less likely to seek social support, compared to other strategies (Dehue et al., 2008; Kowalski et al., 2008; Parris, Varjas, Meyers, & Cutts, 2011; Slonje & Smith, 2008). Individuals that are bullied in multiple ways tend to cope even less effectively (Skrzypiec, Slee, Murray-Harvey, & Pereira, 2011).

It appears that the use of ineffective coping strategies maintains (cyber)bullying (Andreou, 2001; Bijttebier & Vertommen, 1998; Craig et al., 2007; Hunter & Boyle, 2004; Kanetsuna, Smith, & Morita, 2006; Kristensen & Smith, 2003; Mahady Wilton et al., 2000; Perry, Hodges, Egan, Juvonen, & Graham, 2001; Skrzypiec et al., 2011), and that the negative effects of cyberbullying are influenced by the coping style victims use (e.g., ineffective coping appears to yield depression- and health complaints) (Neary & Joseph, 1994; Völlink, Bolman, Dehue, & Jacobs, 2013). For example, the more adolescents engage in cyber aggression, the more loneliness they feel, the lower their global self-worth is, the fewer mutual friendships they have, and the lower their ratings of social acceptance and popularity by peers are (Schoffstall & Cohen, 2011). To increase knowledge about coping strategies used in cyberbullying, it is useful to look at coping strategies employed in cyberbullying and in daily life. For example some victims wait for the problem to go away (Livingstone, Haddon, Görzig, & Olafsson, 2011) or use emotion-focused coping (e.g., crying, expressing emotions) when they believed that they could do nothing to change the stressful situation. These coping strategies appear to not differ significantly, and knowledge about traditional bullying can, to some extent, be applied to cyberbullying (Riebel et al., 2009). Furthermore, coping strategies used in response to daily stressors are good predictors for coping strategies used in response to cyberbullying (Völlink et al., 2013). To reduce victimisation and its negative effects, it thus appears that adolescents need to improve their current coping strategies. They need to employ effective coping strategies that not only help them to mentally deal with (cyber) bullying, but also contribute to the prevention and discontinuation of (cyber) bullying. Therefore, the primary programme goals were reducing the number of: (1) cyberbully victims; and (2) depressive and anxious victims as a consequence of cyberbullying. Secondary goals were a decrease in: (3) victims truanting from school; (4) victims with suicidal thoughts; and (5) an increase in determinants related to cyberbully victims' behaviour, such as self-esteem, self-efficacy, rational helpful beliefs, and effective coping.

Step 2: Matrices of change objectives

Next, the focus shifts from the needs assessment to the formation of a change model (Figure 7.1). In this step intended change in behaviour should be further delineated into specific sub-behaviours: the performance objectives (POs). The POs should be crossed with relevant determinants in order to create a matrix of change objectives (COs) (Bartholomew et al., 2011).

Performance objectives

First, we translated the risk behaviour ineffective coping into a programme outcome: after the intervention, cyberbully victims will cope in an adequate and effective manner with (cyber)bullying experiences. This programme outcome is a broad conceptualisation of what a participant has to do in order to reach the programme's goals. Therefore, participants have to perform specific sub-behaviours, called performance objectives (POs). The POs, and accordingly the content of the intervention, were based on a literature search, focus group interviews with the target group and the linkage group – including the research team, a healthcare coordinator of a school community, a trainer who works with bullied children, and a project leader and director of a website addressing bullied children – formed for this project, a review of relevant (cyber)bullying websites, discussions in an online group about cyberbullying and cybersafety (YouthRiskOnline/Embracecivility), and a Delphi study among 70 international experts in the field of cyberbullying and coping (Jacobs, Völlink, Dehue, & Lechner, 2014). In total, eleven performance objectives were formed for this intervention. For an overview of all POs see the first column of Table 7.1.

Based on discussions with the linkage group, it was decided to develop an online translation of the "Pleasure at school" training (PaS) (Faber et al., 2006). Victims apparently have negative self-related attitudes, thoughts (Cook, Williams, Guerra, Kim, & Sadek, 2010), and self-blaming attributions (Bauman, 2009) after a bully experience. PaS is partly based on principles of Rational Emotive (Behavioural) Therapy (RE(B)T) (Ellis, 1984, 1995), and uses the 5G-schema (Ringrose & Nijenhuis, 1986) to raise awareness in the relation between a thought, feeling, and behaviour, and to replace irrational thoughts with more rational thoughts.

According to RE(B)T, evaluative thoughts mediate the view people have about events that happen and the emotional, behavioural, and inferential reactions to these events (Ellis, 1995; MacInnes, 2004). PaS has proven effective in reducing bullying behaviour, anxiety and psychological problems (Faber et al., 2006) in adolescents. Similarly, RE(B)T has proven effective in the treatment of problems related to cyberbullying (Aricak et al., 2008; Baker & Tanrıkulu, 2010; Hinduja &

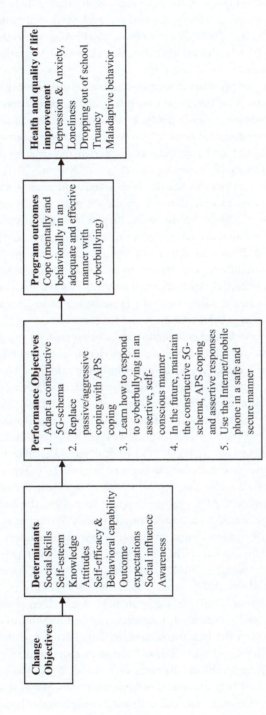

FIGURE 7.1 Change model of Online Pestkoppenstoppen.

Patchin, 2007) and bullying (Kim, Leventhal, Koh, Hubbard, & Boyce, 2006; Perren et al., 2010), such as anxiety, depression, and behavioural problems in adolescents (Banks & Zionts, 2008; Gonzalez et al., 2004). Adolescents therefore learn how to recognise (PO 1), dispute (PO 2) and replace (PO 3) irrational thoughts with rational thoughts.

After thoughts, the 5G-schema focuses on emotions. Relational bully victims often have problems with the correct encoding and interpretation of emotions (Woods, Wolke, Nowicki, & Hall, 2009). It is important for an adolescent's social and cognitive development to correctly perceive and attribute emotions (Nowicki Jr & Duke, 1994). The understanding and experiencing of emotions of others seems to inhibit anti-social behaviour (Kokkinos & Kipritsi, 2011), and adolescents who are able to perceive, handle, understand, and express their emotions tend to experience better social relationships and are more socially accepted (Austin, Saklofske, & Egan, 2005). Furthermore, despite bully victims probably being afraid, their most common reactions to victimisation are interest and joy (Mahady Wilton et al., 2000). Emotional displays of joy and interest can provide the bully with positive social reinforcement, leading to continued victimisation. Therefore, (cyber)bully victims need to learn more about emotions and emotion regulation and need to receive health education and emotional self-management competencies (Patchin & Hinduja, 2011) (PO 4).

The next aspect the 5G-schema focuses on is behaviour. As explained before, whether an adolescent becomes a long-term victim of (cyber)bullying seems to depend on how (s)he copes with (cyber)bullying attempts. Sometimes, the coping strategies employed reduce stress, but the victim fails to confront the bully (Mahady Wilton et al., 2000) leading to possible continuation of the bullying. Victims of cyberbullying therefore should become increasingly aware of the ineffectiveness of their current coping style (PO 5). They need knowledge of reactive and preventive strategies (PO 6) and should change their ineffective coping strategies into effective coping strategies (PO 7) (Tenenbaum et al., 2011). In this paper, all effective coping strategies are named Active Problem Solving (APS) strategies. APS strategies appear to resolve the bullying situation and allows the victim to act assertively (Mahady Wilton et al., 2000). For example, cyberbully victims should try to get help from bystanders, because one quarter of cyberbullying occurs in the presence of witnesses (Mishna, Cook, Gadalla, Daciuk, & Solomon, 2010). They should also block or ignore the cyberbully (Price & Dalgleish, 2010), or seek social support (Tokunaga, 2010). Seeking social support from family is likely to help (Fanti, Demetriou, & Hawa, 2012). Therefore, adolescents need information regarding who to ask for help, how to seek help, and the benefits of seeking help (Price & Dalgleish, 2010). Furthermore, having social skills is associated with reductions in victimisation and fewer internalising problems (Kochenderfer-Ladd, 2004). Cross et al. (2011) for example suggested that students should develop their social skills and learn effective ways of addressing relational difficulties online and offline, in order to prevent and reduce cyberbullying. Additionally, interventions should also focus on improving peer relationships in general (Price & Dalgleish, 2010), because social acceptance (Boulton, Smith, & Cowie, 2010) and integration (Jones, Manstead, & Livingstone, 2011) moderate the impact and consequences of different forms of cyberbullying. Moreover, victims and adolescents not involved in bullying most frequently indicated assertiveness as an intervention strategy (Camodeca & Goossens, 2005). Therefore, interventions should also teach (cyber)bully victims non-aggressive responses, and how to cope in an assertive and pro-social manner (PO 8 and 9).

A specific risk factor for cyberbullying is the little control exerted over personal information (Casas et al., 2013). A lot of cyberbully victims frequently use the Internet, most of the time in a risky manner (Baker & Tanrıkulu, 2010; Smith et al., 2008; Vandebosch & Van Cleemput, 2009). They share passwords, openly display personal information (e.g., addresses, phone numbers) and communicate with strangers (Hinduja & Patchin, 2009; Valcke, De Wever, Van Keer, & Schellens, 2011). Adolescents should therefore receive cyber safety education, learn to treat each other with respect (both online and offline), and become aware of the importance to regularly change their passwords and never sharing personal information (Ang & Goh, 2010) (PO 11).

Determinants

The next step in IM is an analysis of the most relevant (i.e., important, changeable) determinants (Bartholomew et al., 2011) of each PO, by asking what factors determine whether a victim would or is able to perform each PO. The methods used to obtain these determinants were the above mentioned literature review, focus group interviews, a Delphi study on the determinants of ineffective and improved coping with cyberbullying (Jacobs, Völlink, et al., 2014), and a study of protocols of (cyber)bullying interventions. Further, several behaviour-oriented theories were applied, such as social cognitive theory, theory of planned behaviour, transtheoretical model, and goal-setting theory. This resulted in a large list of determinants. The most relevant determinants can be found in the second column of Table 7.1. The aims of this intervention did not include environmental levels (e.g., parents, teachers or schools). Therefore, only determinants on the individual level were identified.

Change objectives

A matrix was developed to combine performance objectives and their hypothesised determinants into Change Objectives (COs) (Bartholomew et al., 2011). In total, we formed 50 COs. Examples of COs are "Individual describes characteristics of irrational and rational thoughts" and "Individual becomes aware of current ineffective (aggressive/passive) coping style" (see third column Table 7.1). All COs were used in the selection of theoretical methods and applications (step 3) that will change the determinants.

TABLE 7.1 POs, determinants, COs, theoretical methods and practical applications of Online Pestkoppenstoppen

Performance objectives	Determinant	Change objective	Theoretical Method	Practical application
1. Monitor and evaluate thoughts after (cyber)bully experience.	Knowledge	Describe irrational thoughts' differing characteristics.	1. Providing cues 2. Tailoring	Participant receives tailored and non-tailored cues from DG that help in recognising irrational thoughts.
	Self-efficacy & Behavioural capability	Demonstrate how to recognise thoughts.	1. Providing cues 2. Tailoring	VMs demonstrate how to use cues in recognising irrational thoughts and gives participant examples of recognising thoughts, amount of examples tailored to self-efficacy.
	Outcome expectations	Expect to be able to recognise and dispute irrational unhelpful thoughts.	1. Repeated exposure 2. Modelling	DG explains and VM demonstrates how to recognise irrational thoughts. Identification tips are provided. Participant is reminded several times to be aware of irrational thoughts.
	Awareness	Be aware of irrational thoughts after (cyber)bully experience.	1. Consciousness raising 2. Tailoring	DG reflects on tailored irrational thoughts of participant. DG and video model explain the 5G-schema.
2. Gain insight into relationship irrational thoughts, negative emotions and behaviour.	Knowledge	Explain relation between (cyber)bully event, thoughts, feelings, behaviour and consequence.	1. Chunking 2. Advanced organisers 3. Tailoring	Participant receives explanation (and tailored examples) of (negative) 5G-schemas depicting each G.
	Self-efficacy & Behavioural capability	Demonstrate how to label thoughts (irrational/rational).	1. Guided practice 2. Tailoring 3. Modelling	DG and video model explain and demonstrate how to label thoughts and give participant the opportunity to practice the labelling of thoughts. Feedback is provided. Amount of practice and example is tailored to self-efficacy.
	Awareness	Be aware of relationship irrational thoughts and negative behaviour.	1. Consciousness raising 2. Tailoring	Participant receives tailored examples of negative 5G-schemas that are transformed into positive 5G-schemas by changing the irrational thoughts.

Performance objective	Determinant	Change objective	Methods	Practical application
3. Replace irrational unhelpful thoughts with rational helpful thoughts.	Knowledge	Define rational thoughts and explain how rational thoughts induce a positive 5G-schema.	1. Persuasive communication 2. Chunking 3. Tailoring	Participant receives examples of rational thoughts, explanations of why these thoughts will help, and positive 5G-schemas tailored to self-efficacy and coping style.
	Attitude	Feel positive about monitoring, evaluating, disputing and replacing irrational thoughts with rational thoughts.	1. Arguments	VMs explain positive effects after monitoring, evaluating, disputing and replacing irrational thoughts with rational thoughts.
	Self-efficacy & Behavioural capability	Demonstrate how to dispute and replace irrational thoughts with rational thoughts.	1. Modelling 2. Guided practice 3. Direct experiences 4. Tailoring	VMs (amount of videos is tailored to self-efficacy) demonstrate disputing and replacing irrational thoughts. Participant and DG practices the replacement of thoughts and receives feedback.
	Outcome expectations	Expect to be able to dispute and replace irrational thoughts with rational thoughts.	1. Modelling 2. Guided practice 3. Repeated exposure 4. Active learning	DG explains and VM demonstrates how to replace irrational thoughts with rational thoughts. An overview of replaced thoughts is provided. Rational thoughts should be installed as screensaver prompts, stickers or as a list above the participant's bed. Replacing thoughts is practiced with feedback.
	Self-regulation	Plan to replace thoughts in daily life.	1. Goal-setting	Participant chooses (a) goal(s) related to skills learned in the first advice.
4. Recognise and regulate emotions.	Knowledge	Define emotion regulation strategies.	1. Tailoring 2. Persuasive communication	DG explains importance of emotion recognition and regulation. Participant receives emotion regulation techniques tailored to participant's score on the YSR's aggression and/or social problem scale and is encouraged to use them.
	Attitude	Feel positive about regulating emotions.	1. Arguments 2. Direct experience 3. Tailoring	DG explains to participant with high scores on YSR aggression/social problems why emotion regulation is helpful in (cyber)bullying situations. Participant is encouraged to try the emotion regulation exercises and is asked if (s)he feels the relaxation.

(Continued)

TABLE 7.1 (Continued)

Performance objectives	Determinant	Change objective	Theoretical Method	Practical application
	Self-efficacy & Behavioural capability	Demonstrate how to recognise and regulate emotions and impulsivity.	1. Guided practice 2. Tailoring	Participant with high scores on YSR aggression/social problems watches VM using emotion regulation techniques and receives practice, guidance and feedback in using these techniques. All participants receive models explaining and demonstrating recognition of emotions.
	Outcome expectations	Expect that regulating/recognising emotions lead to better outcomes.	1. Direct experience 2. Arguments	Participant should experience relaxation and calmness after regulating emotions. VMs provide arguments for the usefulness of recognising emotions.
	Self-regulation	Form plans to regulate emotions in daily life.	1. Active learning 2. Implementation intentions	Participant combines sentences into plans for emotion regulation techniques in daily life.
5. Gain insight into ineffective (aggressive/passive) coping style and negative outcomes.	Knowledge	Define ineffective (aggressive/passive) coping strategies and negative outcomes.	1. Tailoring 2. Persuasive communication 3. Consciousness raising 4. Modelling	Participant receives tailored examples of ineffective coping strategies and negative outcomes (in comics, written/spoken text and VMs).
	Awareness	Be aware of current ineffective coping style.	1. Consciousness raising 2. Tailoring	DG reflects on participant's current coping strategies and negative outcomes.
6. Gain insight into APS coping and positive outcomes.	Knowledge	Define APS coping strategies and positive outcomes.	1. Persuasive communication 2. Advanced organisers	Participant receives examples and overview of tailored and non-tailored APS coping strategies and positive outcomes.
	Attitude	Feel positive about APS coping.	1. Arguments 2. Tailoring	Positive effects of APS coping are explained. Tailored on YSR scores, participant receives instructions and positive effects of different social skills, and is encouraged to practice.
	Outcome expectations	Expect positive outcomes associated with APS coping.	1. Direct experience 2. Modelling	VM provides and DG explains positive experiences with APS coping. Participant is encouraged to practice the APS skill and think about positive effects.

7. Replace aggressive/passive coping with APS coping.	Social Influence	Explain social influence in APS coping.	1. Information about others' approval	DG describes influence of participant's APS behaviour on other adolescents, what they might think, and the dynamics of a bullying situation.
	Awareness	Be aware of positive effects of APS coping.	1. Consciousness raising 2. Framing	DG describes APS coping and positive effects.
	Social skills	Demonstrate social skills needed for APS coping.	1. Set tasks on gradient of difficulty 2. Tailoring 3. Goal setting	Participant receives additional extra social skills lessons tailored on YSR scores. Social skill lessons are linked with plans to use the skills in daily life.
	Self-esteem and self-confidence	Demonstrate and explain importance of self-esteem and self-confidence in APS coping.	1. Persuasive communication 2. Modelling	DG explains and importance of, and VMs demonstrate self-esteem/confidence in APS coping.
	Self-efficacy & Behavioural capability	Demonstrate how to use APS coping, apply social cognition and conflict resolution.	1. Set tasks on a gradient of difficulty 2. Tailoring 3. Enactive mastery experiences 4. Set tasks on a gradient of difficulty	Participant receives APS coping models, explanation and practice in different social skills. Conflict resolution is broken up in sub-skills. Feedback and additional lessons are provided tailored to the progress measured.
	Social influence	Recognise importance of seeking social support.	1. Shifting focus	DG lists helpful help-behaviours of peers/parents/teacher when experiencing cyberbullying.
	Self-regulation	Plan to use APS coping strategies.	1. Guided practice 2. Modelling 3. Persuasion 4. Planning coping responses/Implementation intentions	VM demonstrates and DG explains how to form plans, positive effects are provided and participant practices forming own action/coping plans with feedback.

(Continued)

TABLE 7.1 (Continued)

Performance objectives	Determinant	Change objective	Theoretical Method	Practical application
8. Gain insight into assertive behaviour (and nvc patterns*) and its outcomes in relation to (cyber) bullying.	Knowledge	Lists effective nvc patterns.	1. Using Imagery 2. Modelling	Participant receives examples of nvc in assertiveness and starting conversations, and is encouraged to feel the difference after applying this knowledge.
	Attitude	Feel positive about assertive behaviour.	1. Belief selection 2. Persuasive communication	DG explains positive effects of assertive behaviour, participant is encouraged to think about positive effects of assertive behaviour.
	Outcome expectations	Expect positive outcomes associated with assertive behaviour and nvc.	1. Arguments 2. Modelling 3. Consciousness raising	DG describes positive effects of assertive behaviour. VM and DG demonstrate assertive responding and positive effects. Participant is encouraged to reflect on assertive responding.
9. Replace ineffective (aggressive/passive) behaviour (and nvc*) with effective (assertive) behaviour (and nvc*).	Social skills	Demonstrate social skills needed for assertive behaviour.	1. Set task on a gradient of difficulty	Participant receives explanation and practice in assertive responses in three steps, which can be used online and offline.
	Self-esteem	Demonstrate self-esteem in assertive behaviour and nvc.	1. Persuasive communication 2. Modelling	DG and VM explain and demonstrate assertive reactions (with and without assertive nvc*).
	Knowledge	List assertive behaviours.	1. Elaboration 2. Use Imagery	Participant receives descriptions of assertive behaviours and how to perform it. Practice is provided by displaying images of "assertive" or strong characters, and participants are encouraged to imagine feeling like this character.
	Attitude	Feel positive about adapting assertive behaviour.	1. Belief selection 2. Arguments	DG explains positive effects after adapting assertive behaviour, participant is encouraged to think about positive effects of (adapting) assertive behaviour.

Objective	Determinant	Performance objective	Methods	Application
	Self-efficacy & Behavioural capability	Demonstrate when and how to display assertive behaviour and nvc.	1. Guided practice 2. Repeated exposure 3. Tailoring	Participant receives VMs and comics demonstrating assertive behaviour tailored to coping style measured.
	Social influence	Recognise social influence in assertive behaviour and nvc.	1. Shifting focus	DG acknowledges that others' presence can have influence on responding in an assertive manner.
	Awareness	Be aware of positive effects associated with assertive behaviour.	1. Consciousness raising 2. Framing	DG explains that assertive reactions lead to positive outcomes. Participant is encouraged to think about the lessons they have learned.
	Self-regulation	Plan to use assertive reactions and behaviour.	1. Planning coping responses 2. Implementation intentions	Participant first forms assertive responses from predefined lists. Next, participant forms coping plans with these assertive responses, choosing from predefined lists.
10. Maintain the constructive 5G-schema, APS coping and assertive responses.	Attitude	Feel committed to maintaining constructive 5G-schema, APS coping and assertive behaviour.	1. Arguments 2. Tailoring	DG encourages participant to practice all lessons in daily life, with warnings for possible failure, but with the message "Do not give up, practice makes perfect". Feedback is provided about progress.
	Self-efficacy & Behavioural capability	Demonstrate how to maintain constructive 5G-schema, APS coping and assertive behaviour.	1. Goal setting 2. Planning coping responses	Participant forms plans linking APS to daily life (difficult) situations, aided by DG.
	Outcome expectations	Expect positive outcomes after maintaining constructive 5G-schema, APS coping and assertive behaviour.	1. Persuasive communication	DG explains positive effects of APS coping and stresses the importance of keep using this coping strategy.
	Self-regulation	Evaluate and/or adjust plans to use the skills learned concerning 5G-schema, APS coping and assertive responding lessons.	1. Tailoring 2. Active learning 3. Implementation intentions	Participant evaluates own plans, and adjusts if necessary.

(Continued)

TABLE 7.1 (Continued)

Performance objectives	Determinant	Change objective	Theoretical Method	Practical application
11. Prevent and solve negative cyber bully experiences by using the Internet and mobile phones in a safe and secure manner.	Knowledge	List security and safety advices for the Internet and mobile phones.	1. Prompts	Participant receives prompts concerning safe Internet/mobile phone use.
	Attitude	Feel positive about safe and secure use of the Internet and mobile phones.	1. Arguments	DG explains positive effects of safety tips and guidelines for safe Internet and mobile phone use.
	Self-efficacy & Behavioural capability	Demonstrate how to use the Internet and mobile phones in a secure manner.	1. Modelling	DG explains and demonstrates (via screenshots) how to form safe passwords, and provides information how to protect yourself on the Internet.
	Outcome expectations	Expect positive outcomes after using the Internet and mobile phones in a secure manner.	1. Arguments	DG explains to participant that safe use of the Internet and mobile phone leads to less cyberbullying.
	Awareness	Become aware of own insecure and unsafe use of the Internet and mobile phones.	1. Consciousness raising 2. Loss frame	DG explains that unsafe Internet use heightens the chance of becoming a cyberbully victim. Participant is encouraged to think about own Internet-behaviour
	Self-regulation	Form plans to keep using the Internet in a secure manner	1. Goal setting 2. Implementation intentions	Participant chooses plans related to the safe use of Internet and resetting passwords regularly.

*DG = Digital Guide; VM = Video model; YSR = Youth Self-Report (Achenbach, 1991); APS = Active, Problem-Solving coping; Nvc = non-verbal communication

Step 3: Theory-based methods and practical strategies

A theoretical method is a general process that is supposed to influence change in behavioural determinants, based on theories. A practical application is a specific technique for practical use of theoretical methods, in ways that are applicable to the intervention population and context in which the intervention will be used (Bartholomew et al., 2011). When a method is translated into a practical application, sufficient understanding of the theory behind the method and its theoretical parameters that determine the effectiveness is needed (Kok, Schaalma, Ruiter, Van Empelen, & Brug, 2004). For example, to influence determinants such as self-efficacy, modelling (Bandura, 1986, 1993) can be used as a theoretical method. A practical strategy would be to use a role model demonstrating how to react assertively to a difficult situation. Theoretical parameters for modelling state that modelling is effective when the individual is able to identify with the model, the model demonstrates adequate skills and is reinforced for the behaviour displayed (Kok et al., 2004).

To identify theoretical methods, parameters, and practical strategies: (1) the literature was searched for behaviour change techniques (Bartholomew et al., 2011); (2) the IM book was used to find theoretical methods that influence specific determinants; (3) existing (cyber)bullying interventions were compared; (4) the PaS training (Faber et al., 2006) was used; and (5) focus group interviews were held, asking the members of the target group what they believed were effective strategies (Jacobs, Goossens, Dehue, Völlink, & Lechner, 2014). In Table 7.1, besides the POs, determinants and COs, we describe the application(s) and the theoretical method selected for changing the determinant related to the POs. An overview of theoretical methods and practical applications used in the *Online Pestkoppenstoppen* intervention is shown in the fifth column of Table 7.1. An elucidation of the most important methods follows next.

Computer tailoring

As mentioned before, tailoring appears to be a successful health promotion technique (Krebs et al., 2010; Noar et al., 2007). Tailoring is the combination of strategies and information intended to reach one specific person by providing personalised feedback based on unique characteristics of a person. These characteristics are assessed individually and are related to the outcome of interest (Kreuter, Farrell, Olevitch, & Brennan, 2000). The use of tailored information results in more improvement in behaviour over time compared to the use of generic information (De Vries, Kremers, Smeets, Brug, & Eijmael, 2008; Noar et al., 2007). Tailored messages are better read, saved and remembered than non-tailored messages (Brug, Oenema, & Campbell, 2003). There are two types of tailoring; dynamic tailoring (DT), assessing intervention variables prior to each feedback; and static tailoring (ST), assessing intervention variables at one baseline moment. Although research indicates that DT interventions outperform ST interventions (Krebs et al., 2010), this intervention mostly tailors statically, because several variables used for tailoring are also used for the measurement of effectiveness, and thus need to be assessed prior to each piece of advice. Tailoring is a general technique used throughout the complete intervention and is also combined with the other methods used. See Table 7.2 for an overview of all variables used for tailoring. The intervention is, for example, tailored to personality (as measured by the Big 5 Questionnaire – Short form [McManus, Livingston, & Katona, 2006]), because personality may determine a participant's behaviour within a specific context, and this behaviour (e.g., reactions, interpretations) can influence the reoccurrence of that event (Caspi & Bem, 1990). For example neuroticism appears to lead to more bullying and victimisation, agreeableness and conscientiousness lead to less bullying, and extraversion leads to more bullying and less to victimisation (Bollmer, Harris, & Milich, 2006).

Chunking

A chunk is a pattern of stimuli consisting of separate parts, but that is perceived as a whole. With chunking, labels or acronyms are assigned to the intervention's material in order to aid memory (Bartholomew et al., 2011). Because working memory is relatively small, chunking can be used to increase its effectiveness (Garrison, Anderson, & Archer, 2001) by providing smaller pieces of information at a time. The 5G-schema is divided into 5 different chunks: each "G" describes a different process, and all the "G"s together explain how an event can lead to a certain consequence. Each "G" receives attention in the intervention, starting in the first piece of advice with the relation between an event, a thought and a feeling. In the second and third pieces of advice, the focus shifts to behaviour with reminders about the importance of thoughts and feelings.

Consciousness raising

Consciousness raising is used to increase a participant's awareness about: (1) the thoughts (s)he has after a (cyber)bullying event; (2) his/her own negative 5G-schemas; (3) ineffective coping styles and negative outcomes; and (4) effective coping styles and positive outcomes. Based on answers about irrational thoughts and coping styles, the participant receives tailored feedback concerning his/her irrational thoughts, 5G-schemas, and current coping responses. This feedback may increase awareness, which in turn may help the participant to see why the current way of thinking and/or coping is not helpful or effective. It is important that the participant receives information about problem solving immediately (Bartholomew et al., 2011). Therefore, the participant immediately receives information about how to recognise, dispute, and replace thoughts after becoming aware of his/her 5G-schema, and how to change ineffective coping into effective coping after becoming aware of his/her ineffective coping.

TABLE 7.2 Questionnaires and variables used to tailor the content of the intervention to the characteristics of the participant

Questionnaire	Advice 1	Advice 2	Advice 3
17 Deviant cyber behaviours (Ysebaert, Dehue, & Völlink, 2008) (ST)	Digital guide reflects on participant's experienced cyberbullying.	Digital guide reflects on participant being a bully and tailors behaviour (e.g., "Because you bully them", "Do you call them names?" or "Did you do something not nice to someone else?").	When participant receives additional lesson in coping behaviour, digital guide gives tailored reflection on participant being a bully and tailors behaviour (e.g., "Because you bully them", "Do you call them names?" or "Did you do something not nice to someone else?").
Bullying (ST)	Digital guide reflects on also being bullied offline when participant answered "Yes" on being bullied offline question.		
Irrational thoughts [self-developed] (ST)	1. Participant receives tailored help-questions that aid in recognising and disputing irrational thoughts. 2. Participant receives own irrational thoughts and is encouraged to choose rational thoughts.		1. Total scores on T0, T1 and T2 are compared. Participant receives tailored feedback messages about progress and is given the opportunity to receive additional lessons when progress is not sufficient. 2. In case the participant receives additional lesson in working with the 5G-schema, participant receives tailored help-questions to dispute and recognise irrational thoughts.
Cyberspecific Coping Questionnaire [self-developed] (ST)	Participant receives examples of 5G-schemas tailored to aggressive, passive or aggressive/passive coping style.	1. Participant receives tailored aggressive, passive or aggressive/passive comic stories and videos, and guidance in how change behaviour into APS coping. 2. Digital guide gives tailored reflection of participant's coping behaviour.	Total scores on T0, T1 and T2 are compared. Participant receives tailored feedback about progress and is given the opportunity to receive additional lesson when progress was not sufficient.

(Continued)

TABLE 7.2 (Continued)

Questionnaire	Advice 1	Advice 2	Advice 3
Self-efficacy (Bandura, 1986, 1993) (DT)	1. Self-efficacy in recognising emotions determines amount of practice (judging 8, 6, 5 or 4 pictures of emotional faces). 2. Self-efficacy in working with the 5G-schema determines number of example (tailored) 5G-schemas (8, 6, 4 or 2 examples). 3. Self-efficacy in recognising irrational thoughts determines number of example video-clips (4, 3, 2 or 1) and recognition-practice (11, 10, 4 or 2 thoughts). 4. Self-efficacy in replacing irrational thoughts with rational thoughts determines amount of example video-clips (3, 2, 1 or 1).		Beside progress on irrational thoughts and coping style, participant also receives self-efficacy questions about working with the 5G-schema and coping. When self-efficacy is low, participant is given the opportunity to receive additional lessons about the 5G-schema and coping.
Youth Self-Report (Achenbach, 1991) (ST)	1. Participant with high norm-scores on YSR scale "Somatic complaints"; "Delinquent behaviour" and "Depression" receives (emphatic) reflections of problem behaviour and pieces of advices for help.		Total scores on T1 and T2 for YSR-scales "Delinquent behaviour"; "Social problems", "Withdrawn behaviour" and "Aggression" are compared. Participant receives positive feedback when problem behaviour is decreased.

2. Participant with:

- high norm–scores on YSR "Social problems" receives extra lessons in "Starting a conversation", "Asking questions", "Expressing opinions", "Theory of mind", and "Body language".

- high norm–scores on YSR scale "Withdrawn behaviour" receives extra lessons in "Starting a conversation", "Asking questions", "Expressing opinions", and "Planning skills".

- high norm–scores on YSR "Aggression" receives extra lessons in "Theory of mind" and "Emotion regulation".

- high norm–scores on multiple scales receive a combination of these lessons.

3. In the extra lessons, empathic reflections and guidance is given for participant with high scores on YSR scale "Somatic complaints", "Delinquent behaviour" and "Depression".

1. During active problem-solving coping lessons participant receives empathic reflections and guidance when scores are high/low on B5Q-scales" "Introversion", "Agreeableness" and "Neuroticism".

2. In the extra lessons participant receives empathic reflections and guidance when scores are high/low on B5Q-scales" "Introversion", "Agreeableness" and "Neuroticism".

Big Five Questionnaire – short form (McManus et al., 2006) (ST)

(Continued)

TABLE 7.2 (Continued)

Questionnaire	Advice 1	Advice 2	Advice 3
Additional questions (DT)	1. "Which thought would you choose to replace Tim's/Linda's irrational thought?" is tailored to a positive example in which Tim/Linda has a (the chosen) rational thought and reacts effectively to a cyberbully-experience. 2. "Would you like to know how to start a conversation?" determines if participant receives examples of conversation starters.	1. Chosen helping thoughts (piece of advice 1) are displayed at the start of piece of advice 2. 2. "Did you use these thoughts?" determines feedback participant receives. 3. "Do you want examples of using these tips online?" and in case participant answers "yes", "How many examples do you want?" determine if and how many examples participant receives. 4. Compiling plans to use when something unpleasant happens online. 5. Compiling sentences and plans that can be used as assertive reactions. 6. Gender determines if participant receives The Hulk or Catwoman as example of a strong person with strong body language. 7. Specific feedback is provided during the formation of plans concerning bystanders. 8. Specific feedback is given on answers during the extra lessons.	1. All plans made in piece of advice 1 and 2 are displayed. Participant evaluates every single plan and indicates why the plan did not work. If evaluated as "not working well", participant is offered the option to adjust the play. 2. Comics that display the steps of conflict resolution are tailored to gender. 3. Chosen helpful thoughts from piece of advice 1 are displayed again during conflict resolution. 4. Participant can indicate whether (s)he wants to receive additional lessons in non-verbal communication, humour and emotion regulation. 5. When the participant receives additional lessons in working with the 5G-schema, participant is offered to choose new helping thoughts. 6. New (piece of advice 3) or old (piece of advice 1) chosen thoughts are displayed in an extra lesson on coping behaviour. 7. New formed plans are displayed in an extra lesson on coping behaviour. 8. Participant indicates which safety-information (s)he wants to receive. 9. Participant forms safety-plans, which are displayed at the end of piece of advice 3.

Note: DT: Dynamic tailoring; ST: Static tailoring

Guided practice

Guided practice is prompting the participant to rehearse and repeat the desired behaviour, discuss the experience and provide feedback (Bartholomew et al., 2011). This method is used to increase self-efficacy and behavioural capability. Additionally, it is used to overcome barriers. In this intervention, the participant receives either video-models demonstrating the desired skill, or comics and digital guides demonstrating and explaining the desired skill, followed by opportunities to practice the skill. Several insight questions are asked in relation to performing the skills, upon which the digital guides give feedback.

Providing information

Providing information is used to increase a participant's knowledge, skills, and attitudes, using arguments and persuasive communication (Bartholomew et al., 2011). According to the Elaboration Likelihood Model (Petty & Cacioppo, 1986), good arguments are effective in reaching stable change in attitudes only when the message is processed through the central route. This happens when the message is personally relevant and not too discrepant from the participant's beliefs (Bartholomew et al., 2011). The participant receives general (e.g., what are the dynamics of a bullying situation, what to do and not to do online) and tailored (e.g., questions that aid recognising irrational thoughts and changing aggressive/ passive coping into active and problem solving coping) information. To check whether the participant remembers the correct information, questions are asked interspersed with feedback. Additionally, to prevent the participant from paying attention to information (s)he already knows, at some points in the intervention (s)he can choose which information (s)he wants to read. Furthermore, all important information is summarised on the personal page and sent to the participant's e-mail inbox.

Modelling

In modelling a person serves as an appropriate model for others that is reinforced for the desired behaviour assuming that the behaviour of the model will be imitated (Bandura, 1997). Modelling is included in this intervention as a method to increase a participant's self-efficacy and behavioural capability to carry out the desired behaviour change, because it is proven to be an effective teaching tool (Woolfolk, 2010). For example, previous research indicated that video-counselling – in which a real human speaks and asks questions – can be a promising technique for health interventions (Jackson, Stotland, Caughey, & Gerbert, 2011). In line with the parameters of modelling, the video-models are coping models (i.e., who previously experienced the health problem, but who learned to deal with it effectively), the participant is able to identify with the models, and the models are being reinforced for positive behaviour (Bartholomew et al., 2011). The short videos were professionally recorded (Vandelanotte & Mummery, 2011). In several video-clips, models demonstrate and explain how to perform a behaviour (e.g., recognising, disputing and replacing irrational thoughts, coping behaviours).

Implementation intentions and coping plans

Research indicates that planning is a powerful self-regulatory tool in the process of behaviour change (Sniehotta, Scholz, & Schwarzer, 2005; Sniehotta, Schwarzer, Scholz, & Schüz, 2005). When people plan, they mentally simulate the linking of concrete responses to future situations, replacing spontaneous reactions for pre-planned actions. There are two types of plans: action plans (Leventhal, Singer, & Jones, 1965), or implementation intentions (Gollwitzer & Sheeran, 2008), and coping plans (Sniehotta, Schwarzer, et al., 2005). In action planning, individuals link goal-directed behaviour to certain environmental cues by specifying when, where and how to act (Sniehotta, Schwarzer, et al., 2005) in if-then statements (Sheeran, Webb, & Gollwitzer, 2005). As a result, environmental cues should activate – without conscious intent – the initiation of action (Sniehotta, Schwarzer, et al., 2005). In coping planning, individuals anticipate possible risk situations beforehand by already defining suitable and effective response behaviour linked to these potential barriers (Sniehotta, Schwarzer, et al., 2005). Implementation intentions, action and coping plans are found to be effective in translating various intentions into actions (Reuter et al., 2010; van Osch, Lechner, Reubsaet, Wigger, & De Vries, 2008; Wiedemann, Lippke, Reuter, Ziegelmann, & Schwarzer, 2011), and appear to be working synergistically in adolescents (Araújo-Soares, McIntyre, & Sniehotta, 2009). In the intervention, the participant makes a combination of implementation intentions and coping plans. A closed-ended plan setting procedure is used to prevent inadequate goals; from a pre-defined list, the participant chooses the context *if* (either difficult situations or situations in daily life), and action *then* (applications of learned skills, from a predefined list).

Step 4: Producing programme components and materials

Taking the end products of the previous steps into account, we decided to develop one intervention containing three web-based sessions containing tailored pieces of advice addressing mostly personal and psychological determinants. A programme plan including the scope, sequence and programme materials was developed (Bartholomew et al., 2011), which is described below. During the process of producing programme components and materials, intended programme participants and the linkage group were consulted to determine the preferences for programme design by conducting focus group interviews and short voting sessions.

Scope and sequence

Based on brainstorms and voting sessions with members of the target group, we named the intervention *Online Pestkoppenstoppen* (Stop Bullies Online or Stop

Online Bullies, figure 7.2) with three web-based tailored pieces of advice named: (1) *Think strong, feel better*; (2) *Stop the bully now!*; and (3) *You are doing well, can you do better?*. Each piece of advice is preceded by several questionnaires – measuring tailoring and effect variables – that take approximately half an hour to complete, and each piece of advice takes approximately 45 minutes to complete. The pieces of advice are offered over three months, and e-mails and text messages are used to remind the participant of participation. Figure 7.3 provides a flowchart of the web-based tailored pieces of advice and questionnaires.

Selection

Because the literature indicated that an explicit approach (e.g., "did you experience cyberbullying?") systematically underestimates the problem (Dehue et al., 2008; Walrave & Heirman, 2011), an implicit approach was used; the individual rates his or her experience with different cyberbullying behaviours. Individuals are included in the intervention if they had experiences with at least one of the cyberbullying behaviours at least "once a month" during the last half year. Cyberbullies and adolescents who did not experience the 17 deviant cyber behaviours are excluded from participation. Next, the individual (= participant) fills in his or her (nick)name, age, e-mail address, mobile phone number, and a login code that is provided to him/her in an information letter. The e-mail address and mobile phone number will be used to remind participants of participation before the start of each piece of advice, during the process of filling in the questionnaires, and during the process of completing each piece of advice.

Materials

Below, we describe the different materials developed for the intervention.

FIGURE 7.2 Logo Stop the bully now!

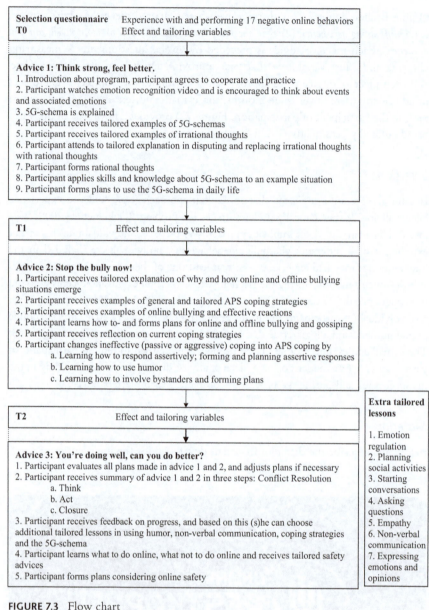

Selection questionnaire T0	Experience with and performing 17 negative online behaviors Effect and tailoring variables

Advice 1: Think strong, feel better.
1. Introduction about program, participant agrees to cooperate and practice
2. Participant watches emotion recognition video and is encouraged to think about events and associated emotions
3. 5G-schema is explained
4. Participant receives tailored examples of 5G-schemas
5. Participant receives tailored examples of irrational thoughts
6. Participant attends to tailored explanation in disputing and replacing irrational thoughts with rational thoughts
7. Participant forms rational thoughts
8. Participant applies skills and knowledge about 5G-schema to an example situation
9. Participant forms plans to use the 5G-schema in daily life

T1	Effect and tailoring variables

Advice 2: Stop the bully now!
1. Participant receives tailored explanation of why and how online and offline bullying situations emerge
2. Participant receives examples of general and tailored APS coping strategies
3. Participant receives examples of online bullying and effective reactions
4. Participant learns how to- and forms plans for online and offline bullying and gossiping
5. Participant receives reflection on current coping strategies
6. Participant changes ineffective (passive or aggressive) coping into APS coping by
    a. Learning how to respond assertively; forming and planning assertive responses
    b. Learning how to use humor
    c. Learning how to involve bystanders and forming plans

T2	Effect and tailoring variables

Advice 3: You're doing well, can you do better?
1. Participant evaluates all plans made in advice 1 and 2, and adjusts plans if necessary
2. Participant receives summary of advice 1 and 2 in three steps: Conflict Resolution
    a. Think
    b. Act
    c. Closure
3. Participant receives feedback on progress, and based on this (s)he can choose additional tailored lessons in using humor, non-verbal communication, coping strategies and the 5G-schema
4. Participant learns what to do online, what not to do online and receives tailored safety advices
5. Participant forms plans considering online safety

Extra tailored lessons

1. Emotion regulation
2. Planning social activities
3. Starting conversations
4. Asking questions
5. Empathy
6. Non-verbal communication
7. Expressing emotions and opinions

FIGURE 7.3 Flow chart

Personal page

After selection/logging in, the participant is redirected to the personal page (Figure 7.4), from which (s)he: (1) can proceed or continue with the questionnaires and/or pieces of advice; (2) can find for each piece of advice pictures, video-clips, comics, summaries, formed helpful thoughts, plans and sentences to use; and (3) has access to the extra tailored social skill lessons of piece of advice 2.

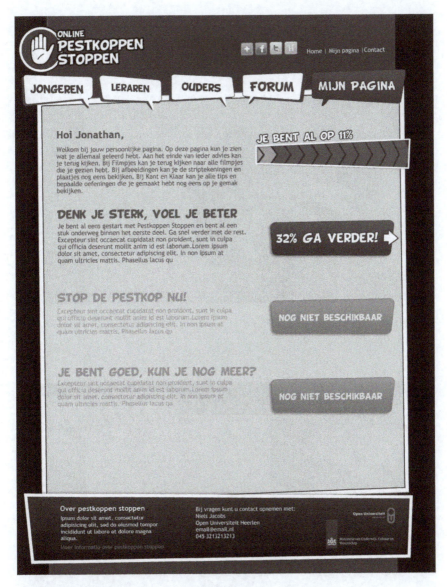

FIGURE 7.4 Personal page of Stop the bully now!

Assessing tailoring and effect measures

Before receiving each web-based tailored piece of advice, the participant answers several questionnaires (T0, T1 and T2) to assess the effect and tailoring variables. Gender of the participant was used to tailor gender of the guides and contexts (e.g., girls will see Noa, Jessica and a girl's bedroom [Figure 7.5a], and boys will see Levi, Mike and a boy's bedroom [Figure 7.5b]).

FIGURE 7.5A Girl's guide and bedroom.

FIGURE 7.5B Boy's guide and bedroom.

Piece of advice 1 "Think strong, feel better."

After the baseline measure (T0), the participant starts with the first piece of advice. The participant learns to: (1) work with the 5G-schema in order to recognise (PO 1), dispute (PO 2) and replace (PO 3) irrational thoughts with rational thoughts; (2) carefully examine emotions in response to certain events (PO 4); and (3) form action plans to use the 5G-schema in daily life (PO 10) (Figure 7.6).

Piece of advice 2 "Stop the bully now!"

A month after the start, the participant begins with the second questionnaire (T1) and piece of advice. The participant: (1) receives knowledge about the dynamics of online and offline bullying situations; (2) receives general APS coping strategies (PO 6); (3) learns and forms implementation intentions for responding towards online and offline bullying (PO 7 and PO 10); (4) becomes aware of ineffective coping style (PO 5); (5) is offered tailored examples of and guidance in APS coping (PO 6 and PO 7); (6) learns about responding assertively (PO 8 and PO 9); (7) forms implementation intentions and coping plans regarding assertive responses (PO 10); and (8) receives information about the use and benefits of humour and bystanders (PO 6). Observing victimisation on its own can

FIGURE 7.6 The 5G-schema

have negative consequences on psychological wellbeing (Rivers, Poteat, Noret, & Ashurst, 2009). Therefore, the participant forms implementation intentions and coping plans regarding how to react and involve bystanders in (cyber)bullying situations (PO 10).

Additional lessons

Additional social skill lessons (PO 7 and PO 9) were offered to improve specific skills associated with problem behaviours. The lessons are tailored to the participant's score on several Youth Self-Report (YSR) scales (Achenbach, 1991). The participant can choose if, when and which extra lessons (s)he wants to complete. For several extra lessons implementation intentions and coping plans are formed (PO 10). An overview of all lessons tailored to norm scores (above the 93% clinical range on YSR subscales) can be found in Table 7.3.

The Youth Self-Report (Achenbach, 1991) has nine syndrome scales (i.e., anxious/depressed, withdrawn/depressed, somatic complaints, social problems, thought problems, attention problems, rule-breaking behaviour, aggressive behaviour, and other problems). Based on the literature, the results of the Delphi study concerning relevant coping determinants (Jacobs, Völlink, et al., 2014) and the PaS training (Faber et al., 2006), it was decided that extra social skill lessons would be tailored to the scores on "withdrawn/depressed", "social problems" and "aggressive behaviour".

TABLE 7.3 Social lessons based on YSR subscales with norm scores

	YSR Social Problems		YSR Withdrawn/ Depressed		YSR Aggression	
	Male > 7	Female > 7	Male > 6	Female > 7	Male > 12	Female > 13
Starting conversations	X	X	X	X		
Asking questions	X	X	X	X		
Express feelings and opinions	X	X	X	X		
Empathy/social cognition	X	X			X	X
Non-verbal communication	X	X				
Planning to become more socially active			X	X		
Emotional regulation					X	X

Concerning the "withdrawn/depressed" scale, adolescents displaying socially withdrawn behaviour are shy, sad, want to be alone and often will not talk (Achenbach, 1991). They may increase the risk for negative social development, because these adolescents miss important developmental opportunities (Harrist, Zaia, Bates, Dodge, & Pettit, 1997). Adolescents who feel withdrawn from their peers may become socially isolated. In the literature, there are a number of interventions that teach socially isolated adolescents important skills. Oden and Asher (2011), for example, offered socially isolated adolescents instructions and practice in participating in a game, cooperating with other adolescents (e.g., taking turns and sharing materials), communication (e.g., talking and listening) and validating or supporting others (e.g., giving attention or help). Ladd (1981) argues that popular adolescents greet peers, ask for information, extend invitations and give more information than unpopular counterparts. In an intervention study, adolescents were therefore trained in verbal skills (asking questions and offering support to peers) by receiving instructions, rehearsing, and receiving feedback in the training. In a review by Rook (1984), several actions that facilitate social bonding are mentioned: more self-disclosure, more responsiveness to others, a less cynical approach to social interactions, and improving social skills. Concluding from these findings, socially withdrawn adolescents apparently need to learn how to make friends, how to cooperate, communicate, ask questions, and how to show validation or support. They also need to develop interest in other people (and their interests) and they need to self-disclose more. Therefore, adolescents scoring above the 93% clinical range on the scale "withdrawn/depressed" receive lessons in starting conversations, asking questions, expressing feelings and opinions, and planning to become more sociable.

Concerning the "social problems" scale, adolescents with social problems are clingy, act young, do not get along with peers, are clumsy and prefer to play with younger adolescents (Achenbach, 1991). People who suffer from social problems often find it difficult to initiate, negotiate and maintain social interactions (Frith, 2004). They also experience challenges in social cognition and empathy (Blacher, Kraemer, & Schalow, 2003), using and interpreting verbal and non-verbal behaviours in communication (Frith, 2004), and sharing of affective experiences (Gutstein & Whitney, 2002). Instructions in social interaction skills appear to be more effective than teaching communication skills (Mathur, Kavale, Quinn, Forness, & Rutherford, 1998). Adolescents who score above the 93% clinical range on the scale "social problems" therefore will receive lessons in starting conversations, asking questions, express feelings and opinions, empathy/social cognition, and non-verbal communication.

Concerning the "aggressive behaviour" scale, aggressive adolescents argue a lot, are mean, destroy things, get in fights and demand attention (Achenbach, 1991). Furthermore, adolescents who engage in cyber aggression appear to have negative social competence, and experience social problems at the individual, interaction, relationship and group levels of social functioning (Schoffstall & Cohen, 2011). The more they engage in cyber aggression, the more they report loneliness and lower global self-worth. There have been interventions aimed at aggressive adolescents. Guerra and Slaby (1990) for example, designed an intervention that teaches aggressive adolescents moral reasoning skills and social perspective-taking skills. Furthermore, social-cognitive skills involved in the process of solving specific social problems and generalised social beliefs about supporting the use of aggression were remediated. In order to be able to fully apply the skills in social problems, as well as the evaluation and application of one's general beliefs in these situations, the control of impulsive responding is needed. This self-control, or self-regulation, allows individuals to resist temptation and hold back from acting on impulses (DeWall, Baumeister, Stillman, & Gailliot, 2007). Other interventions that target aggressive people included lessons in a broad set of social skills such as social problem solving (Feindler, Marriott, & Iwata, 1984; Lochman, 1992; Sarason & Ganzer, 1973; Sarason & Sarason, 1981), communication skills, social perspective taking (Sarason & Sarason, 1981), cognitive self-control and behavioural contracting (Feindler et al., 1984). For example, lessons in perspective taking is an effective part of prevention and therapy programmes aimed at young offenders engaging in violence and bullying (Abraham & Michie, 2008; Chalmers & Townsend, 1990). It thus appears that interventions aimed at aggressive behaviour focus on aggressive beliefs, cognitive distortions, arousal (recognition/identification of situations/bodily sensations, etc.), management, generating other (better) reactions, impulsivity, conflict resolution, problem-solving, and empathy enhancement/social perspective taking. Therefore, adolescents scoring above the 93% clinical range on the scale "aggression" receive lessons in empathy/social cognition and emotion regulation.

Piece of advice 3 "You are doing well, can you do better?"

Two months after the start, the participant starts with the third questionnaire (T2) and follow-up piece of advice. The participant evaluates all plans made in pieces of advice 1 and 2 on usability, and if necessary adjusts the plans (PO 10). All skills of pieces of advice 1 and 2 are summarised into three steps (i.e., 1. Think; 2. Act; 3. Closure). These three steps together form the skill conflict resolution, which is associated with reductions in victimisation and fewer internalising problems (Kochenderfer-Ladd, 2004). Tailored on progress, the participant receives feedback (on irrational thoughts, coping responses and YSR scores), and if needed, additional lessons (5G-schema, coping styles, humour, non-verbal communication and emotion regulation). Finally, the participant learns and plans how to use the Internet and mobile phone in a safe and secure manner (PO 11).

Development

The web-based tailored pieces of advice were developed using special software (Nettailor, Evident, the Netherlands), a programme that has been developed specifically for web-based tailored interventions, using digital guides in the delivery of the intervention. Research indicates that the integration of an intervention into a website enhances participants' outcomes and retention (Brug et al., 2005). Therefore, the web-based tailored pieces of advice were integrated into a website (http://www.pestkoppenstoppen.nl). On this website information about the intervention can be found. After logging in, participants can read general information and watch YouTube video clips about (cyber)bullying, follow the web-based tailored pieces of advice and/or answer the questionnaires.

Digital guides

The Nettailor software allows for the use of digital guides or animated interface agents: embodied characters that exhibit various types of life-like behaviours (e.g., speech, emotions, gestures, head and body movements). The use of agents is beneficial, because a system with agents is perceived as more entertaining than a system without agents (Dehn & Van Mulken, 2000). Results from the literature can be interpreted as guidelines for developing the appearance of an agent. For example, the presence of a realistic agent displaying human-like behaviour was rated positively on likeability and comfortability, and displays with faces attracted more attention than displays without faces (Dehn & Van Mulken, 2000). The more an agent had a human-like face, the more it received positive social judgments, greater homophily attribution, and higher competency and trustworthiness ratings (Gong, 2008). Furthermore, users are more influenced by an agent whose appearance is similar to themselves. Stereotypes and expectations can therefore be used to create an ideal social model for a specific subgroup (Baylor, 2009).

Similarly, guidelines for developing the number of agents and their behaviours were also found. Users learn more and are significantly more motivated when working with multiple agents (e.g., two motivator and expert agents) compared to working with one mentor agent (Baylor & Kim, 2005). In addition, users judge agents expressing positive emotions as more facilitating and engaging than agents expressing negative emotions, and empathic agents lead to higher interest and self-efficacy (Kim, Baylor, & Shen, 2007). Agents should (1) present accurate information with a confident experience when the user's goal is to acquire knowledge or skills; (2) present sometimes inaccurate information with a lack of experience when the user's self-efficacy is low; and (3) be proactive in providing information, leading to significantly higher recall scores compared to responsive agents (Kim & Baylor, 2006). Furthermore, the more an agent has a human-like voice, the more understanding, positive evaluations and positive behavioural intent users reported (Gong & Nass, 2007). Human voices lead to greater perceived agent credibility in the context of a learning environment (Baylor & Ryu, 2003).

Based on these findings, and based on discussions with the target group (Jacobs, Goossens, et al., 2014), it was decided to develop five agents. Most members of the target group indicated that they preferred to talk about (cyber)bullying to peers and an older "brother or sister". Therefore, four agents were designed as coping models; two agents (one male and one female) as members of the participant's in-group (same age and similar clothing style) and two agents (also one male and one female) as members of a somewhat older peer-group. One agent was designed as an expert/mentor model in the form of an older female schoolteacher. Different voice actors were used to record all information provided by the agents.

Videos

For the 41 recorded videos, a professional adult actor (well known among adolescents), seven young actresses, and three young actors were used. Videos were recorded at a school yard, in a classroom, in the school's canteen, in a film studio that was decorated as (boy's/girl's) bedroom and in a big corridor. The videos' topics were, for example, recognising, disputing, and replacing irrational thoughts (Figure 7.7), and aggressive, passive, assertive, active and problem solving reactions towards bullying, and planning.

Pictures

All pictures (27), comics (11) and animations (4) that were used in the intervention to illustrate certain information were selected or drawn by the first author.

Pretest of the interventions

Part of the focus group interviews conducted for the development of this intervention were pre- and pilot tests (Jacobs, Goossens, et al., 2014). Members of the target group were instructed to go to the website, complete the questionnaires and follow the pieces of advice. Next, six focus group interviews were held with a total of 41 participants from 4 schools. Based on the results from the pretests, pilot tests and focus group interviews, several adjustments were made: lay-out issues were resolved, bugs were repaired, and both the number of questions and the amount of content were reduced.

Step 5: Adoption and implementation

A plan for the adoption, implementation and continuation of the web-based tailored pieces of advice was developed. To facilitate adoption and implementation, a linkage group was formed (Bartholomew et al., 2011). The intervention was developed in such a way that the potential for adoption, implementation, and continuation is enhanced. For example, intervention users can find, register and use the intervention online. Therefore, the implementation of the intervention does not need additional human actions. The only actions needed and costs associated with the implementation, adoption and continuation are recruiting participating schools or individuals, hosting the website, preparing the intervention for implementation after the research has been conducted, and keeping the information up to date. Hence, the intervention can easily reach a large number of adolescents and at very low costs.

FIGURE 7.7 An actor explaining how to recognize, dispute and replace irrational thoughts with rational thoughts.

Step 6: Planning for evaluation

The evaluation of the programme – which is described below – was planned. The research on the effectiveness of the intervention *Online Pestkoppenstoppen* has been approved by the Medical Ethics Committee of the Atrium Hospital of Heerlen (NL39072.096.12; METC nr. 12-T-126), and is registered in the Dutch Trial Register (NTR3613).

Design and procedure

A three-group (experimental group, general information group and waiting list control group) randomised control trial (RCT) will be conducted to evaluate the efficacy of the intervention, with self-assessed measures at baseline (T0), before piece of advice two (T1), before piece of advice three (T2), a half year post start (T3) and 1 year post start (T4). Statements about the effectiveness of the three tailored web-based pieces of advice compared to general information can be made by comparing the experimental group with the general information group. The waiting list control group allows for controlling internal validation issues such as aging. However, this group does not receive measurements at T4. The timing and distribution of the measuring moments between the three conditions can be found in Figure 7.8. After the research, both the waiting list control group and general information group will be allowed to use the intervention.

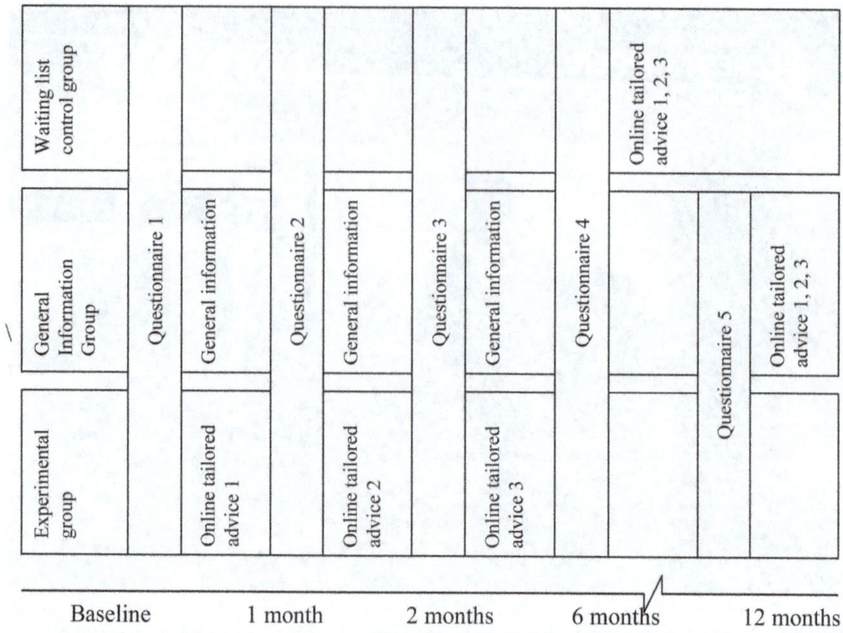

	Baseline	1 month	2 months	6 months	12 months
Waiting list control group					Online tailored advice 1, 2, 3
General Information Group	Questionnaire 1	General information · Questionnaire 2	General information · Questionnaire 3	General information · Questionnaire 4	Questionnaire 5 · Online tailored advice 1, 2, 3
Experimental group	Online tailored advice 1	Online tailored advice 2	Online tailored advice 3		

FIGURE 7.8 Timing and distribution of measurement moments.

Participants will be recruited via contacting all secondary vocational education schools in the Netherlands. When schools give their consent to participation, randomisation will follow. Schools will be stratified on three categories; a) size (small, medium or large); b) location of school (urban or rural); and c) type of education (theoretical or both theoretical and vocational). Schools will be matched and randomly assigned to one of the three intervention conditions. After randomisation, all participants will attend a lesson at school in which the research will be explained. Participants receive a written information letter and informed consent, which has to be signed by both the participant and his or her parent(s). Next, participants have to visit the website and complete the selection questionnaire. When a participant meets the inclusion criteria, registration will follow and the research and intervention procedure will start (see Figure 7.2 and 7.3).

A back-up plan was created in case the above mentioned method of recruiting did not provide a sufficient number of participants. In case of insufficient participants, adolescents are recruited by placing a message on several popular websites often visited by adolescents and/or their parents. Additionally, recruitment messages are sent via Facebook, LinkedIn, and Twitter. In this message individual adolescents are recruited to participate in the research by asking them to send us an e-mail with their name, age, name of school, and level of education. Next, they receive instructions (written and on video), a written information letter, and informed consent for them and their parents. In case parents read the message, they are asked to let their child participate in the research. Only after the adolescent provides us with the signed informed consents from them and their parents, will a login code be sent to the participant with which (s)he can access the intervention and/or research.

Measurement instruments

To evaluate the effectiveness of the intervention, several concepts will be measured via self-reported questionnaires. The primary outcomes of this study are frequency of (cyber)bullying, psychological wellbeing, problem behaviour, school performance and truancy. These will be assessed at baseline (T0), 6 (T3) and 12 months (T4) follow-up. The secondary outcomes of this study (i.e., moderators or working mechanisms (mediators) of the intervention) are irrational thoughts, self-efficacy, coping with cyberbullying and self-esteem. These will be assessed at baseline (T0), after 1 (T1), 2 (T2), 6 (T3) and 12 months (T4) follow-up. At baseline, several moderators will be measured as well (i.e., demographic characteristics such as gender, age, educational level). In addition, a process evaluation at T3 will be conducted to examine potential moderators.

Discussion

The aim of this chapter was to give a detailed description of the systematic development of the three web-based tailored pieces of advice for cyberbully victims that aimed at increasing psychological wellbeing, and decreasing victimisation, problem behaviour, school problems and truancy. In this intervention, cyberbully victims learn how to recognise, dispute and replace irrational thoughts with rational thoughts. Furthermore, their ineffective coping strategies are replaced with effective coping strategies, and they learn how to use the Internet and mobile phone in a safe and secure manner. The intervention is delivered online, via digital guides in digital environments. Digital guides provide information, ask questions, and show videos, pictures, comics and animations.

This intervention has several strengths. First, in developing, implementing and evaluating a systematic approach (Bartholomew et al., 2011), the Intervention Mapping approach is used. In the process of developing the intervention, empirical evidence, theories, guidelines and recommendations from the cyberbullying and bullying intervention and prevention literature were used to build a solid framework. Second, the intervention aims to change multiple determinants that were found in a study done by Jacobs, Völlink, et al., (2014). Third, guidelines and recommendations from other, not related to (cyber)bullying, intervention studies and theories were used, combined with results from focus groups interviews with the target groups. Fourth, this intervention is tailored to the specific needs of the target group: cyberbully victims are often unwilling to tell a teacher, parent or other adult that they need help. Therefore, they may feel more comfortable finding help anonymously (M. Webb et al., 2008) on the Internet (Ahlfors, 2010). Furthermore, we tried to incorporate all preferences of the target group as indicated in the pre-tests and pilot tests. Fifth, web-based computer tailored interventions can be used any time (Oenema et al., 2008), can reach a lot of people in a relatively cheap way (Cobiac et al., 2009), and allow for tailoring (De Vries & Brug, 1999), which has the potential for a successful health promotion technique (Krebs et al., 2010; Noar et al., 2007). Sixth, the planned RCT allows several important conclusions to be drawn. Finally, a process evaluation allows us to draw conclusions about several working mechanisms.

This intervention may also be subjected to limitations. First, it was difficult to reduce the amount of questions in the questionnaires we used for evaluation purposes. In the focus group interviews, members of the target group clearly stated that too many questions will lead to drop-out, because answering many questions is experienced as boring and fatiguing (Jacobs, Goossens, et al., 2014). Furthermore, too many questions may cause no-saying or yes-saying and response fatigue (for a review, see [Choi & Pak, 2005]), leading to less reliable results. Second, the intervention may contain too much information. Based on the literature, it was decided to include the 5G-schema, coping strategies, social skills, planning and safety instructions. In focus group interviews, members of the target-group mentioned the large amount of information making it difficult to remember everything. Third, besides the process evaluation, we cannot check the degree of usage on the experimental and general information. This may hamper the interpretation of the results. Therefore, we have added process evaluation questions, in which we ask the participants if they have read the information.

In conclusion, the *Online Pestkoppenstoppen* programme seems to be a promising start in solving cyberbullying problems. The results of the evaluation studies, which will be reported in other papers, may contribute to the knowledge about how to stop online victimisation and how to use tailoring and web-based interventions in this purpose. The results can be used as input for other web-based and computer-tailored interventions aimed at cyberbully victims. If the studies point out that the intervention is effective in its purpose, we have an intervention ready for implementation on a large scale.

Note

1 This chapter is an extended version of an article published in BMC Public Health: Jacobs, N. C. L., Völlink, T., Dehue, F., & Lechner, L. (2014). Online Pestkoppenstoppen: systematic and theory-based development of a web-based tailored intervention for adolescent cyberbully victims to combat and prevent cyberbullying. BMC Public Health, 14(1), 396. doi:10.1186/1471-2458-14-396

References

Abraham, C., & Michie, S. (2008). A taxonomy of behavior change techniques used in interventions. *Health Psychology: Official Journal of the Division of Health Psychology, American Psychological Association, 27*(3), 379–87. doi:10.1037/0278-6133.27.3.379

Achenbach, T. M. (1991). *Integrative guide for the 1991 CBCL/4–18, YSR, and TRF profiles.* Department of Psychiatry, University of Vermont Burlington.

Ahlfors, R. (2010). Many sources, one theme: Analysis of cyberbullying prevention and intervention websites. *Journal of Social Sciences, 6*(4), 515–522. doi:10.3844/jssp.2010.515.522

Andreou, E. (2001). Bully/victim problems and their association with coping behaviour in conflictual peer interactions among school-age children. *Educational Psychology, 21*(1), 59–66. doi:10.1080/01443410125042

Ang, R. P., & Goh, D. H. (2010). Cyberbullying among adolescents: the role of affective and cognitive empathy, and gender. *Child Psychiatry and Human Development, 41*(4), 387–97. doi:10.1007/s10578-010-0176-3

Araújo-Soares, V., McIntyre, T., & Sniehotta, F. F. (2009). Predicting changes in physical activity among adolescents: the role of self-efficacy, intention, action planning and coping planning. *Health Education Research, 24*(1), 128–39. doi:10.1093/her/cyn005

Aricak, T., Siyahhan, S., Uzunhasanoglu, A., Saribeyoglu, S., Ciplak, S., Yilmaz, N., & Memmedov, C. (2008). Cyberbullying among Turkish adolescents. *Cyberpsychology & Behavior: The Impact of the Internet, Multimedia and Virtual Reality on Behavior and Society, 11*(3), 253–61. doi:10.1089/cpb.2007.0016

Austin, E. J., Saklofske, D. H., & Egan, V. (2005). Personality, well-being and health correlates of trait emotional intelligence. *Personality and Individual Differences, 38*(3), 547–558. doi:10.1016/j.paid.2004.05.009

Baker, Ö. E., & Tanrıkulu, İ. (2010). Psychological consequences of cyber bullying experiences among Turkish secondary school children. *Procedia – Social and Behavioral Sciences, 2*(2), 2771–2776. doi:10.1016/j.sbspro.2010.03.413

Bandura, A. (1986). *Social foundations of thought and action: a social cognitive theory.* Englewood Cliffs, NJ: Prentice Hall.

Bandura, A. (1993). Perceived self-efficacy in cognitive development and functioning. *Educational Psychologist, 28*(2), 117–148.

Bandura, A. (1997). *Self-efficacy: The exercise of control.* New York: W. H. Freeman.

Banks, T., & Zionts, P. (2008). REBT Used with Children and Adolescents who have Emotional and Behavioral Disorders in Educational Settings: A Review of the Literature. *Journal of Rational-Emotive & Cognitive-Behavior Therapy, 27*(1), 51–65. doi:10.1007/s10942-008-0081-x

Barlińska, J., Szuster, A., & Winiewski, M. (2013). Cyberbullying among adolescent bystanders: Role of the communication medium, form of violence, and empathy. *Journal of Community & Applied Social Psychology, 23*(1), 37–51. doi:10.1002/casp.2137

Bartholomew, L. K., Parcel, G. S., Kok, G., Gottlieb, N. H., & Fernández, M. E. (2011). *Planning health promotion programs: an Intervention Mapping Approach.* San Francisco: Jossey-Bass.

Bauman, S. (2009). Cyberbullying in a Rural Intermediate School: An Exploratory Study. *The Journal of Early Adolescence, 30*(6), 803–833. doi:10.1177/0272431609350927

Baylor, A. L. (2009). Promoting motivation with virtual agents and avatars: role of visual presence and appearance. *Philosophical Transactions of the Royal Society of London. Series B, Biological Sciences, 364*(1535), 3559–65. doi:10.1098/rstb.2009.0148

Baylor, A. L., & Kim, Y. (2005). Simulating instructional roles through pedagogical agents. *International Journal of Artificial Intelligence in Education, 15*(2), 95–115.

Baylor, A. L., & Ryu, J. (2003). The effects of image and animation in enhancing pedagogical agent persona. *Journal of Educational Computing Research, 28*(4), 373–394. doi:10.2190/V0WQ-NWGN-JB54-FAT4

Beran, T., & Li, Q. (2005). Cyber-harassment: a study of a new method for an old behavior. *Journal of Educational Computing Research, 32*(3), 265–277. doi:10.2190/8YQM-B04H-PG4D-BLLH

Beran, T., & Li, Q. (2007). The relationship between cyberbullying and school bullying. *Journal of Student Wellbeing, 1*(2), 15–33.

Bijttebier, P., & Vertommen, H. (1998). Coping with peer arguments in school-age children with bully/victim problems. *British Journal of Educational Psychology, 68*(3), 387–394.

Blacher, J., Kraemer, B., & Schalow, M. (2003). Asperger syndrome and high functioning autism: Research concerns and emerging foci. *Current Opinion in Psychiatry, 16*(5), 535–542.

Bollmer, J. M., Harris, M. J., & Milich, R. (2006). Reactions to bullying and peer victimization: Narratives, physiological arousal, and personality. *Journal of Research in Personality, 40*(5), 803–828. doi:10.1016/j.jrp.2005.09.003

Boulton, M. J., Smith, P. K., & Cowie, H. (2010). Short-term longitudinal relationships between children's peer victimization/bullying experiences and self-perceptions evidence for reciprocity. *School Psychology International, 31*(3), 296–311.

Brug, J., Oenema, A., & Campbell, M. (2003). Past, present, and future of computer-tailored nutrition education. *The American Journal of Clinical Nutrition, 77*(4), 1028S–1034S. Retrieved from http://ajcn.nutrition.org/content/77/4/1028S.abstract

Brug, J., Oenema, A., Kroeze, W., & Raat, H. (2005). The internet and nutrition education: challenges and opportunities. *European Journal of Clinical Nutrition, 59*, S130–S139.

Camodeca, M., & Goossens, F. A. (2005). Aggression, social cognitions, anger and sadness in bullies and victims. *Journal of Child Psychology and Psychiatry, and Allied Disciplines, 46*(2), 186–97. doi:10.1111/j.1469-7610.2004.00347.x

Campbell, M. A., Spears, B., Slee, P., Butler, D., & Kift, S. (2012). Victims' perceptions of traditional and cyberbullying, and the psychosocial correlates of their victimisation. *Emotional and Behavioural Difficulties, 17*(3–4), 389–401. doi:10.1080/13632752.2012.704316

Casas, J. A., Del Rey, R., & Ortega-Ruiz, R. (2013). Bullying and cyberbullying: Convergent and divergent predictor variables. *Computers in Human Behavior, 29*(3), 580–587. doi:10.1016/j.chb.2012.11.015

Caspi, A., & Bem, D. J. (1990). Personality continuity and change across the life course. In L. A. Pervin (Ed.), *Handbook of personality: theory and research* (pp. 549–575). New York: Guilford Press.

Chalmers, J. B., & Townsend, M. A. R. (1990). The effects of training in social perspective taking on socially maladjusted girls. *Child Development, 61*(1), 178–190.

Choi, B. C. K., & Pak, A. W. P. (2005). A catalog of biases in questionnaires. *Preventing Chronic Disease, 2*(1), A13.

Cobiac, J., Vos, T., & Barendregt, J. (2009). Cost-effectiveness of interventions to promote physical activity: a modelling study. *PLoS Med, 6*(7), e1000110. doi:10.1371/journal.pmed.1000110

Cook, C. R., Williams, K. R., Guerra, N. G., Kim, T. E., & Sadek, S. (2010). Predictors of bullying and victimization in childhood and adolescence: a meta-analytic investigation. *School Psychology Quarterly, 25*(2), 65–83.

Craig, W., Pepler, D., & Blais, J. (2007). Responding to Bullying: What Works? *School Psychology International, 28*(4), 465–477. doi:10.1177/0143034307084136

Cross, D., Monks, H., Campbell, M. A., Spears, B., & Slee, P. (2011). School-based strategies to address cyber bullying. *Centre for Strategic Education Occasional Papers., 119*, 1–12.

Dehn, D. M., & Van Mulken, S. (2000). The impact of animated interface agents: a review of empirical research. *International Journal of Human-Computer Studies, 52*(1), 1–22. doi:10.1006/ijhc.1999.0325

Dehue, F., Bolman, C., & Völlink, T. (2008). Cyberbullying: youngsters' experiences and parental perception. *Cyberpsychology & Behavior: The Impact of the Internet, Multimedia and Virtual Reality on Behavior and Society, 11*(2), 217–23. doi:10.1089/cpb.2007.0008

De Vries, H., & Brug, J. (1999). Computer-tailored interventions motivating people to adopt health promoting behaviours: Introduction to a new approach. *Patient Education and Counseling, 36*(2), 99–195. doi:10.1016/S0738-3991(98)00127-X

De Vries, H., Kremers, S. P. J., Smeets, T., Brug, J., & Eijmael, K. (2008). The effectiveness of tailored feedback and action plans in an intervention addressing multiple health behaviors. *American Journal of Health Promotion, 22*(6), 417–425. doi:10.4278/ajhp.22.6.417

DeWall, C. N., Baumeister, R. F., Stillman, T. F., & Gailliot, M. T. (2007). Violence restrained: Effects of self-regulation and its depletion on aggression. *Journal of Experimental Social Psychology, 43*(1), 62–76. doi:http://dx.doi.org/10.1016/j.jesp.2005.12.005

Dooley, J. J., Shaw, T., & Cross, D. (2012). The association between the mental health and behavioural problems of students and their reactions to cyber-victimization. *European Journal of Developmental Psychology, 9*(2), 275–289. doi:10.1080/17405629.2011.648425

Ellis, A. (1984). The essence of RET. *Journal of Rational-Emotive & Cognitive-Behavior Therapy, 2*(1), 19–25.

Ellis, A. (1995). Changing Rational-emotive therapy (RET) to Rational, emotive behavior therapy (REBT). *Journal of Rational-Emotive & Cognitive-Behavior Therapy, 13*(2), 85–89.

Faber, M., Verkerk, G., van Aken, M., Lissenburg, L., & Geerlings, M. (2006). Plezier op school: sterker naar de brugklas. *Kind En Adolescent Praktijk, 5*(1), 31–39. doi:10.1007/bf03059577

Fanti, K. A., Demetriou, A. G., & Hawa, V. V. (2012). A longitudinal study of cyberbullying: Examining risk and protective factors. *European Journal of Developmental Psychology, 9*(2), 168–181.

Feindler, E. L., Marriott, S. A., & Iwata, M. (1984). Group anger control training for junior high school delinquents. *Cognitive Therapy and Research, 8*(3), 299–311.

Frith, U. (2004). Emanuel Miller lecture: Confusions and controversies about Asperger syndrome. *Journal of Child Psychology and Psychiatry, 45*(4), 672–686.

Garrison, R. D., Anderson, T., & Archer, W. (2001). Critical thinking, cognitive presence, and computer conferencing in distance education. *American Journal of Distance Education, 15*(1), 7–23.

Gavin, L. A., & Furman, W. (1989). Age differences in adolescents' perceptions of their peer groups. *Developmental Psychology, 25*(5), 827.

Gollwitzer, P. M., & Sheeran, P. (2008). *Implementation intentions.* Bibliothek der Universität Konstanz.

Gong, L. (2008). How social is social responses to computers? The function of the degree of anthropomorphism in computer representations. *Computers in Human Behavior, 24*(4), 1494–1509. doi:10.1016/j.chb.2007.05.007

Gong, L., & Nass, C. (2007). When a talking-face computer agent is half-human and half-humanoid: Human identity and consistency preference. *Human Communication Research, 33*(2), 163–193. doi:10.1111/j.1468-2958.2007.00295.x

Gonzalez, J. E., Nelson, J. R., Gutkin, T. B., Saunders, A., Galloway, A., & Shwery, C. S. (2004). Rational Emotive Therapy with children and adolescents: A meta-analysis. *Journal of Emotional and Behavioral Disorders, 12*(4), 222–235. doi:10.1177/10634266040120040301

Green, L. W., & Kreuter, M. W. (2005). *Health program planning: an educational and ecological approach.* McGraw-Hill New York.

Gross, E. F. (2004). Adolescent Internet use: What we expect, what teens report. *Journal of Applied Developmental Psychology, 25*(6), 633–649. doi:http://dx.doi.org/10.1016/j.appdev.2004.09.005

Guerra, N. G., & Slaby, R. G. (1990). Cognitive mediators of aggression in adolescent offenders: 2. Intervention. *Developmental Psychology, 26*(2), 269–277. Retrieved from http://www.sciencedirect.com/science/article/pii/S0012164902013207

Gutstein, S. E., & Whitney, T. (2002). Asperger syndrome and the development of social competence. *Focus on Autism and Other Developmental Disabilities, 17*(3), 161–171.

Harrist, A. W., Zaia, A. F., Bates, J. E., Dodge, K. A., & Pettit, G. S. (1997). Subtypes of Social Withdrawal in Early Childhood: Sociometric Status and Social-Cognitive Differences across Four Years. *Child Development, 68*(2), 278–294. doi:10.1111/j.1467-8624.1997.tb01940.x

Havas, J., de Nooijer, J., Crutzen, R., & Feron, F. (2011). Adolescents' views about an internet platform for adolescents with mental health problems. *Health Education, 111*(3), 164–176. doi:10.1108/09654281111123466

Hemphill, S. A., Kotevski, A., Tollit, M., Smith, R., Herrenkohl, T. I., Toumbourou, J. W., & Catalano, R. F. (2012). Longitudinal predictors of cyber and traditional bullying perpetration in Australian secondary school students. *The Journal of Adolescent Health: Official Publication of the Society for Adolescent Medicine, 51*(1), 59–65. Retrieved from http://linkinghub.elsevier.com/retrieve/pii/S1054139X11006525?showall=true

Hinduja, S., & Patchin, J. W. (2007). Offline consequences of online victimization. *Journal of School Violence, 6*(3), 89–112. doi:10.1300/J202v06n03_06

Hinduja, S., & Patchin, J. W. (2008). Cyberbullying: An exploratory analysis of factors related to offending and victimization. *Deviant Behavior, 29*(2), 129–156. Retrieved from http://www.informaworld.com/10.1080/01639620701457816

Hinduja, S., & Patchin, J. W. (2009). *Bullying beyond the schoolyard: Preventing and responding to cyberbullying.* California: Corwin Press.

Hinduja, S., & Patchin, J. W. (2010). Bullying, cyberbullying, and suicide. *Archives of Suicide Research, 14*(3), 206–221. Retrieved from http://www.informaworld.com/10.1080/13811118.2010.494133

Hunter, S. C., & Boyle, J. M. E. (2004). Appraisal and coping strategy use in victims of school bullying. *British Journal of Educational Psychology, 74*(1), 83–107. doi:10.1348/000709904322848833

Jackson, R. A., Stotland, N. E., Caughey, A. B., & Gerbert, B. (2011). Improving diet and exercise in pregnancy with Video Doctor counseling: a randomized trial. *Patient Education and Counseling, 83*(2), 203–209.

Jacobs, N. C. L., Goossens, L., Dehue, F., Völlink, T., & Lechner, L. (2014). *Dutch cyberbullying victims' experiences, perceptions, attitudes and motivations related to (coping with) cyberbullying: Focus group interviews.* Manuscript submitted for publication.

Jacobs, N. C. L., Völlink, T., Dehue, F., & Lechner, L. (2014). Determinants of adolescents' ineffective and improved coping with cyberbullying: a Delphi study. *Journal of Adolescence, 37*(4), 373–385. doi:http://dx.doi.org/10.1016/j.adolescence.2014.02.011

Jones, S. E., Manstead, A. S. R., & Livingstone, A. G. (2011). Ganging up or sticking together? Group processes and children's responses to text-message bullying. *British Journal of Psychology, 102*(1), 71–96. doi:10.1348/000712610x502826

Kanetsuna, T., Smith, P. K., & Morita, Y. (2006). Coping with bullying at school: children's recommended strategies and attitudes to school-based interventions in England and Japan. *Aggressive Behavior, 32*(6), 570–580. doi:10.1002/ab.20156

Katzer, C., Fetchenhauer, D., & Belschak, F. (2009). Cyberbullying: Who are the victims? *Journal of Media Psychology: Theories, Methods, and Applications, 21*(1), 25–36. doi:10.1027/1864-1105.21.1.25

Kim, Y., & Baylor, A. L. (2006). Pedagogical agents as learning companions: The role of agent competency and type of interaction. *Educational Technology Research and Development, 54*(3), 223–243.

Kim, Y., Baylor, A. L., & Shen, E. (2007). Pedagogical agents as learning companions: the impact of agent emotion and gender. *Journal of Computer Assisted Learning, 23*(3), 220–234.

Kim, Y. S., Leventhal, B. L., Koh, Y.-J., Hubbard, A., & Boyce, W. T. (2006). School bullying and youth violence: causes or consequences of psychopathologic behavior? *Archives
of General Psychiatry, 63*(9), 1035–41. doi:10.1001/archpsyc.63.9.1035

Kochenderfer-Ladd, B. (2004). Peer Victimization: The Role of Emotions in Adaptive and Maladaptive Coping. *Social Development, 13*(3), 329–349. doi:10.1111/j.1467-9507.2004.00271.x

Kok, G., Schaalma, H., Ruiter, R. A. C., Van Empelen, P., & Brug, J. (2004). Intervention
Mapping: Protocol for applying health psychology theory to prevention programmes.
Journal of Health Psychology, 9(1), 85–98. doi:10.1177/1359105304038379

Kokkinos, C. M., & Kipritsi, E. (2011). The relationship between bullying, victimization,
trait emotional intelligence, self-efficacy and empathy among preadolescents. *Social
Psychology of Education, 15*(1), 41–58. doi:10.1007/s11218-011-9168-9

Kowalski, R. M., Limber, S. P., & Agatston, P. W. (2008). *Cyber Bullying: Bullying in the
digital age* (p. 218). Malden: Blackwell Publishing.

Krebs, P., Prochaska, J. O., & Rossi, J. S. (2010). A meta-analysis of computer-tailored interventions for health behavior change. *Preventive Medicine, 51*(3–4), 214–221. doi:10.1016/
j.ypmed.2010.06.004

Kreuter, M., Farrell, D., Olevitch, L., & Brennan, L. (2000). *Tailoring health messages: cus-
tomizing communication with computer technology.* Mahwah, NJ: Erlbaum.

Kristensen, S. M., & Smith, P. K. (2003). The use of coping strategies by Danish children
classed as bullies, victims, bully/victims, and not involved, in response to different
(hypothetical) types of bullying. *Scandinavian Journal of Psychology, 44,* 479–488.

Ladd, G. W. (1981). Effectiveness of a social learning model for enhancing children's social
interaction and peer acceptance. *Child Development, 52,* 171–178.

Låftman, S. B., Modin, B., & Östberg, V. (2013). Cyberbullying and subjective health: A
large-scale study of students in Stockholm, Sweden. *Children and Youth Services Review,
35*(1), 112–119. doi:http://dx.doi.org/10.1016/j.childyouth.2012.10.020

Lazarus, R. S., & Folkman, S. (1987). Transactional theory and research on emotions and
coping. *European Journal of Personality, 1*(3), 141–169. doi:10.1002/per.2410010304

Lenhart, A., Purcell, K., Smith, A., & Zickuhr, K. (2010). *Social media & mobile internet use
among teens and young adults.* Washington, DC: Pew Research Center, Pew Internet &
American Life Project.

Leventhal, H., Singer, R., & Jones, S. (1965). Effects of fear and specificity of recommenda-
tion upon attitudes and behavior. *Journal of Personality and Social Psychology, 2*(1), 20–29.

Lewinsohn, P. M., Hops, H., Roberts, R. E., & Seeley, J. R. (1993). Adolescent psychopathology: I. Prevalence and incidence of depression and other DSM-III – R disorders
in high school students. *Journal of Abnormal Psychology, 102*(1), 133–144. doi:10.1037/
0021-843X.102.1.133

Livingstone, S., Haddon, L., Görzig, A., & Olafsson, K. (2011). Risks and safety on the
internet: the perspective of European children: full findings and policy implications
from the EU Kids Online survey of 9–16 year olds and their parents in 25 countries.
London: EU Kids Online.

Lochman, J. E. (1992). Cognitive-behavioral intervention with aggressive boys: Three-year
follow-up and preventive effects. *Journal of Consulting and Clinical Psychology, 60*(3), 426.

MacInnes, D. (2004). The theories underpinning rational emotive behaviour therapy: Where's
the supportive evidence? *International Journal of Nursing Studies, 41*(6), 685–695. Retrieved
from http://linkinghub.elsevier.com/retrieve/pii/S0020748904000343?showall=true

Mahady Wilton, M. M., Craig, W. M., & Pepler, D. J. (2000). Emotional regulation
and display in classroom victims of bullying: Characteristic expressions of affect,
coping styles and relevant contextual factors. *Social Development, 9*(2), 227–245.
doi:10.1111/1467-9507.00121

Mathur, S.R., Kavale, K.A., Quinn, M.M., Forness, S.R., & Rutherford, R.B. (1998). Social skills interventions with students with emotional and behavioral problems: A quantitative synthesis of single-subject research. *Behavioral Disorders, 23*(3), 193–201.

McManus, I.C., Livingston, G., & Katona, C. (2006). The attractions of medicine: the generic motivations of medical school applicants in relation to demography, personality and achievement. *BMC Medical Education, 6*, 11.

Michie, S., Johnston, M., Francis, J., Hardeman, W., & Eccles, M. (2008). From theory to intervention: Mapping theoretically derived behavioural determinants to behaviour change techniques. *Applied Psychology, 57*(4), 660–680. doi:10.1111/j.1464-0597.2008.00341.x

Mishna, F., Cook, C., Gadalla, T., Daciuk, J., & Solomon, S. (2010). Cyber bullying behaviors among middle and high school students. *American Journal of Orthopsychiatry, 80*(3), 362–374. doi:10.1111/j.1939-0025.2010.01040.x

Mitchell, K.J., Ybarra, M.L., & Finkelhor, D. (2007). The relative importance of online victimization in understanding depression, delinquency, and substance use. *Child Maltreatment, 12*(4), 314–324.

Neary, A., & Joseph, S. (1994). Peer victimization and its relationship to self-concept and depression among schoolgirls. *Personality and Individual Differences, 16*(1), 183–186. doi:10.1016/0191-8869(94)90122-8

Noar, S.M., Benac, C.N., & Harris, M.S. (2007). Does tailoring matter? Meta-analytic review of tailored print health behavior change interventions. *Psychological Bulletin, 133*(4), 673–693.

Nowicki Jr, S., & Duke, M.P. (1994). Individual differences in the nonverbal communication of affect: The Diagnostic Analysis of Nonverbal Accuracy Scale. *Journal of Nonverbal Behavior, 18*(1), 9–35.

Oden, S., & Asher, S.R. (1977). Coaching children in social skills for friendship making. *Child Development, 48*(2), 495–506.

Oenema, A., Brug, J., Dijkstra, A., Weerdt, I., & Vries, H. (2008). Efficacy and use of an Internet-delivered computer-tailored lifestyle intervention, targeting saturated fat intake, physical activity and smoking cessation: A randomized controlled trial. *Annals of Behavioral Medicine, 35*(2), 125–135. doi:10.1007/s12160-008-9023-1

Olweus, D. (2012). Cyberbullying: An overrated phenomenon? *European Journal of Developmental Psychology, 9*(5), 520–538. doi:10.1080/17405629.2012.682358

Parris, L., Varjas, K., Meyers, J., & Cutts, H. (2011). High school students' perceptions of coping with cyberbullying. *Youth & Society, 44*(2), 284–306. doi:10.1177/0044118X11398881

Patchin, J.W., & Hinduja, S. (2011). Traditional and nontraditional bullying among youth: A test of general strain theory. *Youth & Society, 43*(2), 727–751. doi:10.1177/0044118x10366951

Paul, S., Smith, P.K., & Blumberg, H.H. (2012). Revisiting cyberbullying in schools using the quality circle approach. *School Psychology International, 33*(5), 492–504. doi:10.1177/0143034312445243

Perren, S., Corcoran, L, Cowie, H., Dehue, F., Garcia, D., Mc Guckin, C., Sevcikova, A., Tsatsou, P., Völlink, T. (2012). Tackling cyberbullying: Review of empirical evidence regarding successful responses by students, parents and schools. *International Journal of Conflict and Violence, 6*(2).

Perren, S., Dooley, J., Shaw, T., & Cross, D. (2010). Bullying in school and cyberspace: Associations with depressive symptoms in Swiss and Australian adolescents. *Child and Adolescent Psychiatry and Mental Health, 4*(1), 1–10. doi:10.1186/1753-2000-4-28

Perry, D.G., Hodges, E.V.E., Egan, S.K., Juvonen, J., & Graham, S. (2001). Determinants of chronic victimization by peers: A review and new model of family influence. In J. Juvonen & S. Graham (Eds.), *Peer harassment in school: The plight of the vulnerable and victimized.* (pp. 73–104). New York, NY: Guilford Press.

Petty, R. E., & Cacioppo, J. T. (1986). The elaboration likelihood model of persuasion. In *Communication and Persuasion* (pp. 1–24). New York, NY: Springer.

Price, M., & Dalgleish, J. (2010). Cyberbullying: Experiences, impacts and coping strategies as described by Australian young people. *Youth Studies Australia, 29*(2), 51–59.

Raskauskas, J., & Stoltz, A. D. (2007). Involvement in traditional and electronic bullying among adolescents. *Developmental Psychology, 43*(3), 564–75. doi:10.1037/0012-1649.43.3.564

Reuter, T., Ziegelmann, J. P., Wiedemann, A. U., Geiser, C., Lippke, S., Schüz, B., & Schwarzer, R. (2010). Changes in intentions, planning, and self-efficacy predict changes in behaviors: An application of latent true change modeling. *Journal of Health Psychology, 15*(6), 935–947. doi:10.1177/1359105309360071

Riebel, J., Jäger, R. S., & Fischer, U. C. (2009). Cyberbullying in Germany – an exploration of prevalence, overlapping with real life bullying and coping strategies. *Psychology Science Quarterly, 51*(3), 298–314.

Ringrose, H. J., & Nijenhuis, E. H. (1986). *Bang zijn voor andere kinderen*. Groningen: Wolters-Noordhoff.

Rivers, I., Poteat, V. P., Noret, N., & Ashurst, N. (2009). The mental health implications of witness status. *School Psychology Quarterly, 24*(4), 211–223.

Rook, K. S. (1984). Interventions for loneliness: A review and analysis. *Preventing the Harmful Consequences of Severe and Persistent Loneliness,* 47–79.

Sarason, I. G., & Ganzer, V. J. (1973). Modeling and group discussion in the rehabilitation of juvenile delinquents. *Journal of Counseling Psychology, 20*(5), 442–449.

Sarason, I. G., & Sarason, B. R. (1981). Teaching cognitive and social skills to high school students. *Journal of Consulting and Clinical Psychology, 49,* 908–918.

Schneider, S. K., O'Donnell, L., Stueve, A., & Coulter, R. W. S. (2012). Cyberbullying, school bullying, and psychological distress: a regional census of high school students. *American Journal of Public Health, 102*(1), 171–177. doi:10.2105/AJPH.2011.300308

Schoffstall, C. L., & Cohen, R. (2011). Cyber aggression: The relation between online offenders and offline social competence. *Social Development, 20*(3), 587–604.

Sheeran, P., Webb, T. L., & Gollwitzer, P. M. (2005). The interplay between goal intentions and implementation intentions. *Personality and Social Psychology Bulletin, 31*(1), 87–98.

Skrzypiec, G., Slee, P., Murray-Harvey, R., & Pereira, B. (2011). School bullying by one or more ways: Does it matter and how do students cope? *School Psychology International, 32*(3), 288–311. doi:10.1177/0143034311402308

Slonje, R., & Smith, P. K. (2008). Cyberbullying: another main type of bullying? *Scandinavian Journal of Psychology, 49*(2), 147–54. doi:10.1111/j.1467-9450.2007.00611.x

Slonje, R., Smith, P. K., & Frisén, A. (2013). The nature of cyberbullying, and strategies for prevention. *Computers in Human Behavior, 29*(1), 26–32. doi:10.1016/j.chb.2012.05.024

Smith, P. K., Mahdavi, J., Carvalho, M., Fisher, S., Russell, S., & Tippett, N. (2008). Cyberbullying: its nature and impact in secondary school pupils. *Journal of Child Psychology and Psychiatry, and Allied Disciplines, 49*(4), 376–85. doi:10.1111/j.1469-7610.2007.01846.x

Smith, P. K., Salmivalli, C., & Cowie, H. (2012). Effectiveness of school-based programs to reduce bullying: a commentary. *Journal of Experimental Criminology, 8*(4), 433–441. doi:10.1007/s11292-012-9142-3

Snakenborg, J., Van Acker, R., & Gable, R. A. (2011). Cyberbullying: prevention and intervention to protect our children and youth. *Preventing School Failure, 55*(2), 88–95. doi:10.1080/1045988x.2011.539454

Sniehotta, F. F., Scholz, U., & Schwarzer, R. (2005). Bridging the intention–behaviour gap: Planning, self-efficacy, and action control in the adoption and maintenance of physical exercise. *Psychology & Health, 20*(2), 143–160.

Sniehotta, F. F., Schwarzer, R., Scholz, U., & Schüz, B. (2005). Action planning and coping planning for long-term lifestyle change: theory and assessment. *European Journal of Social Psychology, 35*(4), 565–576. doi:10.1002/ejsp.258

Tenenbaum, L. S., Varjas, K., Meyers, J., & Parris, L. (2011). Coping strategies and perceived effectiveness in fourth through eighth grade victims of bullying. *School Psychology International, 32*(3), 263–287. doi:10.1177/0143034311402309

Tokunaga, R. S. (2010). Following you home from school: A critical review and synthesis of research on cyberbullying victimization. *Computers in Human Behavior, 26*(3), 277–287. doi:10.1016/j.chb.2009.11.014

Valcke, M., De Wever, B., Van Keer, H., & Schellens, T. (2011). Long-term study of safe Internet use of young children. *Computers & Education, 57*(1), 1292–1305. doi:http://dx.doi.org/10.1016/j.compedu.2011.01.010

Vandebosch, H., & Van Cleemput, K. (2009). Cyberbullying among youngsters: profiles of bullies and victims. *New Media & Society, 11*(8), 1349–1371. doi:10.1177/1461444809341263

Vandelanotte, C., & Mummery, W. K. (2011). Qualitative and quantitative research into the development and feasibility of a video-tailored physical activity intervention. *International Journal of Behavioral Nutrition and Physical Activity, 8*(1), 70.

Van der Vegt, A. L., den Blanken, M., & Jepma, I. J. (2007). *Nationale scholierenmonitor: meting voorjaar 2007. onderwijsvernieuwingen.roser.nl.* Retrieved from http://www.rijksoverheid.nl/

Van Osch, L., Lechner, L., Reubsaet, A., Wigger, S., & De Vries, H. (2008). Relapse prevention in a national smoking cessation contest: Effects of coping planning. *British Journal of Health Psychology, 13*(3), 525–535. doi:10.1348/135910707x224504

Völlink, T., Bolman, C. A. W., Dehue, F., & Jacobs, N. C. L. (2013). Coping with cyberbullying: Differences between victims, bully-victims and children not involved in bullying. *Journal of Community & Applied Social Psychology, 23*(1), 7–24. doi:10.1002/casp.2142

Wade, A., & Beran, T. (2011). Cyberbullying: The new era of bullying. *Canadian Journal of School Psychology, 26*(1), 44–61.

Walrave, M., & Heirman, W. (2011). Cyberbullying: Predicting victimisation and perpetration. *Children & Society, 25*(1), 59–72. doi:10.1111/j.1099-0860.2009.00260.x

Webb, M., Burns, J., & Collin, P. (2008). Providing online support for young people with mental health difficulties: challenges and opportunities explored. *Early Intervention in Psychiatry, 2*(2), 108–113. doi:10.1111/j.1751-7893.2008.00066.x

Webb, T. L., Joseph, J., Yardley, L., & Michie, S. (2010). Using the internet to promote health behavior change: a systematic review and meta-analysis of the impact of theoretical basis, use of behavior change techniques, and mode of delivery on efficacy. *Journal of Medical Internet Research, 12*(1), e4. doi:10.2196/jmir.1376

Wiedemann, A. U., Lippke, S., Reuter, T., Ziegelmann, J. P., & Schwarzer, R. (2011). How planning facilitates behaviour change: Additive and interactive effects of a randomized controlled trial. *European Journal of Social Psychology, 41*(1), 42–51. doi:10.1002/ejsp.724

Woods, S., Wolke, D., Nowicki, S., & Hall, L. (2009). Emotion recognition abilities and empathy of victims of bullying. *Child Abuse & Neglect, 33*(5), 307–311. doi:10.1016/j.chiabu.2008.11.002

Woolfolk, A. (2010). *Educational Psychology.* Boston: Allyn & Bacon.

Ybarra, M. L. (2004). Linkages between depressive symptomatology and Internet harassment among young regular Internet users. *Cyberpsychology & Behavior: The Impact of the Internet, Multimedia and Virtual Reality on Behavior and Society, 7*(2), 247–57. doi:10.1089/109493104323024500

Ybarra, M. L., Diener-West, M., & Leaf, P. J. (2007). Examining the overlap in internet harassment and school bullying: Implications for school intervention. *The Journal of*

Adolescent Health: Official Publication of the Society for Adolescent Medicine, 41(6), S42–S50. doi:http://dx.doi.org/10.1016/j.jadohealth.2007.09.004

Ybarra, M. L., & Mitchell, K. J. (2004). Online aggressor/targets, aggressors, and targets: a comparison of associated youth characteristics. *Journal of Child Psychology and Psychiatry, and Allied Disciplines, 45*(7), 1308–16. doi:10.1111/j.1469-7610.2004.00328.x

Ybarra, M. L., Mitchell, K. J., Wolak, J., & Finkelhor, D. (2006). Examining characteristics and associated distress related to Internet harassment: findings from the Second Youth Internet Safety Survey. *Pediatrics, 118*(4), e1169–77. doi:10.1542/peds.2006-0815

Ysebaert, D. W., Dehue, F., & Völlink, T. (2008). *De relatie tussen persoonlijkheidskenmerken en cyberpesten* (Unpublished master's thesis). Open Universiteit, Heerlen, Nederland.

8

NONCADIAMOINTRAPPOLA!
[LET'S NOT FALL INTO THE TRAP!]

Online and school-based program to prevent cyberbullying among adolescents

Ersilia Menesini, Benedetta Emanuela Palladino and Annalaura Nocentini

Introduction

From the bullying interventions literature, we can see that many programs devised to combat traditional bullying can arguably be extended to tackle cyberbullying without major changes; for instance, we can incorporate the topic of cyberbullying into traditional anti-bullying awareness-raising and curriculum-based activities and as a whole-school anti-bullying policy (Slonje, Smith, & Frisén, 2013). Considering the overlap between the two phenomena, it is assumed that similar processes concern both bullying and cyberbullying, and therefore if we work on those processes we can reduce and prevent both. However, the peculiarities of the virtual context (such as the possible anonymity of the bully's identity, the ability to share anything online, the absence of direct feedback, the technical countermeasures that we can take online in order to be safe, etc.) have led some researchers to speculate that specific prevention strategies need to be included in an anti-cyberbullying program (Dooley, Pyżalski, & Cross, 2009; Kiriakidis & Kavoura, 2010; Kowalski & Limber, 2007; Tokunaga, 2010; Wingate, Minney, & Guadagno, 2013).

In reviewing literature regarding the efficacy of interventions to combat cyberbullying, we found that it is a relatively new area: there is a paucity of published peer-review studies and most of them don't completely match the standard of evidence (Flay et al., 2005).

We can cluster pre-existing programs into three main groups:

- Anti-bullying programs that are principally devoted to tackling the traditional bullying phenomenon with some effects on cyberbullying such as KiVa (Kärnä et al., 2011) and the ViSC program (Spiel, Wagner, & Strohmeier, 2012);
- Programs developed to deal with online risks without specific modules for face-to-face bullying such as Medienhelden (Wölfer et al., 2013); ConRed (Del Rey-Alamillo Casas, & Ortega-Ruiz, 2012);

- A program focused on both sides of the youth relational world (virtual and real interactions) and on the risks that can arise from them such as *Noncadiamointrappola!* (Menesini, Nocentini, & Palladino, 2012; Menesini & Nocentini, 2012; Palladino, Nocentini, & Menesini, 2012).

The *Noncadiamointrappola!* program has changed its approach and the topics it has covered over the years: it has switched from the second group of this classification (focused only on cyberbullying) to the third (focused on both bullying and cyberbullying) based on results found after implementation of the first edition of the program.

Noncadiamointrappola!: History and development of the program

Noncadiamointrappola!, which means "Let's not fall into the trap!", is a *school-based universal program* developed beginning in 2008 with the aim of preventing bullying and cyberbullying and making positive use of new technologies.

We began this program based on a consideration of the virtual word: while using ICTs involves risk, we must also appreciate the opportunities offered by the new technologies (e.g., the possibility to target a large audience, to be in contact with people even if it is impossible to meet them in person, to find new information, resources, etc.). For this reason, we used ICTs to promote protective factors (e.g., online social support) and to enhance positive behaviours online. In order to promote coping strategies among young students, we included online support activities led by peer educators in each edition of the program, making changes and adding new aspects to keep pace with the times (e.g., we created a Facebook fan page in the second edition).

The program is an evolution of a face-to-face peer support model (Menesini, Codecasa, Benelli, & Cowie, 2003). In *Noncadiamointrappola!*, the *peer-led model is applied in the online setting as well as the face-to-face setting.* In our model we have two main phases: in the first, the program is managed by adults (psychologists and other experts); in the second, the program is led by peer educators (students that assume this role after undergoing specific training). The core schema is the same for all editions:

1) Adults (psychologists and experts) talk with all the students of the experimental classes about the target phenomena (namely the launch of the program and awareness development). Some of the students in each class are invited to become peer educators, assuming a more involved role in the program. They participate in a specific training (the other students of the experimental classes do not).

2) The trained peer educators carry out some activities with their peers. In all editions, they give their support anonymously (using nicknames) to all people requesting help on the webpage of the program.

Every year the program was improved by adding and modifying specific components following the results found in the previous edition (Menesini, Nocentini, & Palladino, 2012; Menesini & Nocentini, 2009; Palladino, Nocentini, & Menesini, 2012) and the more recent literature findings (Ttofi & Farrington, 2011) in order to develop an evidence-based and effective program (Flay et al., 2005).

The entire program was started and carried out with the students' collaboration. In the pilot trial, two schools were involved and students were consulted for the design and development of a webpage (school year 2008/2009). On the webpage, peer educators initiated lines of discussion through an online forum and uploaded some materials (such as posters against bullying) produced in class. The webpage was named "Noncadiamointrappola!". The students chose the name of the program and designed the logo.

Noncadiamointrappola! 1st edition (school year 2009/2010)

During the first year of the program's implementation, the peer educators' activities were principally online while the other students were only involved directly in the first phase of the program, namely the adult-led meeting directed towards the launch of the program and awareness development. The focus of the meeting was mainly on cyberbullying. Unfortunately, evaluation of the effects of the program showed a decrease only in cyberbullying behaviours (not traditional bullying) and only for male peer educators (Menesini et al., 2012). For this reason, we decided to change some aspects of the program in order to improve its efficacy.

Noncadiamointrappola! 2nd edition (school year 2010/2011)

We carried out a new trial to test a modified version of the program. We maintained the same general scheme (i.e., an adult-led phase followed by a peer-led phase) but we decided:

(a) To put equal attention on both bullying and cyberbullying;
(b) To pay greater attention to the victim's role in each step and to involve bystanders. Bullying is a group phenomenon and we wanted to target all the participants' roles (Pöyhönen, Juvonen, & Salmivalli, 2012; Salmivalli, Lagerspetz, Björkqvist, Österman, & Kaukiainen, 1996), especially the "silent majority" who often observe bullying but do not do anything to stop it;
(c) To work on coping strategies that victims and bystanders could use in response to bullying and cyberbullying (What can I do if I witness a cyberbullying situation? How can I respond and what can I do if I become a victim of cyberbullying?). From the literature, we know that teaching coping strategies makes defending behaviours more likely to occur (Pozzoli & Gini, 2013);
(d) To implement specific, face-to-face activities led by peer educators with the other classmates. In the first edition, we found that the effects of the program

were significant only for peer educators. Based on these findings, we assumed that activities led by peer educators could be a source of support for the other classmates and a way to allow the peer educators to become agents of change in their class, influencing the group dynamics;

(e) To request greater collaboration from curricular teachers on the class activities led by peer educators in an effort to use a more ecological approach in our program. The activities were determined for each school and class according to the curricular programs (e.g., high school seniors specialising in didactics and education created a short movie on cyberbullying starting from specific in-depth lessons about emotions [taught by psychology teachers] and the writing of a screenplay [taught by Italian language teachers]; computer science students created a set of rules for the safe use of e-mail and social networks [taught by computer studies teachers]). Classroom activities were designed to create "products" to be used in other editions or classes;

(f) To create a Facebook group complementing the webpage forum. While in the webpage forum people could find anonymous peer support (from peer educators) and professional support (from psychologists), the Facebook group was used to communicate with peer educators and to share with everyone the resources offered by the program.

In the second edition of the program, we found a significant decrease in bullying, victimisation, and cybervictimisation in the experimental group as compared to the control group (Menesini et al., 2012). Moreover, in the experimental group we noticed a significant increase in adaptive coping strategies and a significant decrease in maladaptive coping strategies. These changes mediated the changes in the behavioural variables. In particular, the decrease in avoidance predicted the decrease in victimisation and cybervictimisation in the experimental group. In the peer educator group, the increase in problem solving predicted the decrease in cybervictimisation. The exclusion of the rest of the experimental group from this result was likely due to the specific, intensive training focused on problem-solving strategies the peer educators received. The other students in the experimental classes did not work on problem solving during the face-to-face activities.

Noncadiamointrappola! The 3rd, current edition

Trying to improve the efficacy of the program, the research findings from the second edition helped us to design activities for the program and to focus on the processes sustaining the phenomena we want to address.

Bullying and cyberbullying are complex behaviours influenced by the interplay between individual and social-contextual factors. In planning and developing an anti-bullying/cyberbullying intervention that can lead to a change in the underlying processes, it is important to consider both the individual characteristics and contextual variables that serve to perpetuate these phenomena.

Bullying is often considered a social type of aggression because it involves a group of peers in which each member plays a specific role. Besides the traditional roles of bully, victim, and bully-victim, other participant roles have been identified: assistants, supporters, outsiders, and the victim defenders (Salmivalli et al., 1996). This group dynamic shows that bystanders have the potential to influence the situation in different ways: they can reinforce the bully by joining in or passively accepting the situation or, conversely, they can distance themselves from the bullies or defend the victims. Research has shown that bystanders can be trapped in a social conflict; they may claim to be against bullying but might also want to defend themselves and maintain their own status (Salmivalli, 2010). There are several mechanisms that are relevant to understanding why bystanders may have difficulty defending the victims. Primarily, diffusion of responsibility occurs when an event happens in front of a group of people, and bystanders feel less individual responsibility (Salmivalli, 2010). Other contributing factors include that it's easier to be on the side of the bullies, the dominant group in the class, and that often the bystanders' behaviours are influenced by the attitudes of the majority of the class (Gini, Pozzoli, Borghi, & Franzoni, 2008). From a social point of view, bystanders are easier to influence than bullies and victims because they often have anti-bullying attitudes despite the difficulties they perceive in intervening in bullying situations. Literature on victims' support and on the bystander role has underlined the value of involving the group and, specifically, the uninvolved children (i.e., the so-called "silent majority") in order to change the dynamics of bullying and to stop negative behaviours (Menesini et al., 2003; Salmivalli, 2010).

An approach focused on peer involvement appears to be relevant and suitable for use in anti-bullying and anti-cyberbullying programs (Cowie & Wallace, 2000; Shiner, 1999). Peer education and peer support models are based on the assumption that peers have significant influence on each other. The group's norms and behaviours are most likely to change when liked and trusted group members take the lead to initiate individual and contextual changes (Shiner, 1999; Turner & Shepherd, 1999). Regarding the effectiveness of this approach, peer-led models have shown controversial results. In a recent meta-analysis on the effectiveness of school-based programs aimed at reducing bullying, the authors concluded that "work with peers was significantly associated with an increase in victimization" (Ttofi & Farrington, 2011, p.45). The phrase "work with peers" tends to cover a wide range of peer support activities (Smith, Salmivalli, & Cowie, 2012). While the evidence shows these peer-led models can vary in effectiveness, many of these models are perceived positively by pupils, who are aware of the program's contribution to their sense of safety at school (Cowie, Hutson, Oztug, & Myers, 2008; Cowie & Oztug, 2008). Peer-led methods provide training in a range of interpersonal and social skills and can educate students on how to take responsibility for their own actions. Many studies have suggested that peer support systems and peer education can provide benefits to users of such models, to peer supporters, and to schools in general (Birnbaum, Crohn, Maticka-Tyndale, & Barnett, 2010; Cowie, Naylor, Talamelli, Chauhan, & Smith, 2002; Naylor & Cowie, 1999; Menesini, &

Nocentini, 2012). From the results of previous editions of the *Noncadiamointrappola!* program (Menesini, Nocentini, & Palladino, 2012), we know that within a peer-led model, the role that peer educators assume is particularly important in relation to the effects of the program itself (Menesini & Nocentini, 2012).

Another important step when making a program aimed at preventing bullying and cyberbullying is the identification of the individual processes in order to intercept them and activate mechanisms of change. What can we do to encourage a bystander's intervention in a bullying or cyberbullying situation? How can the victims and bystanders cope with these situations? We know that empathy and attitudes against bullying predict bystander intervention (Cappadocia, Pepler, Cummings, & Craig, 2012) and problem-solving coping strategies. Perceived normative peer pressure for bystanders is also positively associated with actively helping a victim (Pozzoli & Gini, 2010). Furthermore, having positive attitudes towards the victim leads students to feel greater personal responsibility for intervention, and both positive attitudes and feelings of responsibility are positively associated with students' choice to adopt "approaching coping strategies" that make defending behaviour more likely to occur (Pozzoli & Gini, 2013). Defending victims of bullying is also associated with the expectation that the victim will feel better as a result and that the student will value such an outcome (Pöyhönen et al., 2012). Generally speaking, encouraging students to practice safer strategies to support and defend their victimised peers allows them to self-protect against the possible negative consequences of defending. This might be true especially for the students who tend to remain passive while witnessing bullying. Furthermore, as Rigby asserts (2000), even small acts of support may possess high meaning for the victim.

In summary, the association between different coping styles and various victim/bystander behaviours suggests that improving the use of adaptive strategies could further reduce the incidence of bullying and cyberbullying. Moreover, the moral component of active help (feelings of personal responsibility for intervention and empathy) should be explicitly addressed in order to increase the likelihood of active bystanding behaviours. Again, it is important to keep in mind that bullying is a group phenomenon (Salmivalli, 2010); trying to change individual cognitions, coping strategies, and values without simultaneously addressing the whole group does not appear a promising approach. Intervention programs must create a context that enables students to support and defend their victimised peers. This type of intervention may dispel social norms that block bystanders from helping the victim.

In the *Noncadiamointrappola!* program 3rd edition (school years 2011/2012 and 2012/2013) we maintained the same general method, keeping the peer-led model and the effective components of the previous edition (i.e., promoting adaptive coping strategies), while we better defined some aspects of the program (e.g., the activities led by peers) and added some new components that appeared to be effective as interventions (e.g., cooperative work) (Ttofi & Farrington, 2011).

The main reason for revising the program was the need to implement uniform face-to-face activities led by peer educators instead of defining specific activities for each type of school according to the curricular programs: these often change and it's difficult to find teachers of the core subject of study that are available to deliver the program. This change of approach was also needed because only a standardised program can be easily implemented in other contexts, matching the standard of evidence required for an evidence-based program ready for dissemination (Flay et al., 2005). The new activities led by peer educators were based on cooperative work with the other classmates and specifically focused on empathy and problem solving, targeting the point of view of the victim and the bystander in order to address the processes that can lead to a change in the role of these figures (Cappadocia, Pepler, Cummings, & Craig, 2012; Freis & Gurung, 2013; Pozzoli & Gini, 2013; Ttofi & Farrington, 2011).

We decided to focus on a specific age group as a target of the program: students in their first year of high school (in Italy, it corresponds to 9th grade, 14- to 15-year-old students). This decision was driven by several considerations about individual, relational, and academic variables. First and foremost, going from middle school to high school involves an important developmental transition with changes in friends, teachers, subjects, and location, and in the first year of high school, there are higher rates of grade retention and dropouts, two strictly related phenomena (Jimerson, Anderson, & Whipple, 2002; Palladino, Nocentini, Ciucci, & Menesini, 2011). Especially in adolescence, aggressive behaviour and the quality of peer relations may be proximal factors that significantly affect performance, grade retention, and early school dropout (French & Conrad, 2001; Kokko, Tremblay, Lacourse, Nagin, & Vitaro, 2006). Physical aggression, antisocial behaviour, and achievement predict school dropout and physical violence. Furthermore, peer experiences at the group level (i.e., peer rejection, low social preference scores) are connected directly or with a mediating role to school dropout (Véronneau & Vitaro, 2007) and negative early adolescent peer affiliations increase the risk of school dropout (Farmer et al., 2003). In order to establish positive, non-aggressive relations among peers, to increase the likelihood of having a good class environment, and to avoid school failure, an intervention focused on bullying and cyberbullying appears to be most relevant in the first year of high school.

We maintained the role of peer educators but laid out their activities in a different way in order to create a peer support model in the virtual context and a more cooperative approach in the face-to-face context. This change was due to several reasons: first, cooperative group work is one of the most effective components of anti-bullying programs (Ttofi & Farrington, 2011), and we decided to extend this component to our face-to-face intervention section; second, given the shift to a more focused age group (first-year high school students), a pure peer education approach in which some trained students "teach" the others about bullying and cyberbullying seemed less interesting than a peer support model.

Following the literature's indications (Pozzoli & Gini, 2013; Ttofi & Farrington, 2011), we maintained an ecological approach, focusing on the individual (peer educators), class, and school level. Beyond individual characteristics, the context also plays a significant role in bullying, and taking the context into account is consistent with a more ecologically valid approach to the phenomenon: anti-bullying intervention should address the individuals involved, their peer group, and the whole school community. Specifically, we included a training unit for teachers in parallel with the students' meetings in the first part of the program in order to promote higher involvement of adults. We also created new joint activities for teachers and students focused on the revision of the school rules regarding bullying and cyberbullying during the second phase managed by the trained "peer" (teachers and students).

Evaluation of 3rd edition program efficacy and participant engagement

We carried out two different trials of the 3rd edition of the *Noncadiamointrappola!* program involving different participants, classes, and schools in order to test the efficacy of the program in reducing bullying, victimisation, cyberbullying, and cybervictimisation. The main aim of our work was to match as much as possible the standard of evidence defined by *Prevention Science* (Flay et al., 2005) in order to define our program as "evidence-based". Specifically, to identify an intervention as efficacious: (a) it should have been tested in at least two rigorous trials that (b) involved defined samples from defined populations; (c) used psychometrically sound measures and data collection procedures; (d) analysed data with rigorous statistical approaches; (e) showed consistent positive effects (without serious iatrogenic effects); and (f) reported at least one significant long-term follow-up.

Participants

The experimental schools were selected using a self-selection process and the classes were selected by the school staff. There was a call made by the Province of Lucca and by the Ufficio Scolastico Regionale (the regional section of Ministry of Education, University and Research- MIUR) to participate in the program in June, which was sent to all of the high schools in Lucca and Florence (in the form of mailed letters to the schools' principals). No school agreed to participate with a random selection, so we were unable to have a randomised control trial (RCT) design. For this reason, we paired schools that asked to participate only as experimental schools with other control schools selected specifically for having classes with the same type of curriculum (e.g., we paired a vocational school for mechanics with a technical school for computer scientists, etc.). In September, we directly asked specific schools to participate as control schools.

First quasi-experimental trial – school year 2011/2012

Participants were 622 adolescents enrolled in 9th grade in 8 high schools in Tuscany (provinces of Lucca and Florence). 29.3% of the students attended lyceum high schools, 13.5% attended technical institutes, and 57.2% attended vocational high schools. The majority of students were Italian (85.88%), 6% came from Eastern Europe (mainly from Albania and Romania), and the others were from other parts of the world. 76% of the sample passed the previous grade and were attempting the first year of high school for the first time while 24% had failed previously and were engaging in a repeated attempt to pass the 9th grade.

The experimental group was composed of 451 adolescents (57% male; mean age = 14.79; SD = 1.12) in 22 classes in 5 high schools. Ninety-two students (53.3% male) decided to assume a more involved role in the program and become peer educators.

The control group was composed of 171 students (69% male; mean age = 15.28; SD = 1.15). Three schools agreed to participate as part of the control group, which consisted of a total of 9 classes.

Second quasi-experimental trial – school year 2012/2013

In the second quasi-experimental trial, 461 adolescents participated (52% male). They were all enrolled in 9th grade across 7 high schools in a province of Lucca. The majority of students were Italian (85.89%), 7.6% came from East Europe (mainly Albania), and the others were from various other parts of the world. 49.1% of the students attended lyceum high schools, 20% attended technical institutes, and 30.9% attended vocational high schools.

The experimental group was composed of 234 adolescents (28.6% male; mean age = 15.60; SD = .92, age range = 14–18 years) in 10 classes of 4 high schools. Thirty-nine students (20.5% male) decided to become peer educators. The control group was composed of 227 students in 10 classes belonging to three schools (76.2% male; mean age = 15.57; SD = .88, age range = 14–18 years).

For both trials, students in the control group did not receive any kind of intervention. The control group participants just answered the same questionnaires at the same time as the experimental group's participants. Those questionnaires were administered in class by trained researchers during school time. The consent procedure for research consisted of approval by the school, the class council, and parents: 100% of the families agreed to their child's participation in the research.

The program steps

For the experimental group, the steps of the program in *Noncadiamointrappola!* 3rd edition were the following (see also Figure 8.1):

a) Initial assessment (questionnaire administration in November);
b) Specific course on ICT, online risks, bullying and cyberbullying focusing on what a school can do to stop the two phenomena (two meetings lasting two hours each in each experimental school). Admission was free for all teachers of the experimental schools. The final aim was to start a joint revision (with students) of the school rules and policy on bullying and cyberbullying;

c) Launch of the program and awareness development. Presentation of the program to the participating classes trying to raise awareness and communication on issues related to bullying and cyberbullying (two hours, two classes combined). We used videos and other materials developed in the previous edition. The meeting was followed by another meeting with a "postal police" psychologist (Italian police specialising in online crimes) focused on the criminal implications of bullying and cyberbullying;

d) Selection of peer educators from each participating class through self-nomination (5–6 students in each class). In each class, we asked the participants directly to assume the peer educator role;

e) Day training for peer educators (8 hours). Focus on communication skills, social skills in real and virtual interactions, victim's and bystander's emotions, empathy and coping strategies, and especially problem solving;

f) Face-to-face peer educator-led activities (2 meetings of 2 hours each) on: a) victim's and bystanders' feelings and emotions and empathy; b) how to cope in bullying and cyberbullying situations from the victim and bystander point of view (What can I do if I see a bullying/cyberbullying episode or if I'm a victim/cybervictim?). Problem-solving strategies were used in order to determine a plethora of possible solutions and choose which one was best. The activities were carried out in small groups led by peer educators. Each student had a specific role they had to act out in order to cooperate and complete the activity. The groups created posters about each part of the activities and the photos of the posters were published on the *Noncadiamointrappola!* Facebook group. At the end of the activities the students presented their posters to the other classmates and together the class discussed the emotions they worked on and solutions they found;

g) Online peer educators' intervention. We created a rotation schedule whereby all online peer educators worked for a period of two weeks as forum moderators and publishers (http://www.squarciagola.net/cyberbullismo/) and as publishers on a Facebook group (called Noncadiamointrappola). Registration on the website was required to answer or post something in the forum, though it was possible to read the threads as a "website guest" without registration;

h) Final assessment: the same questionnaire was re-administered at the end of May/beginning of June to evaluate the final situation.

Measures

Bullying and victimisation

The Florence Bullying/Victimization Scales were used (Palladino, 2013). Each scale consists of 10 items asking how often the respondent had experienced particular behaviours as both perpetrator and victim during the past couple of months. Each item covered a certain behaviour and was stated in terms of both perpetration and victimisation (e.g., "I threatened someone" and "I beat and pushed someone"

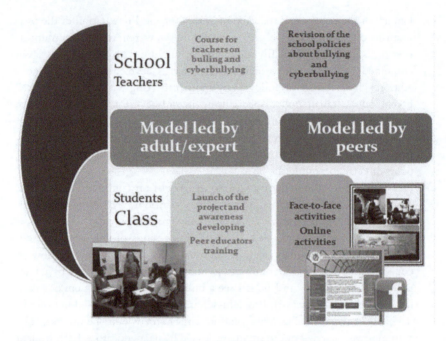

FIGURE 8.1 The steps of the Noncadiamointrappola! Program

for bullying; "I was threatened" and "I was beaten and pushed" for victimisation). Each item was evaluated on a 5-point scale from "never" to "several times a week". Both scales were composed of three subscales: (a) physical (four items), (b) verbal (three items), and (c) indirect (three items) bullying/victimisation. First and second order confirmatory factor analysis (CFA) showed good fit indices for both scales (Palladino, 2013). The alpha coefficients were good both for the first trial and the second trial (range: $\alpha = .67$ to $\alpha = .82$): demonstrating good internal consistency pre- and post-intervention.

Cyberbullying and cybervictimisation

The Florence Cyberbullying/Cybervictimization Scales were used (Palladino, Nocentini, & Menesini, n.d.). They are composed of two scales, one for cyberbullying and one for cybervictimisation. Each scale consists of 14 items, asking how often in the past couple of months respondents had experienced several behaviours. Each item covered certain behaviour and was stated in terms of both perpetration and victimisation. For example an item about *violent videos/photos/pictures by mobile phone* was defined for cybervictimisation as "receiving videos/photos/pictures of embarrassing or personal situations on internet (e-mail, websites, YouTube, Facebook)" and for cyberbullying as "sharing videos/photos/pictures of embarrassing or personal situations on internet (e-mail, websites, YouTube, Facebook)". Each item was evaluated on a 5-point scale from "never" to "several times a week". Both scales were composed of four subscales: (a) Written-Verbal (four items), (b) Visual (three items), (c) Impersonation (four items), and (d) Exclusion (three items). First and second order CFA showed good fit indices for both scales. The alpha coefficients are good both for the first trial and the second trial (range: $\alpha = .75$ to $\alpha = .92$): demonstrating good internal consistency pre- and post-intervention.

Participants' engagement with the program

Specific scales were developed. We asked the students in the experimental classes to rate the involvement, commitment, and collaboration of peer educators, classmates, teachers, and themselves on a 0 to 10 Likert scale. We decided on this range according to the Italian school achievements scores. The scales showed high levels of reliability: alpha coefficients ranged from $\alpha = .93$ to $\alpha = .98$. For all the categories of participants (peer educators, teachers, etc.) we calculated the mean of three items.

Results

We first tested for differences between the control and experimental groups for both trials in the pre-test data collection using a one-way ANOVA with four groups: control group for the 1st trial, control group for the 2nd trial, experimental group for the 1st trial, and experimental group for the 2nd trial. No differences were found for bullying ($F_{(3, 804)} = 1.169$; n.s.), victimisation ($F_{(3, 804)} = .448$; n.s.), cyberbullying ($F_{(3, 804)} = 2.228$; n.s.), and cybervictimisation ($F_{(3, 804)} = 1.910$; n.s.).

To analyse the effects of the program we conducted repeated measures ANOVA for the two trials separately in order to analyse the longitudinal differences (pre- and post-intervention) in bullying, victimisation, cyberbullying, and cybervictimisation (*within* factor) between the control and experimental group (*between* factor).

Bullying and victamisation

First trial results: Victimisation and bullying results showed significant main effects of time (victimisation $F_{(1, 620)} = 30.141$; $p \leq .001$; $\eta^2_p = .046$; bullying $F_{(1, 620)} = 6.307$; $p \leq .05$; $\eta^2_p = .010$) and significant interaction time × group (victimisation $F_{(1, 620)} = 23.029$; $p \leq .001$; $\eta^2_p = .046$; bullying $F_{(1, 620)} = 12.314$; $p \leq .001$; $\eta^2_p = .019$). No significant main effect of group was found (victimisation $F_{(1, 620)} = 1.411$ n.s.; bullying $F_{(1, 620)} = 1.151$ n.s.).

Second trial results: For victimisation and bullying, results showed significant main effects of group (victimisation $F_{(1, 459)} = 7.044$; $p \leq .001$; $\eta^2_p = .015$; bullying $F_{(1, 459)} = 27.889$; $p \leq .001$; $\eta^2_p = .057$) and significant interaction time*group (victimisation $F_{(1, 459)} = 10.610$; $p \leq .001$; $\eta^2_p = .023$; bullying $F_{(1, 459)} = 23.100$; $p \leq .001$; $\eta^2_p = .048$). We only found a significant main effect of time for victimisation (victimisation $F_{(1, 459)} = 13.992$; $p \leq .001$; $\eta^2_p = .030$; bullying $F_{(1, 459)} = 2.180$ n.s.).

Cyberbullying and cybervictimisation

First trial results: For cybervictimisation and cyberbullying, results showed significant main effects of group (cybervictimisation $F_{(1, 620)}$ = 7.896; p ≤ .01; η^2_p = .013; cyberbullying $F_{(1, 620)}$ = 14.508; p ≤. 001; η^2_p = .023) and significant interaction time*group (cybervictimisation $F_{(1, 620)}$ = 21.793; p ≤ .001; η^2_p = .034; cyberbullying $F_{(1, 620)}$ = 30.750; p ≤ .001; η^2_p = .047). We only found a significant main effect of time for cybervictimisation (cybervictimisation $F_{(1, 620)}$ = 14.299; p ≤ .001; η^2_p = .023; cyberbullying $F_{(1, 620)}$ = .384 n.s.).

Second trial results: For cybervictimisation and cyberbullying, results showed significant main effects of group (cybervictimisation $F_{(1, 459)}$ = 8.706; p ≤ .01; η^2_p = .019; cyberbullying $F_{(1, 459)}$ = 24.315; p ≤ .001; η^2_p = .050) and significant interaction time*group (cybervictimisation $F_{(1, 459)}$ = 19.254; p ≤ .001; η^2_p = .040; cyberbullying $F_{(1, 459)}$ = 12.893; p ≤ .001; η^2_p =.027). We only found a significant main effect of time for cybervictimisation (cybervictimisation $F_{(1, 459)}$ = 15.742; p ≤ .001; η^2_p = .033; cyberbullying $F_{(1, 459)}$ = 1.180 n.s.).

Figures 8.2 and 8.3 show that while in both control groups the four program target variables were quite stable for the suffered forms and tended to increase during the year for the perpetrated forms, in experimental groups (first and second trial) a significant decrease in victimisation, bullying, cybervictimisation, and cyberbullying was found.

Participants' engagement in the program

In Figure 8.4 you can see students' mean scores about the level of engagement of their peer educators, their classmates, themselves, and their teachers in the program.

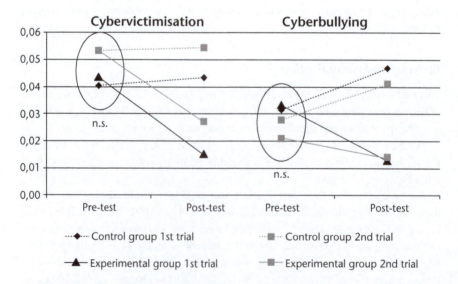

FIGURE 8.2

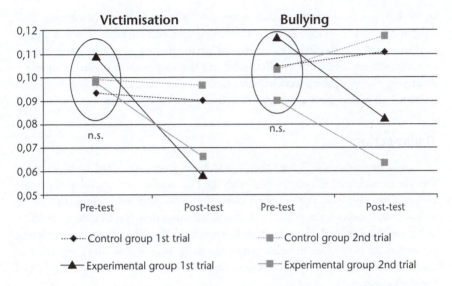

FIGURE 8.3 Trends about cybervictimisation and cyberbullying in each one of the four groups (control group-1st trial; control group-2nd trial; experimental group-1st trial and experimental group-2nd trial): means pre- and post-test.

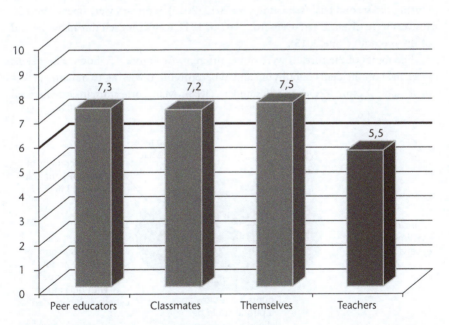

FIGURE 8.4 Mean scores about the engagement in the program of peer educators, classmates, themselves and teachers. The thick line is the cut-off for a passing grade in the Italian school system of achievement evaluation.

In the Italian school system, a score below 6 is an unsatisfactory achievement (not a passing grade), the range 6–7 was a passing grade, and the range 7–8 was a good evaluation. While the students rated their personal engagement in the program, the engagement of their peer educators, and the engagement of their classmates positively, the low rating students gave their teachers' engagement highlights the students' view that the teachers did not commit enough to the program.

Online activity

In *Noncadiamointrappola!* 3rd edition, the website forum remained open for three months in each trial in conjunction with the face-to-face activities that were carried out by peer educators in their class. Peer educators were nominated to be website moderators for two weeks at a time, meaning they had more responsibility and more features available to them in this period, such as the possibility of deleting or modifying posts (e.g., impolite posts), blocking users, and so on. They also had the task of answering posts and trying to support and help all the people who asked for their assistance.

During the first trial (school year 2011/2012), 10 new threads were opened and 66 answers were given. The number of "views" of the webpage threads (views meaning reading posts without leaving any comments) was very high: there were from 180 to 1464 views for each thread by the end of the program (June 2012). During the second trial (scholastic year 2012/2013), 9 threads were opened and 52 answers were given. There were from 167 to 1311 views for each thread by the end of the program (June 2013).

The topics of the threads were quite different. As Figure 8.5 shows, discussions were held on incidents of bullying and cyberbullying involving two main participant roles: victims (21%) and bystanders (16%). Many other discussions focused

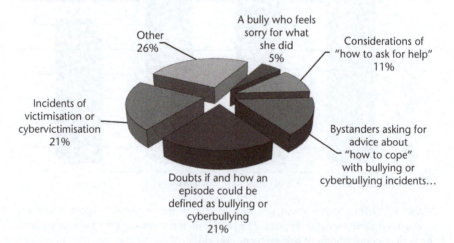

FIGURE 8.5 Topics of the threads in the forum discussions

on the possible misunderstandings of incidents (21%): how can one understand if it is a bullying/cyberbullying situation or just joking? Less frequent were the considerations on how a victim can cope with situations (11%) and, only in one case, a bully demonstrated she was sorry about what she did: she asked for advice on what she could do to change the situation. The "other" category consists of reports about other important adolescence issues (e.g., romantic relationships) and personal considerations (e.g., "Is it acceptable to annoy those who are different?").

Discussion and conclusion

This chapter aimed to describe the progress of *Noncadiamointrappola!* 3rd edition and give an empirical evaluation of the program. On the whole, results clearly confirm the efficacy of the program: we found a significant decrease in bullying, victimisation, cyberbullying, and cybervictimisation in the experimental group in comparison to the control group (although the effect size is not very strong). Different from the first and the second editions (Menesini et al., 2012; Palladino et al., 2012; Menesini & Nocentini, 2012), we found effects in each one of the four target variables in the experimental classes, and these results were confirmed in two independent trials.

Another aspect of the evaluation of a program as evidence-based is related to its effectiveness (Spiel & Strohmeier, 2012). A program is effective if it provides manuals, appropriate training, and technical support; if it has been evaluated under real-world conditions in studies that included sound measurement of the level of implementation and engagement of the target audience; and if it has indicated the practical importance of intervention outcome and has clearly demonstrated to whom intervention findings can be generalised.

In the *Noncadiamointrappola!* program 3rd edition, the same level of implementation (fidelity) for all participants was assured by the relatively small sample involved: the same trainers delivered every step of the program and every class attended the same standardised face-to-face activities (the same amount of time was spent on the same topic). However, the participants' varying levels of engagement with the program has yet to be analysed. Students' feedback on their perception of their own and others' engagement reveal some aspects of the program that still to need to be addressed. We tried to use a more ecological approach in our program, but the students' feelings about the real involvement, commitment, and collaboration of the teachers reveal that, in their perception, only the students themselves were personally engaged with the program. We feel that this perception may have some value: for instance, despite our effort to try to involve teachers, only a few of them participated in the course focused on bullying, ICTs, and online risks. While we have in each class on average more than ten teachers of different subjects, no more than one or two teachers from each class participated in the meetings. Mainly, they were the representatives that accepted the inclusion of their classes in the program leading the project and helping us in the organizational aspects. It's likely that the students' unsatisfactory judgment of the teachers' engagement is related to the low number of teachers involved rather than the personal engagement of those that were active in the program. This result can be seen as a partial failure of the effort we made to have a more ecological approach to the phenomena of bullying and cyberbullying. On the other hand, it can also be seen as an indirect feedback about the validity of the general model we adopted: a peer-led model.

The debate on the efficacy of peer-led models (peer education and peer support) is still open in the literature (Smith et al., 2012; Ttofi & Farrington, 2011, 2012). While it was suggested that "work with peers" should be avoided (Ttofi & Farrington, 2011), empirical results from the 2nd (Palladino et al., 2012) and 3rd (current) edition of the *Noncadiamointrappola!* program suggest just the opposite. It is possible that these discrepant findings were brought about by the fact that "work with peers" consisted of rather different approaches, components, and types of intervention in each study. That is, each approach covered a wide range of peer support activities (Smith, Salmivalli, & Cowie, 2012). From the results of the different editions of the *Noncadiamointrappola!* program (Menesini, Nocentini, & Palladino, 2012), we know that the role of the peer educators is highly relevant within a peer-led model. If this role leads only to a process of personal change that does not involve the other students, this approach can have limited effects (1st edition; Menesini & Nocentini, 2009). On the contrary, if the peer educators are supported in their capacity to promote initiatives and active participation of other students, the process of change could involve the entire class (Palladino et al., 2012). With adolescents, an approach focused on peer involvement *theoretically* appears to be relevant and suitable to be used in anti-bullying and anti-cyberbullying programs (Shiner, 1999; Cowie, & Wallace, 2000). Our results suggest that this is also true *empirically*. A final consideration about the peer-led models should be the cost-benefit analysis of such programs that are usually highly profitable for schools and communities. In our program, the use of ICT as a means to support students can lead to a great impact: it is possible for students both in the school and from other places to find help. Using these online activities, peer educators can be agents of change for many other people and not only for their classmates or schoolmates.

In the results section, we highlighted the online activities carried out through the webpage. The peer educators moderated the web forum, dealt with online threats, and supported people who requested help for three months in each trial. As we expected, the people more involved as victims and bystanders came to the website to ask for advice or support. Only one bully asked for some suggestion on how to cope. Specifically, in the thread she stressed that she had seen how hurt the victim was and that she did not think she had behaved that badly. A significant amount of threads were devoted to questions about how to recognise an incident as bullying or cyberbullying. More than one student was quite worried about having done harm accidentally and they stressed the difficulty of recognising the boundaries between a joke and bullying or cyberbullying. At this age it is likely very difficult to focus on the consequences of one's behaviour.

One of the most important features in the digital space is visibility: the possibility of disseminating a post, thought, or picture just by publishing it online. The amount of views received by the *Noncadiamointrappola!* threads is quite impressive. It is always possible to read the discussion posted on the webpage but it is possible to write a response only during the three months every year when the peer educators are devoted to working online. Unfortunately, it is not possible to know who reads the discussion but we can argue that the peer educators' suggestions and the support they gave arrived, indirectly, to more people than expected.

Acknowledgments

The authors wish to thank the Province of Lucca for the financial support of the program and the schools, teachers and students for their collaboration.

References

Birnbaum, M., Crohn, K., Maticka-Tyndale, E., & Barnett, J. P. (2010). Peer-led interventions to reduce HIV risk of youth: A review. *Evaluation and Program Planning, 33*(2), 98–112.

Cappadocia, M. C., Pepler, D., Cummings, J. G., & Craig, W. (2012). Individual motivations and characteristics associated with bystander intervention during bullying episodes among children and youth. *Canadian Journal of School Psychology, 27*(3), 201–216. doi:10.1177/0829573512450567

Cowie, H., Hutson, N., Oztug, O., & Myers, C. (2008). The impact of peer support schemes on pupils' perceptions of bullying, aggression and safety at school. *Emotional and Behavioural Difficulties, 13*(1), 63–71. doi:10.1080/13632750701814708

Cowie, H., Naylor, P., Talamelli, L., Chauhan, P., & Smith, P. K. (2002). Knowledge, use of and attitudes towards peer support: a 2-year follow-up to the Prince's Trust survey. *Journal of Adolescence, 25*(5), 453–467. doi:10.1006/jado.2002.0498

Cowie, H., & Oztug, O. (2008). Pupils' perceptions of safety at school. *Pastoral Care in Education, 26*(2), 59–67. doi:10.1080/02643940802062501

Cowie, H., & Wallace, P. (2000). *Peer support in action.* London: Sage.

Del Rey-Alamillo, R., Casas, J. A., & Ortega-Ruiz, R. (2012). The ConRed Program, an evidence-based practice. *Comunicar, 20*(39), 129–138. doi:10.3916/C39-2012-03-03

Dooley, J. J., Pyżalski, J., & Cross, D. (2009). Cyberbullying versus face-to-face bullying. *Zeitschrift Für Psychologie / Journal of Psychology, 217*(4), 182–188. doi:10.1027/0044-3409.217.4.182

Farmer, T. W., Estell, D. B., Leung, M.-C., Trott, H., Bishop, J., & Cairns, B. D. (2003). Individual characteristics, early adolescent peer affiliations, and school dropout: an examination of aggressive and popular group types. *Journal of School Psychology, 41*(3), 217–232. doi:10.1016/S0022-4405(03)00046-3

Flay, B. R., Biglan, A., Boruch, R. F., Castro, F. G., Gottfredson, D., Kellam, S., . . . Ji, P. (2005). Standards of evidence: Criteria for efficacy, effectiveness and dissemination. *Prevention Science, 6*(3), 151–175. doi:10.1007/s11121-005-5553-y

Freis, S. D., & Gurung, R. A. R. (2013). A Facebook analysis of helping behavior in online bullying. *Psychology of Popular Media Culture, 2*(1), 11–19. doi:10.1037/a0030239

French, D. C., & Conrad, J. (2001). School dropout as predicted by peer rejection and antisocial behavior. *Journal of Research on Adolescence, 11*(3), 225–244. doi:10.1111/1532-7795.00011

Gini, G., Pozzoli, T., Borghi, F., & Franzoni, L. (2008). The role of bystanders in students' perception of bullying and sense of safety. *Journal of School Psychology, 46*(6), 617–38. doi:10.1016/j.jsp.2008.02.001

Jimerson, S. R., Anderson, G. E., & Whipple, A. D. (2002). Winning the battle and losing the war: Examining the relation between grade retention and dropping out of high school. *Psychology in the Schools, 39*(4), 441–457. doi:10.1002/pits.10046

Kärnä, A., Voeten, M., Little, T. D., Poskiparta, E., Alanen, E., & Salmivalli, C. (2011). Going to scale: a nonrandomized nationwide trial of the KiVa antibullying program for grades 1–9. *Journal of Consulting and Clinical Psychology, 79*(6), 796–805. doi:10.1037/a0025740

Kiriakidis, S. P., & Kavoura, A. (2010). Cyberbullying: a review of the literature on harassment through the Internet and other electronic means. *Family & Community Health, 33*(2), 82–93. doi:10.1097/FCH.0b013e3181d593e4

Kokko, K., Tremblay, R. E., Lacourse, E., Nagin, D. S., & Vitaro, F. (2006). Trajectories of prosocial behavior and physical aggression in middle childhood: Links to adolescent school dropout and physical violence. *Journal of Research on Adolescence, 16*(3), 403–428. doi:10.1111/j.1532-7795.2006.00500.x

Kowalski, R. M., & Limber, S. P. (2007). Electronic bullying among middle school students. *The Journal of Adolescent Health, 41*(6), S22–30. doi:10.1016/j.jadohealth.2007.08.017

Menesini, E., Codecasa, E., Benelli, B., & Cowie, H. (2003). Enhancing children's responsibility to take action against bullying: Evaluation of a befriending intervention in Italian middle schools. *Aggressive Behavior, 29*(1), 1–14. doi:10.1002/ab.80012

Menesini, E., & Nocentini, A. (2009). Cyberbullying definition and measurement: some critical considerations. *Zeitschrift fur Psychologie/Journal of Psychology, 217*(4), 230–232.

Menesini, E., & Nocentini, A. (2012). Peer education intervention: face-to-face versus online. In A. Costabile & B. Spears (Eds.), *The impact of technology on relationships in educational settings* (pp. 139–150). London: Routledge.

Menesini, E., Nocentini, A., & Palladino, B. E. (2012). Empowering students against bullying and cyberbullying: Evaluation of an Italian peer-led model. *International Journal of Conflict and Violence, 6*(2), 313–320.

Naylor, P., & Cowie, H. (1999). The effectiveness of peer support systems in challenging school bullying: the perspectives and experiences of teachers and pupils. *Journal of Adolescence, 22*(4), 467–479.

Palladino, B. E. (2013). *Evidence-based intervention against bullying and cyberbullying: measurement of the constructs, evaluation of efficacy and mediation processes* (Unpublished doctoral dissertation) University of Florence.

Palladino, B. E., Nocentini, A., Ciucci, E., & Menesini, E. (2011). I diversi volti del fallimento scolastico: ruolo dei predittori individuali e relazionali. *Giornale Di Psicologia Dello Sviluppo – Journal of Developmental Psychology, 98*, 95–103.

Palladino, B. E., Nocentini, A., & Menesini, E. (n.d.). *Psychometric properties of Florence CyberBullying-cyberVictimization Scales (FCBVSs).* Manuscript submitted for publication.

Palladino, B. E., Nocentini, A., & Menesini, E. (2012). Online and offline peer led models against bullying and cyberbullying. *Psicothema, 24*(4), 634–639.

Pöyhönen, V., Juvonen, J., & Salmivalli, C. (2012). Standing up for the victim, siding with the bully or standing by? Bystander responses in bullying situations. *Social Development, 21*(4), 722–741. doi:10.1111/j.1467-9507.2012.00662.x

Pozzoli, T., & Gini, G. (2010). Active defending and passive bystanding behavior in bullying: the role of personal characteristics and perceived peer pressure. *Journal of Abnormal Child Psychology, 38*(6), 815–27. doi:10.1007/s10802-010-9399-9

Pozzoli, T., & Gini, G. (2013). Why do bystanders of bullying help or not? A multidimensional model. *The Journal of Early Adolescence, 33*(3), 315–340. doi:10.1177/0272431612440172

Rigby, K. (2000). Effects of peer victimization in schools and perceived social support on adolescent well-being. *Journal of Adolescence, 23*(1), 57–68.

Salmivalli, C. (2010). Bullying and the peer group: A review. *Aggression and Violent Behavior, 15*(2), 112–120. doi:10.1016/j.avb.2009.08.007

Salmivalli, C., Lagerspetz, K., Björkqvist, K., Österman, K., & Kaukiainen, A. (1996). Bullying as a group process: Participant roles and their relations to social status within the group. *Aggressive Behavior, 22,* 1–15.

Shiner, M. (1999). Defining peer education. *Journal of Adolescence, 22,* 555–566.

Slonje, R., Smith, P. K., & Frisén, A. (2013). The nature of cyberbullying, and strategies for prevention. *Computers in Human Behavior, 29*(1), 26–32. doi:10.1016/j.chb.2012.05.024

Smith, P. K., Salmivalli, C., & Cowie, H. (2012). Effectiveness of school-based programs to reduce bullying: a commentary. *Journal of Experimental Criminology, 8*(4), 433–441. doi:10.1007/s11292-012-9142-3

Spiel, C., & Strohmeier, D. (2012). Evidence-based practice and policy: When researchers, policy makers, and practitioners learn how to work together. *European Journal of Developmental Psychology, 9*(1), 150–162.

Spiel, C., Wagner, P., & Strohmeier, D. (2012). Violence prevention in Austrian schools: Implementation and evaluation of a national strategy. *International Journal of Conflict and Violence, 6*(2), 176–186.

Tokunaga, R. S. (2010). Following you home from school: A critical review and synthesis of research on cyberbullying victimization. *Computers in Human Behavior, 26*(3), 277–287. doi:10.1016/j.chb.2009.11.014

Ttofi, M. M., & Farrington, D. P. (2011). Effectiveness of school-based programs to reduce bullying: a systematic and meta-analytic review. *Journal of Experimental Criminology, 7,* 27–56. doi:10.1007/s11292-010-9109-1

Ttofi, M. M., & Farrington, D. P. (2012). Bullying prevention programs: the importance of peer intervention, disciplinary methods and age variations. *Journal of Experimental Criminology, 8*(4), 443–462. doi:10.1007/s11292-012-9161-0

Turner, G., & Shepherd, J. (1999). A method in search of a theory: peer education and health promotion. *Health Education Research, 14*(2), 235–47.

Véronneau, M., & Vitaro, F. (2007). Social Experiences with Peers and High School Graduation: A review of theoretical and empirical research. *Educational Psychology, 27*(3), 419–445. doi:10.1080/01443410601104320

Wingate, V. S., Minney, J. A., & Guadagno, R. E. (2013). Sticks and stones may break your bones, but words will always hurt you: A review of cyberbullying. *Social Influence, 8*(2–3), 87–106. doi:10.1080/15534510.2012.730491

Wölfer, R., Schultze-Krumbholz, A., Zagorscak, P., Jäkel, A., Göbel, K., & Scheithauer, H. (2013). Prevention 2.0: Targeting cyberbullying @ school. *Prevention Science: The Official Journal of the Society for Prevention Research, 15*(6), 879–887. doi:10.1007/s11121-013-0438-y

9

CONCLUSION

A critical review of the ICT based interventions

Conor Mc Guckin, Trijntje Völlink and Francine Dehue

Introduction and welcome

Well, you've made it safely to Chapter 9 and the conclusion of the book! We hope that you have enjoyed the chapters, their up-to-the-moment scholarly reviews, critical considerations, and thoughts for the future of this important area – not only for children, parents, carers, and educators – but for wider society too. As the concluding chapter, the focus here is upon integrating the "know-how" from Part I of the book with the advice and knowledge regarding practical applications from Part II. The main questions that will guide the discussion in this chapter are:

1   Are current definitions of cyberbullying adequate in selecting the children who actually need help from the prevention and intervention programs, or did the programme developers adapt the definition? From this, what can we learn about "where we are" and "where we are going"? Do we need to consider a re-definition of "cyberbullying" so as to enhance the practical use of the terminology that we use?

2   The chapters in Part II present an interesting perspective on how we can (or should) focus our efforts in terms of preventative and intervention approaches. For example, the ICT based approaches outlined in Chapter 6 (Friendly ATTAC) and Chapter 7 (Stop the bully online) have a main focus on combating cyberbullying, whereas the ICT based approaches outlined in Chapter 5 (FearNot!) and Chapter 8 (Lets not fall into the trap) have a main focus on combating traditional bullying. So, (a) to what extent do these interventions differ in the use of methods, practical applications, and intervention content?, and (b) based on the research overview of determinants of traditional and cyberbullying (Chapter 3), is it possible to see which of these approaches is more preferable to prevent and combat cyberbullying?

3   Do the interventions described in Part II contribute to decreasing the harmful effects of cyberbullying as described in Chapter 4?

These questions are not exhaustive – nor are they intended to be. Rather, they are simply intended to be a useful structure for us to consider and reflect upon what we have learned from both parts of the book. That is, they are designed to be thinking tools, tools to help us be more inquisitive about the content of the chapters, their application to real-world issues, and useful prompts to help us consider other questions that will naturally arise as we think about and answer these guiding questions.

Prevention and intervention information – where do we get the information – and is it reliable?

Part I of the book clearly demonstrated that many children and young people (CYP) are involved in problems associated with cyberbullying. Involvement in such issues is related to a host of negative consequences – from health and well-being to problematic behaviour – both internalised and externalised (e.g., Gunther and colleagues: Chapter 4). Because adults with a remit to protect CYP from harm and harassment, either in their personal or professional capacities (or both) are seeking information to help them in their important work, we have witnessed the emergence of a plethora of intervention and preventative programmes, approaches, and tools. Whilst this availability of resources is laudable and appreciated, many of those seeking out these resources may lack the critical and analytical thinking tools required to separate the evidence-informed offerings from the more "rash" quick-fix offerings. Well-intentioned but misguided approaches will, at best, probably yield no appreciable reduction in either cyberbullying involvement or its associated sequel. At worst, such approaches may exacerbate the problem.

For the most part, the first port of call for adults seeking new information in this, or indeed any other area, is the Internet. As the old joke goes: on the Internet, no-one knows you're a dog! That is, anyone can upload anything to the Internet and masquerade as anyone they want the observer to identify them as – e.g. an expert authority on that particular subject. Coupled with this, popular approaches to such issues on the Internet attract more attention than research-informed information – thus continuing to propagate the notion that "if this is popular / high up on the search results . . . then it must be good". Using the CyberTraining Project (funded by the EU Lifelong Learning Programme: [Project No.142237-LLP-1–2008–1-DE-LEONARDO-LMP] http://www.adam-europe.eu/adam/project/view.htm?prj=4306#.VbYcTfntlBc), a well-grounded, research-based training manual on cyberbullying for trainers (see Mora-Merchan & Jäger, 2010), Mc Guckin and Crowley (2012) have demonstrated how programme developers can enhance their knowledge of who is accessing their wares and use this information to make evidence-informed decisions. As psychologists, researchers, and academics, we see the terms intervention and prevention in nearly every article that we read, every professional publication that we see, and every piece of student writing that we grade.

We are concerned that we are somehow just using these words without even thinking about their true meaning – their very real potency when we are thinking about approaches that we can advocate to parents, teachers, schools, and society. When we go to the hospital for an operation, we expect the surgeon to have a very sharp and clean scalpel, and to know whereabouts the failing organ is physically located in our body. Two things here are very real and identifiable: the scalpel and the failing body organ – both physically exist. What is crucially different about our attempts to conceptualise and operationalise difficult problems in society, like cyberbullying, is that they must be conceptualised and operationalised clearly enough that we can truly and honestly say that we are as certain as possible that the concept and resulting definition are precise and accurate reflections of the problem at hand. Our requirement is to move beyond lay theories of cyberbullying. Without high levels of rigour here, we end up building intervention and prevention programmes on quicksand. Doomed to failure. This example may, at first, seem obtuse, but the reality is that whilst the surgeon is just operating on one person at any one time with tangible tools for tangible problems, we develop programmes for wide-scale application with the added worry of ensuring that the preparation for the programme (the diagnostic and enabling work) is as clinically clean as possible – one slip of our knife would be catastrophic to the patients that we are interested in helping – young school children and adolescents who look to us for help, support, and an education free from harm and harassment.

In this book, the authors have addressed all of these important issues – how to define a concept that is real and continuing to grow and develop, who is involved in these issues, what are the health and well-being implications of being involved, and, importantly, how do we try to help? By using all of this knowledge to design, test, and recommend intervention and prevention programmes that are evidence-informed, robust, and likely to succeed.

So . . . defining the area

In Chapter 2, Ersilia Menesini and colleagues provided us with a review of where we are in terms of developing a robust understanding of how to operationally define the construct (conceptually, theoretically, and methodologically). As the pivotal issue with regards to how we should develop interventions and preventative programmes, we should consider whether we have reached a destination with regards to defining the area – or whether we are still on a journey – perhaps a never-ending journey – to that destination. Just to remind us, the question posed about definitions was: Is the definition of cyberbullying adequate in selecting the children who actually need help for the intervention programmes, or did the intervention developers adapt the definition? What can we learn from that? Is a re-definition of cyberbullying preferable to enhance its practical use? Despite being of fundamental importance, these are really interesting questions. For example, how often do researchers and those involved in policy or practice development actually stop and think about whether their work is correctly focused, on the right area, or whether the work really does help those that it is intended to help? To help us here, Menesini and colleagues provided a thorough review of the current conceptual, theoretical, and methodological issues which should be considered in relation to the design and implementation of any cyberbullying intervention or prevention effort. Their chapter is of particular value to many readers, as the arguments and debates explored in the chapter also have great relevance to any consideration of traditional bullying.

The authors highlighted the different approaches to defining cyberbullying and indicated that many researchers apply the criteria of traditional bullying (namely repetition, power imbalance, and intent) when identifying cyberbullying. Furthermore, they suggest that, in addition to these criteria, other cyber-specific factors such as the public nature of content, lack of adult supervision, anonymity of perpetrators, and the sometimes permanent accessibility of online content must also be considered as possible criteria for cyberbullying. Appropriately, the authors argue that more work is needed before a wide consensus is reached regarding the most appropriate definitional approach to cyberbullying.

Basing their views on the available research to date, Menesini and colleagues also advance the argument by proposing that intent and power imbalance are essential criteria of cyberbullying, albeit different forms of power may pertain to a cyber-specific context. The inclusion of repetition as an essential criterion is still unclear as the public nature of the content is an important consideration when determining if there is repetition of victimisation or repetition of perpetration. Moreover, the cyber-specific factors of anonymity of the perpetrator(s) and the public nature of the content are regarded by Menesini and colleagues as details which can reveal information regarding the severity of the cyberbullying, but should not be regarded as essential definitional criteria. So, in relation to our purposes here, this demonstrates the importance that we should place on the definitional basis upon which programmes are constructed. In building any structure, a solid foundation is vital to the provision of direction and support to those parts that are most important for stability and support.

Aligned to our need to appropriately define the area under investigation is the need to consider how to accurately measure or assess involvement in cyberbullying issues. For many of us, we begin the process of programme implementation by collecting some form of baseline data regarding how many CYP are involved, who is involved in terms of age or gender demographics, and severity of involvement. To further help us here, also reviewed in Chapter 2 by Menesini and colleagues were the two main approaches to measuring cyberbullying. The first approach was one in which cyberbullying is regarded as a sub-type of bullying and is measured with a global question which measures involvement in cyberbullying. The second approach regards cyberbullying as a separate but related construct (to traditional bullying) and measures this construct using a "scale" approach. The authors argue that the first approach is more person-focused and is particularly appropriate for identifying more severe incidents of cyberbullying because there is greater involvement in the behaviour and, therefore, increased personal awareness. For this reason, the authors suggest that this approach is more fitting when attempting to detect more serious cases of cyberbullying. By contrast, the second approach is more behaviour-focused and can, therefore, detect specific behaviours across a range of frequencies.

Reviewing the evidence that relates to prevalence of cyberbullying, Menesini and colleagues found that some research suggests that cyberbullying is an extension of traditional bullying, and thus we can apply insights from that context to the cyber context. By contrast, other research would indicate that cyberbullying should be regarded as a distinct construct. This has clear implications for preventative measures and interventions, and ultimately, the authors argue that it is important that both the commonalities and distinct features of traditional bullying and cyberbullying are recognised when attempting to intervene, and that moreover, we must not focus on cyberbullying to the exclusion of traditional bullying, but instead address both forms of aggression (is it possible that such a silver bullet exists?). They suggest that it is important to look not only at the surface cyber-specific features of cyberbullying when designing interventions, but also to explore the general processes which underpin all bullying behaviour.

Summary

So, with this in mind regarding defining and measuring the area, can we develop "gold-standard" criteria and applications – akin to Laws and Principles in the natural sciences and disciplines relevant to cyber issues (e.g., Moore's Law [1965] that predicts exponential development of computer processing power)? Considering that we are dealing with human behaviour in a social context and a phenomenon that is continually evolving, the answer is "probably not". However, that is not to say that we should not attempt to analyse the interventions presented in Part II of the book with this type of mindset.

Considering individual, social, and health and well-being factors

As the poet John Donne reminded us, "No man is an island". As humans, we are *the* social animal, seeking out comfort, support, and companionship from other humans. We are at an interesting juncture in our development, in that much of our social interaction is now conducted online – even with people who we have never met in real life. As interesting as this may be, it reminds us of the importance of considering the individual and social determinants that are related to involvement in bullying – both traditional and cyberbullying. From Chapter 3, we learned from Dieter Wolke and colleagues about individual and social determinants of traditional and cyberbullying. The obvious question that arises here is: "To what extent do current (or planned) intervention and prevention programmes pay heed to such important "input" advice, and how could we all grow and develop programmes, in a truly iterative way, to respond to the rapidly emerging knowledge in the area?" That is, just with the importance of applying robust knowledge regarding operationally defining the area (Menesini and colleagues: Chapter 2), to what extent do the developers of programmes seek to develop "evidence-informed" programmes – ones that understand and plan for social and individual factors (Wolke and colleagues: Chapter 3), or wider "ecological" factors (Mc Guckin & Minton, 2014)? From the review by Wolke and colleagues (Chapter 3), we can see important issues that are evident with traditional bullying and that are becoming emergent with cyberbullying – regardless of whether they are two separate (but similar) phenomena, or "two sides of the same coin" (i.e., the engaging debate between Olweus [2012] and Smith [2012]). However, the preponderance of available research is highly suggestive of an overlap between involvement in both types of bully/victim problems. At an evidential level, this gives us tentative support for the need to develop intervention and prevention programmes that can adequately address both forms of bullying – perhaps with the most focus on traditional bullying, as more CYP appear to be involved in this form of bully/victim problem, with a sub-set of these being also caught up in cyberbullying problems.

So, before exploring individual and social determinants of involvement in traditional and cyberbullying, we can see that there is a need to comprehend that, as reported by Juvonen and Gross (2008), when other known risk factors are controlled for, the experience of being bullied at school is related to a seven-fold increase in the risk of being victimised online. Also, and importantly, developers of programmes should be aware of the fact that we have no firm understanding (yet), of whether there is stability/consistency across the actor roles adopted by CYP who are involved in both types of bullying scenarios. That is, does your actor role in traditional bullying "predict" the role adopted in cyberbullying situations? Is there consistency across how CYP are similarly/differently involved in both types of bullying? Despite the fact that we have no ongoing and robust findings in this critical component of planning intervention and prevention programmes, developers would be wise to heed the early suggestions of Ybarra and Mitchell (2004) of how actor status in traditional bullying can possibly help predict actor status in cyberbullying situations – i.e., the "revenge of the nerds hypothesis" (Vandebosch & Cleemput, 2009).

In the review of individual and social determinants of traditional and cyberbullying, Chapter 3 explored the issues across five main groups of risk factors which have been previously considered in relation to traditional bullying (Wolke & Stanford, 1999): (a) demographic characteristics including age, sex, and ethnicity; (b) psychological characteristics including self-esteem, internalising behaviours, empathy, and aggression; (c) family and household factors such as parenting, socioeconomic status, and sibling relationships; (d) school and peer factors such as school climate and peer relationships; and finally (e) availability and use of technology, which considers the frequency, patterns, and nature of children's electronic interactions. For example, in terms of age, Wolke and colleagues reminded us that whilst we know that self-reports of traditional victimisation steadily decreases with age, the relationship between age and cyberbullying is less clear, again due to a lack of consistent findings from the research to date. Similarly, with regards to sex differences, findings regarding cyberbullying are not consistent (e.g., Tokunaga, 2010). Indeed, the chapter also reminded us of the importance of keeping abreast of new knowledge regarding issues that we previously considered as "set" and robust – e.g., recent research has led to a revision of our early knowledge about sex differences regarding traditional bullying. Ethnicity was reported to be a problematic, but important, variable to assess in relation to traditional bullying, with limited evidence available regarding ethnicity and cyberbullying. This gap in current knowledge is critical, as many countries are now much more heterogeneous in terms of population demographics than in recent history. Thus, intervention and prevention programmes really need to be able to get such knowledge so as to assimilate and accommodate this information.

Not surprisingly, we also learned that at a psychological level, CYP who endorse aggressive beliefs are more likely to engage in peer-to-peer aggressive behaviour, as both bullies and bully-victims, with bullying perpetration being strongly linked to delinquent behaviour. From the emerging evidence regarding cyberbullying, it would appear that CYP who cyberbully others score higher on measures of aggression. Considering the overlap between actor status in traditional bullying and cyberbullying, we might not be surprised by some of these emerging findings. As we await further studies that explore the complexity of actor status within and across these types of bullying, we should be acutely aware of the potential for interventions.

That "old chestnut", self-esteem, has been implicated extensively as both a risk factor for involvement in traditional bully-victim problems but also an outcome from being involved in these problems. It can also act as a protective factor. In a true "chicken and egg" scenario, we are unsure of the direction of the effect here – does involvement lead to lower levels of self-esteem, or do lowered levels of self-esteem leave someone more vulnerable to bullying behaviours? Also, there quite often appears to be a "dose effect" in terms of the relationship between involvement in traditional bullying and lower levels of self-esteem. This is an ongoing conundrum and, as psychologists and educators, we should urge caution regarding seeing self-esteem enhancement as being the silver bullet to rectify the situation. Considering that many children have well-adjusted levels of self-esteem, would the application of an intervention or prevention programme that focuses on self-esteem enhancement actually lead to the creation of more narcissistic CYP? As we race towards approaches that can help CYP involved in cyberbullying, we should be cautious of the multi-faceted "truths" about the linkages between actor status and self-esteem. Wolke and colleagues also point out the role of empathy (both affective and cognitive) in traditional bullying episodes, and that we have differing opinions in the literature – for example, that bullies lack social skills and social understanding (Crick & Dodge, 1999) or that bullies are in fact skilled manipulators, who possess good cognitive empathy (Sutton, Smith, & Swettenham, 1999).

From this quick review of salient variables explored in Chapter 3 by Wolke and colleagues, it becomes evident that we are quite advanced in terms of our knowledge about involvement in traditional bullying and important individual and social variables. What is more stark is the fact that despite the increased research attention to cyberbullying over recent years, our knowledge in this area is still very much in its infancy – growing, developing, stumbling, but all the time learning. The unenviable task here for programme developers is to keep up their incredibly hard work in designing programmes that can, whilst paying attention to definitional and measurement issues, accommodate and assimilate the growing body of new knowledge about these important individual and social variables.

Developing the work of Wolke and colleagues in Chapter 3, Gunther and colleagues (Chapter 4) impressed upon us the deleterious behavioural and health and well-being (both physical and psychological) effects of involvement in both traditional bullying and cyberbullying. From the emerging research in the area regarding cyberbullying, we saw evidence to support the suggestion that the effects of involvement in cyberbullying issues are more severe than those of traditional bullying (Campbell, 2005). However, as noted previously in relation to self-esteem, we should exercise due caution here with regards to the findings of studies that are cross-sectional in nature, thus prohibiting any statements about "cause and effect" between actor status regarding involvement and examined correlates (Gini & Pozzoli, 2009; Kowalski, Giumetti, Schroeder, & Lattaner, 2014; Reijntjes, Kamphuis, Prinzie, & Telch, 2010). Gunther and colleagues presented the results of their very interesting and welcome narrative study that explored negative outcomes of (cyber)bullies, traditional and (cyber)victims, (cyber)bully-victims, and online bystanders, and on similarities and differences between negative outcomes of traditional bullying and cyberbullying. In relation to traditional bullying, the review demonstrated the robust evidence that is available from longitudinal studies showing that all actors involved in traditional bullying (victim, bully, bully-victim, bystander) are vulnerable to an array of negative mental health outcomes – both short- and long-term (Sourander et al., 2007; Machmutow, Perren, Sticca, & Alsaker, 2012; Wolke, & Lereya, 2015). The bi-directional nature of involvement in traditional bullying and psychological problems was also highlighted (Reijntjes et al., 2010; Reijntjes, Kamphuis, Prinzie, Boelen, van der Schoot & Telch, 2011). In relation to cyberbullying, the review highlighted the (not surprising) fact that most of the early research of interest here has focused predominantly on cyber victimisation. The narrative review showed that both cyber victimisation and cyberbullying are related to several serious negative outcomes (e.g., anxiety, depression, suicidal ideation).

Of great interest were the results from studies that concurrently explored involvement in traditional and cyber victimisation – the experience of combined victims of traditional and cyberbullying victimisation appears to be more strongly related to mental health problems than the experience for pure traditional or cyber victims. Whilst Gunther and colleagues cautioned interpretations to be understood in relation to the usual difficulty of presenting direct comparisons between research studies (e.g., methodological issues such as definitions and time reference periods), they rightly called for more complex studies to be conducted – ones that could analyse potential moderator and/or mediator effects (e.g., coping strategies, social support, parenting) on the relationship between negative outcomes, cyberbullying and cyber victimisation. From a prevention and intervention perspective, Gunther and colleagues concluded that their narrative study suggested a strong need to address both forms of bullying simultaneously in future programmes. In support of this conclusion, they point out that such combined intervention and prevention approaches (e.g., Olweus, 2012) may be most effective for three very important reasons: (a) the large overlap between involvement in these types of bullying behaviours may make a distinction relevant only for a small group of CYP, (b) CYP victimised by both forms of bullying suffer the most, and (c) previous research has indicated that targeting only one form of bullying causes an increase in another type of bullying (Elledge et al., 2013).

Summary

Unfortunately, the emerging research evidence supports the common belief that CYP involved in cyberbullying are at increased risk of exhibiting behavioural problems as well as health and well-being problems. Even though our knowledge regarding social and individual factors related to involvement in cyberbullying is only just emerging, programme developers have a readily available supply of knowledge from the substantial literature on traditional bullying. No preventative approach or intervention programme can, realistically, attend to all of these issues, whilst also trying to keep true to the issues discussed earlier regarding definitional issues. However, we have enough background knowledge about successful programmes and programme components from the field of traditional bullying, and indeed further afield, to be in a position to ensure that new offerings in the area of cyberbullying are robust and fit for purpose.

Interventions to prevent and combat cyberbullying

We are living in the future. The only thing that we know about the future is that it is unpredictable. We are using technology that has not been properly understood as yet. We are educating CYP for jobs that do not exist yet. We read tantalising headlines about research studies that show the positive effects of new technology on babies and school-age children. We rush to ensure that classrooms are wired and that books and lessons are available as downloads. There are undoubtedly positive aspects of new technology and ICT for CYP (Costabile & Spears, 2012). However, knowledge is not "Bluetoothed" from these exciting ICT devices to the hearts and minds of CYP. In the social arena that we all exist in, knowledge transfer also incorporates the prevailing social conditions of the peer group that we belong to, as well as societal norms about what is acceptable behaviour – and not. With this in mind, this book has brought together expert up-to-the-moment knowledge and critical thought about one of the negative aspects of the increasingly wired world that CYP are developing and living in.

In this contemporary world, where access to the Internet is viewed by CYP (and many adults) as more important than the basic physiological needs identified at the base of Maslow's hierarchy of needs, it is incumbent upon us all to move beyond well-intentioned helping actions to approaches that are objective and transparent. Continually highlighted throughout this book have been the issues that we all need to consider in relation to planning for theoretically informed, methodologically robust, and empirically supported programmes to (a) combat the continued growth of cyberbullying, and (b) offer support to those involved in cyberbullying issues. As we reach this point of the final chapter, we have reviewed the importance of the state-of-the-art knowledge from Part I of the book. Attention now turns towards a similar review of the programmes outlined in Part II of the book.

The FearNot! programme

In Chapter 5, Sapouna and colleagues offered recommendations regarding efforts to counter cyberbullying which were based upon cross-cultural (Germany & UK) research which assessed the FearNot! programme. The programme is designed to address traditional forms of bullying and coping skills among primary school-aged children. The interesting and contemporary nature of the programme is evident in the use of role play, based upon experiential learning, within a virtual environment. A core strength of the programme is that it is informed by evidence demonstrating that experiential learning can be an effective tool in allowing students to address social and emotional problems in school, as they are given the opportunity to take the perspective of another student with respect to thoughts, emotions, and behaviours, and in this way there is an opportunity for empathy to develop. Because there are certain obstacles associated with implementing role play in a school environment, particularly in relation to a sensitive topic such as bullying, the virtual environment provides a "safe space" to test out different coping strategies and responses to a bullying scenario. Commendable is the fact that the components of the programme are directed by the bullying literature, with emphasis on various forms of bullying, the bystander role, and effective/ineffective coping strategies. The participants play the role of a friend of a character who is being bullied and in this way they have the chance to advise their friend in terms of how they can respond to victimisation. Importantly, the participants receive immediate feedback in relation to how the strategy might work for the character. Again, highlighting a central argument of this book is the support offered to the programme through empirical research findings. Comparing a group who participated in the intervention with a control group, the FearNot! programme was assessed using pre- and post-measures of victim status, knowledge of effective coping strategies, and supportive bystander behaviour. Findings indicated that victims in the intervention group were significantly more likely to become "escaped victims" one week following the intervention. Some other differences were culture-specific and may have been due to factors such as varying levels of anti-bullying intervention in both countries prior to beginning the study.

Based on the effectiveness of the FearNot! programme it would appear that it could be adapted to also counter cyberbullying in schools. According to Sapouna and colleagues, some important aspects of the design that need to be considered for such an adaptation include the need to allow students and teachers to be involved in the development of the content and characters, the capacity for virtual characters to express themselves, the provision of sufficiently robust computers, the potential need for teachers to up-skill in relation to computer use, and importantly, the incorporation of this approach as just one component of a whole-school system approach. However, another crucial component that we need to return to is the definition and delineation of cyberbullying/cyber aggression. If cyberbullying is merely an extension or sub-type of traditional bullying, then we can confidently apply the same principles and approaches to countering cyberbullying as we do to traditional bullying. However, we must be cognisant of the unique characteristics of cyberbullying/cyber aggression and design our intervention/prevention efforts accordingly.

A "serious game" approach

Chapter 6 provided a review of the initial stages of the design process for a digital game to counter cyberbullying in Belgian secondary schools. The target population for the intervention are 12- to 14-year-old adolescents, a critical age regarding involvement in cyberbullying. Highlighting the theoretical underpinning of the programme, Van Cleemput and colleagues describe "serious" games as appropriate for encouraging learning and behavioural change among young people because these games carry intrinsic motivation, can facilitate learning and behaviour change through feedback, practice, and reward, and provide an appropriate "fit" for young people. In addition, the authors cite empirical support for the effectiveness of this approach in relation to learning and behavioural change. The chapter focused on the initial phases of design which followed intervention mapping protocol so as to build a programme that could be effective in its aims. The game is primarily focused on the role of the bystander as this is the most common role in cyberbullying scenarios and research has shown that bystander-focused interventions can be particularly effective in terms of bullying reduction. Professional story writers are involved in the development of the story upon which the game is based. With regard to narrative development, the researchers were guided by two key theories: Transportation Theory and the Extended Elaboration Likelihood Model. For instance, Transportation theory suggests that when participants become more engaged with a story their beliefs tend to reflect those of the story more closely and moreover they are less likely to develop counter opinions. Transportation can be affected by factors such as emotional empathy for the characters and lack of distraction from the real-world environment. The Extended Elaboration Likelihood Model also states that transportation can be affected by factors such as the appeal of the storyline and the quality of the production. The characters used in such a game can also be important as an attractive character can be a useful tool of persuasion. Furthermore, the authors have drawn on Social Learning Theory by developing characters who can facilitate social modelling of desirable behaviour. The characters (if relatable for the children) can promote development of self-efficacy through changing their lives for the better. Focus groups were conducted with Belgian secondary school children in order to retrieve feedback on an introductory clip for the game. Thus, from this brief review of the programme, it becomes evident that the spirit and ethos of the programme is in line with what we advocate in terms of demonstrable rigour. Overall, this chapter provided a very useful template for setting out to develop an intervention in a rigorous manner with appropriate attention to relevant theory and empirical evidence.

Online Pestkoppenstoppen (stop bullies online/stop online bullies)

In a very welcome development, one that emphasises the critical issues that have been consistently raised throughout this book and emphasised in this chapter, Jacobs and colleagues reported on the systematic development of a web-based tailored intervention aimed at 12- to 15-year-old adolescents. Extending our learning from the chapters in Part I of the book, their programme seeks to not only impart advice for victims to decrease their victimisation, but also tries to ensure that this advice facilitates increased psychological well-being, and decreases in problem behaviour, school problems, and truancy. Pointing out that victims of cyberbullying prefer to get anonymous help, with a wish for this help to be delivered via the Internet, Jacobs and colleagues also note the added advantage of Internet-delivered interventions like theirs – the 24-hour access that it provides users. Advancing the notion of "gold standard" approaches, their intervention sought to attend to all of the central issues that we have discussed in this chapter; that is, the need to be planned, to be systematic, to have a theory-based approach, and to be evidence-informed. As a model, the approach outlined by Jacobs and colleagues is to be welcomed, and their continued development work with the programme will, hopefully, evidence the planned objectives.

"Noncadiamointrappola!" (Let's not fall into the trap)

Taking as a starting point that there is considerable overlap between involvement in traditional bullying and cyberbullying, Menesini and colleagues gave us a really useful and detailed overview of the development of the "Noncadiamointrappola!" programme. In a truly scientific and iterative manner, the programme has grown and developed since its first version. Making a positive use of new technology whilst focusing on both traditional bullying and cyberbullying, the programme is a welcome addition to the canon of prevention and intervention approaches with its use of the peer-led model. The positive research results supporting the programme are a contribution to what we are advocating in the book – theory driven, empirically tested, practice oriented, and iterative.

Conclusion

So, here we are. We have arrived at the conclusion of this chapter, and also at the end of the book. We really do appreciate all of the hard work that you have had to do whilst engaging with the work presented in both Part I and Part II. At this point, we feel that we would also like to thank the authors of the chapters for their scholarly work and considered thoughts regarding the issues that they have written about for us. Because this is such an important area of interest for researchers, parents, educators, and society in general, we have seen that some of the knowledge regarding cyberbullying is still emerging from the research literature. Despite its infancy, we have seen some important parallels and overlaps with our knowledge from traditional bullying. The authors of the chapters on interventions have remained committed to the need for a scientific approach in terms of developing programmes that have every chance of succeeding, whilst also being creative and imaginative in their efforts to engage CYP. We hope that you have enjoyed this book. We also hope that you feel more educated and supported in your important work. Let's continue our work to ensure that CYP can enjoy education free from harm and harassment.

References

Campbell, M. A. (2005). Cyber bullying: an old problem in a new guise? *Australian Journal of Guidance and Counselling, 15*(1), 68–76. doi:10.1375/ajgc.15.1.68

Costabile, A., & Spears, B. A. (Eds.) (2012). *The impact of technology on relationships in educational settings.* David Fulton (Routledge, Abingdon UK & New York).

Crick, N. R., & Dodge, K. A. (1999). Superiority is in the eye of the beholder: A comment on Sutton, Smith, and Swettenham. *Social Development, 8,* 128–131.

Elledge, L. C., Williford, A., Boulton, A. J., DePaolis, K. J., Little, T. D., & Salmivalli, C. (2013). Individual and contextual predictors of cyberbullying: the influence of children's provictim attitudes and teachers' ability to intervene. *Journal of Youth and Adolescence, 42*(5), 698–710. doi:10.1007/s10964-013-9920-x

Gini, G., & Pozzoli, T. (2009). Association between bullying and psychosomatic problems: a meta-analysis. *Pediatrics, 123*(3), 1059–1065. doi:10.1542/peds.2008-1215

Juvonen, J., & Gross, E. F. (2008). Extending the school grounds?—Bullying experiences in cyberspace. *Journal of School Health, 78*(9), 496–505. doi:10.1111/j.1746-1561.2008.00335.x

Kowalski, R. M., Giumetti, G. W., Schroeder, A. N., & Lattaner, M. R. (2014). Bullying in the digital age: a critical review and meta-analysis of cyberbullying research among youth. *Psychological Bulletin, 140*(4), 1073–1137. doi:10.1037/a0035618

Machmutow, K., Perren, S., Sticca, F., & Alsaker, F. D. (2012). Peer victimization and depressive symptoms: can specific coping strategies buffer the negative impact of cybervictimization? *Emotional and Behavioural Difficulties, 17*(3–4), 403–420. doi:10.10 80/13632752.2012.704310

Mc Guckin, C., & Crowley, N. (2012). Using Google Analytics to evaluate the impact of the CyberTraining project. *Cyberpsychology, Behavior, and Social Networking, 15*(11), 625–629. doi:10.1089/cyber.2011.0460

Mc Guckin, C., & Minton, S. J. (2014). From theory to practice: Two ecosystemic approaches and their applications to understanding school bullying. *Australian Journal of Guidance and Counselling, 24*(1), 36–48.

Moore, G. E. (1965). Cramming more components onto integrated circuits. *Electronics, 38*(8), 114–117.

Mora-Merchan, J. A., & Jäger, T. (Eds.). (2010). *Cyberbullying: A cross-national comparison.* Landau: Verlag Emprische Padagogik.

Olweus, D. (2012). Cyber bullying: an overrated phenomenon? *European Journal of Developmental Psychology, 9*(5), 520–538. doi:10.1080/17405629.2012.682358

Reijntjes, A., Kamphuis, J. H., Prinzie, P., & Telch, M. J. (2010). Peer victimization and internalizing problems in children: a meta-analysis of longitudinal studies. *Child Abuse & Neglect, 34*(4), 244–252. doi:10.1016/j.chiabu.2009.07.00

Reijntjes, A., Kamphuis, J. H., Prinzie, P., Boelen, P. A., van der Schoot, M., & Telch, M J. (2011). Prospective linkages between peer victimization and externalizing problems in children: a meta-analysis. *Aggressive Behavior, 37*(3), 215–222. doi: 10.1002/ab.20374

Smith, P. K. (2012). Cyberbullying: Challenges and opportunities for a research program – A response to Olweus (2012). *European Journal of Developmental Psychology, 9*(5), 553–558. doi:10.1080/17405629.2012.689821

Sourander, A., Jensen, P., Rönning, J. A., Elonheimo, H., Niemelä, S, Helenius, H., Kumpulainen, K., Piha, J., Tamminen, T., Moilanen, I., & Almqvist, F. (2007). Childhood bullies and victims and their risk of criminality in late adolescence. The Finnish from a boy to a man study. *Archives of Pediatrics & Adolescent Medicine, 161*(6), 546–552. doi:10.1001/archpedi.161.6.546

Sutton, J., Smith, P. K., & Swettenham, J. (1999). Social cognition and bullying: Social inadequacy or skilled manipulation? *British Journal of Developmental Psychology, 17*(3), 435–450.

Tokunaga, R. S. (2010). Following you home from school: A critical review and synthesis of research on cyberbullying victimization. *Computers in Human Behavior, 26,* 277–287.

Vandebosch, H., & Van Cleemput, K. (2009). Cyberbullying among youngsters: profiles of bullies and victims. *New Media & Society, 11*(8), 1–23. doi:10.1177/1461444809341263

Wolke, D., & Lereya, T. (2015). Long-term effects of bullying. *Archives of Disease in Childhood.* Advance online publication. doi:10.1136/archdischild-2014-306667

Wolke, D., & Stanford, K. (1999). Bullying in school children. In D. Messer & S. Millar (Eds.), *Developmental Psychology.* London: Arnold Publisher.

Ybarra, L. M., & Mitchell, J. K. (2004). Online aggressor/targets, aggressors, and targets: A comparison of associated youth characteristics. *Journal of Child Psychology and Psychiatry, 45*(7), 1308–1316.

INDEX